SHINING STAR

SHINING STAR

Braving the Elements of
EARTH, WIND & FIRE

PHILIP J. BAILEY

with Keith Zimmerman and Kent Zimmerman

VIKING

VIKING
Published by the Penguin Group
Penguin Group (USA) LLC
375 Hudson Street
New York, New York 10014

USA | Canada | UK | Ireland | Australia | New Zealand | India | South Africa | China
penguin.com
A Penguin Random House Company

First published by Viking Penguin, a member of Penguin Group (USA) LLC, 2014

Photographs courtesy of Philip Bailey

LIBRARY OF CONGRESS CATALOGING-IN-PUBLICATION DATA
Bailey, Philip, 1951- author.
Shining star : braving the elements of Earth, Wind & Fire / Philip J. Bailey with Keith Zimmerman and Kent Zimmerman.
pages cm
Includes index.
ISBN 978-0-670-78588-9
1. Bailey, Philip, 1951- 2. Earth, Wind & Fire (Musical group) 3. Singers—United States—Biography. 4. Soul musicians—United States—Biography. I. Zimmerman, Keith, author. II. Zimmerman, Kent, 1953- author. III. Title.
ML420.B125A3 2014
782.42164092—dc23
2013036978

Printed in the United States of America
1 3 5 7 9 10 8 6 4 2

This book is dedicated to my grandchildren, my children, and their mothers because this has been a journey that we've all taken together. These individuals have been my inspiration and God has been my strength and guiding force. This story is by no means over, but continues to evolve as I fulfill my life's intended purpose. By God's grace, he will say, "Well done."

Special Thanks

Thanks to the original nine members of Earth, Wind & Fire for their contribution to this book. And a very special thanks to Verdine White, Ralph Johnson, Larry Dunn, Al McKay, Perry Jones, Bob Cavallo, Janet Bailey, David Foster, and Maurice White.

I'd also like to thank my soul mate, Valerie Davis, for her love and support while I wrote this book.

Love you, babe

P.B.

Living, Learning, Loving, Giving

ACKNOWLEDGMENTS

To the Denver public school system for giving me an excellent musical foundation.

To all my childhood musical buddies in Denver, Colorado.

My three 6:00 a.m. Saturday morning prayer partners for more than thirty years: Dr. Julius L. West, Pastor Steven Dyson, and Elder John Patton.

This book would not have been possible without Maurice White in my life. I love and appreciate him beyond words.

To my sister, Beverly Ann: This is our story. Thanks for taking care of me while Mom worked, though you were only a year older.

To Jan Miller: Thank you for encouraging me to write this book, even though I wondered if I had much to write about.

To the Zimmerman brothers—Keith and Kent—who now know more about me than most people. It's been a journey worthwhile. Thank you both.

To my editor, Rick Kot, at Viking, for this courageous collaborative adventure.

And last but in no way least, I want to acknowledge my sisters, Francine, Edlene, and Verlon, and my aunt Maxine Jackson.

CONTENTS

PRELUDE

THE CONCEPT

Looking back and upon reflection, Earth, Wind & Fire's premier mission has been to raise people to a higher level of consciousness. Maurice White—our founder, visionary, and mentor—called it "the Concept." He'd sit me down, and we'd talk about it for hours. He stressed the importance of the Concept. He had drawings, charts, and schematics of the band detailing the Concept.

"Always be strong talking about the Concept," he emphasized.

It was 1972 in Los Angeles, the year Motown Records relocated from Detroit to the West Coast. Maurice White's brainchild musical ensemble had already released two albums on Warner Brothers Records, the self-titled *Earth, Wind & Fire* and *The Need to Love* in 1970 and 1971, respectively. They were ambitious, eclectic releases that explored the tenets of soul, jazz, blues, and other facets of American music. Yet when disagreements over direction and leadership clouded the picture, in 1971 Maurice promptly dissolved the Warner lineup. He started over in early 1972, having left Chicago for Southern California. The second time around, he was advised to enlist a group of young, eager players he could guide and who would inject more vitality and energy into the group.

That's how I came to join Earth, Wind & Fire. I was a twenty-one-year-old "country" lad, arriving in Los Angeles from Denver with a pregnant wife and a large duffel bag—big enough to hold my conga drums.

Maurice, the tall, slim, and dapper singer, composer, and drummer of EWF, had auditioned and then assembled an ambitious eight-piece group of mostly anxious rookies. I was the third member to join a lineup that included me as a singer-percussionist, Maurice's lanky brother, Verdine White, on bass, singer Jessica Cleaves from the slick R&B pop group Friends of Distinction, local Los Angeles drummer Ralph Johnson, horn player Ronnie Laws (younger brother of jazz flautist Hubert Laws), guitarist Roland Bautista, and keyboardist Lorenzo (Larry) Dunn, who had migrated to LA alongside me from Denver.

Spring 1972 had sprung some impressive R&B superstars and megahits: Sly and the Family Stone were at their creative peak with "Family Affair." The Staple Singers' "I'll Take You There" was a sexy across-the-board success, and Al Green tore it up with the silky "Let's Stay Together." All three became timeless smash crossover hits on both the R&B and Top 40 charts.

Earth, Wind & Fire had just been signed to Columbia Records. Things were happening pretty fast. We had just wowed the label staff at their national convention and were in the process of recording our Columbia debut album, *Last Days and Time.* Yet when it came time to hit the road and solidify our skills as a working road band in order to spread our musical gospel, we had a ways to go. Maurice had hit many a brick wall getting his band to the performing stage, so to speak. Whenever we had an important gig lined up, particularly on the East Coast, something would go wrong at the last minute, and the tour or the dates would be canceled. There were times when I was on my way to the airport, only to find out at the airline gate that our gigs had fallen through . . . again. It must have been doubly frustrating for Maurice, our fearless leader, though he didn't let on at the time. Later, I was to realize at first hand what a gargantuan and supremely demanding undertaking it took, year in and year out, to keep a band this large out on the road.

Even though we were newly signed to Columbia, these were the shoestring touring days of EWF. We'd load the band and our gear into station wagons and weave our way around the East Coast. We weren't exactly traveling in style, but we were safe; that is, as long as Verdine wasn't driving. We loved Verdine's solid bass lines, but he got the prize for being the worst driver in the band. He would jerk the wheel and head straight into oncoming traffic on busy city streets. Maurice had this big old twelve-passenger green van that we drove around LA. It was the only vehicle we drove besides Maurice's car. You can't imagine how that poor van looked after Verdine had driven it for a few consecutive days, all the dents where he didn't quite make the corners, the paint on its back and sides a mass of scratches and scrapes.

One day we received a call about a performance in Philadelphia. We agreed to do the gig for Georgie Woods, a legendary deejay and promoter who booked concerts at the Uptown Theatre, a 2,000-seater built in 1927 in Philly. The Uptown, at 2240 North Broad Street, was nearly as sacred as Harlem's famed Apollo Theater in New York City. It was part of the so-called chitlin' circuit, which African American acts toured on for years. (I would find out later that we had barely enough money to get to the gig in Philly. We would need to book some extra, fill-in college shows to earn enough money to make it back home to California.)

We were sandwiched in with two other acts on the bill at the Uptown, which also included an eleven-piece funk outfit called New Birth and the velvety R&B vocal group The Manhattans. New Birth, led by composer-producer Harvey Fuqua (who would later produce Marvin Gaye's album *Sexual Healing*), had a male and female lead-singer combo like us, but they also played James Brown–style licks and imitated the Godfather of Soul's vocal lines on one of their songs.

Talk that talk! Get on down! Get on the good foot!

The Manhattans were newly signed to Columbia, just like we were, but they were a more traditional doo-wop-styled harmonizing R&B group. Their latest radio song at the time, "One Life to Live," had a buttery spoken-word groove going, with seductive doo-wop harmonies underneath.

Compared to The Manhattans and New Birth, our music was sure to sound quite revolutionary, and far from what the more traditional black audiences at the Uptown might expect. We often threw in bits of free jazz mixed with African world beats, Afro-Cuban rhythms, and our own brand of layered vocals, which included Jessica's, Maurice's tenor, and my falsetto. Nobody was playing anything like that at the time. We included fusion-styled jams left over from the Warner albums, along with a unique arrangement of David Gates of Bread's "Make It with You." We would throw in an occasional Sly and the Family Stone cover for spice.

Earth, Wind & Fire had a lot of spirit and energy; we were still raw and bodacious. Maurice reminded us, "They're either going to like us or hate us. We don't want anything in between, and we don't want to be middle of the road, like those doo-wop groups." As for our look, Maurice encouraged us to be creative with our wardrobe. No way would we don matching suits like The Spinners, nor did we want to go onstage dressed down in jeans and T-shirts like The Allman Brothers. We aimed for a unique flair, only we didn't have much money for stage clothes. We raided the LA costume stores, the Capezio dance shops, and used-clothing joints in Hollywood, picking up anything that caught our attention as flamboyant and different. We wore long thermal underwear with brightly colored vests and makeshift belts! Our good friend Jean Jones crocheted big floppy knit hats for us—the same kind she knitted for Sly Stone in the early days.

When we arrived for load-in at the Uptown, the other bands on the bill looked at our motley troupe as if we were cuckoo—probably not too differently from how the pioneering hip-hoppers were treated by the older, more established African American music establishment. We paid no attention to the doo-wop bands. We were too much into our thing. The chitlin' circuit concept was old hat; to our young aggregation, it was definitely dated. Maurice had a loftier Concept in mind—one that would signify universal love and spiritual enlightenment.

After we finished our brief sound check, we told Georgie the promoter that we were headed back to our hotel. Georgie and his stage manager got very upset with us—we were breaking the Uptown tradition of brotherhood by bolting for the door early. "We don't do that around here," he explained to us. "Y'all stay here all day long until you hit that stage."

Maurice, thin and lean, had a certain swagger about him—a stylish look that he brought with him from Chicago. Both Maurice and Verdine wore sharp, citified short-brimmed hats, smooth silk shirts, and lean bell-bottom pants. With EWF, Maurice wanted to bring the same sense of theater and flash to the stage. EWF was about more than just playing songs and performing. But how would we distinguish ourselves from the other two bands on the bill that night?

Maurice assembled the entire group inside our cramped dressing room. "Here's what we're going to do," he said in the huddle. "When the curtain opens, we're going to be sitting on the stage, looking right back at the audience."

My response was skeptical. "Are you sure?"

"That's what we're gonna do," Maurice reiterated. "Then slowly we'll each get up and individually go to our instruments and start to play."

When we were introduced by the emcee, as the curtain rose, there we were, stoically sitting on the Uptown's dirty, sticky stage floor, staring back at the audience as if we were the masters of the universe.

We were roundly booed by the crowd.

We still didn't move.

Then came more hostility.

"Get off the stage! You guys stink!"

A typically tough Philly horde.

The audience laughed and heckled the band. But we remained motionless on the floor, in the lotus position as Maurice had coached us, transfixed in meditation mode, staring blissfully at the audience. Maurice reassured us: We should *sit and be silent.* As the hostile Philly crowd began to throw stuff onto the stage, we stared straight ahead, quiet as church mice. I was frightened but obedient to Maurice's vision. As things calmed down to an awkward pause, the crowd saw that we weren't going to budge. Maurice made the first move, playing notes on his *kalimba,* a small handheld hurdy-gurdy-sounding exotic African instrument that he plucked with his thumbs.

We opened our set with "Power," an extended instrumental jam the band had recently written in the recording studio. It started out quiet and peaceful with tinkling notes from Maurice's *kalimba.* Then Roland Bautista stood up, adding a tight but slightly dissonant wah-wah rhythm guitar. Ronnie Laws popped up next, grabbing his soprano saxophone and weaving in some fluid jazzy countermelodies. Then Larry Dunn added spiky clavichord changes from his keyboards. Our drummer, Ralph Johnson, kicked into a tight 4/4 medium-tempo backbeat. Next, Verdine slid into a hypnotic, rolling power bass line. Finally, I ran over to the congas and joined in. As the band kicked into high gear, the audience was now bobbing and moving to our new brand of rhythmic fusion. The EWF spaceship had just taken off, and the crowd stood up. The room was sonically airborne.

We blew the audience's minds that night. By the time the song was over, the crowd was wildly applauding. We'd won them over! As "Reese" (one of Verdine's nicknames for Maurice) was stroking his *kalimba* and leading the band, the people sensed that they were hearing something fresh and innovative, an intriguing extension of the whole pride and power movement and a brand-new human-potential experience. As proud African American men (and one woman), we knew we were onto something and that we had connected with our inner selves onstage as well as with the crowd. By the end of our set, we kept the audience on its feet. The heckling had turned into hoots and stomps, awarding us an encore.

The 1972 Uptown Theatre gig was ground zero for Earth, Wind & Fire. That night set a template for what was to be. We were the ones who broke ranks at that gig in Philly, dressed in colorful, flowing shirts, Capezio ballet shoes, draped in all sorts of chains, bells, and costume jewelry.

When we got back to the hotel in downtown Philadelphia, Maurice called an impromptu band meeting. We sensed something unique and very special had just happened that we needed to affirm together. We had hit our mark. It was a huge tribal, ceremonial moment for us. We had heard the people in the backstage area whispering behind our backs, "Them Negroes are straight crazy."

And maybe we were.

But we were also "strong about the Concept."

1

MOTHER WIT

From my earliest memories, there has always been music. It's as if music had been hardwired into my very being. According to my mother, I was singing in key—and rhythmically—before I was talking. I've always heard music in my head and understood its rhyme schemes, melodic progressions, and harmonic themes. Music makes perfect sense to me. It's an omnipresent force. I hear it in the wind and in the trees. I hear music in the washing machine, with its rhythmic cadences. It's in the squeaking of a wheel that turns round and round. The rattle and hum of machinery creates layers of notes or chord patterns, dissonant but structured.

I believe our essence is revealed the moment we're conceived and then growing inside the womb. As a young child, I assumed that everybody nurtured the same inner musical spirit that I felt. But then I realized that music was my special gift, and not necessarily a calling that everybody else heeded inside his or her inner consciousness. I can't think of a time when music wasn't the Pied Piper of my soul, leading me places, beckoning me, *Over here, over here. Come this way.* I've learned always to follow the music, and so far it's served me well.

My mother, Elizabeth Crossland, was born and raised in Muskogee, Oklahoma, and had one brother, Lilmon, whom we visited in Oklahoma numerous times while I was growing up. My grandparents on my mother's side, Lydia Scott and James Crossland, split up when my mother was young. She was raised by her mother alone. Times were especially hard for black folks in Oklahoma in the pre- and post-Depression eras. A lot of African American families were sharecroppers, and my great-grandparents had certainly experienced slavery in their day.

It was especially a struggle for black working folks to raise more than one child in the 1920s and 1930s. Uncle Lilmon and my mother were raised together until the hard times hit, and my grandparents struggled economically. My mother and uncle would then have to live apart, staying with different relatives over long periods of time. As a result, my mom and Uncle Lilmon had two distinctly different life experiences growing up. Lilmon got the "higher road" over my mother, partly because he was lighter-skinned. Lilmon stayed with relatives who were prominent pastors and teachers, while my mom lived with an aunt and my grandmother Lydia, who weren't nearly so well off.

Uncle Lilmon remained attached to his newly adopted family. He later went on to college, just as his only son later went to college, too. My mother, in contrast, took off during her early teens as soon as she could independently fend for herself. She first moved to Denver to settle in a climate that was more suitable for her asthmatic condition, as mountain air was thought to be a better environment for asthmatics.

In addition, she renewed contact with her father, James, who was stationed in Denver as a member of the air force, where he also worked as a barber. After my mother settled in Colorado, she created an expanded family with various friends and acquaintances, and Denver became her home for the rest of her life.

I was born Philip James Bailey on May 8, 1951, in what was at that time Denver General, but what is now called Denver Medical Hospital. I was raised in Denver by my mother, along with my sister, Beverly, who is one year older than me.

Because of the times in which we were raised, my mother was

ostracized by her peers, as both my sister and I were conceived out of wedlock. I have only vague memories of my biological father, Edward Alverna Bailey. Eddie Bailey already had a wife and children in Denver, not far from where we lived. Back in 1950 my father's wife invited my mother to stay with the two of them. Soon my mom and dad ended up getting involved sexually. As a result, my mother felt guilty, though after Beverly was born, Elizabeth and Eddie's relationship continued, and a year later I came along! Elizabeth gave birth to both of us while she was in her thirties.

In 1951 having children out of wedlock carried a social price. Eddie had three daughters with his first wife, the youngest girl being just a year older than Beverly. As a result, my upbringing was disjointed. I could not resolve the strangeness of my parents' relationship. Plus, there was the awkward circumstance in which Eddie's wife had befriended Elizabeth. Everyone in town knew that Elizabeth was involved with a married man with children. Not only was there shame attached to my mother's good name, but Eddie's original family also had to endure a lot of the scandal and gossip as well.

I was a "miracle baby"—as in, "it's a miracle he survived." I was born premature. In fact, my mom told me that the hospital had noted on my birth certificate that I was probably not going to make it. My situation was so touch-and-go that the doctors told my mother not to get her hopes up too high. I was sickly throughout the early years of my childhood. I remember having to go back and forth frequently to the doctor, because I suffered an acute form of spinal meningitis. I also inherited respiratory problems as a result of my mother's chronic asthma. There were many times when my mother had to rush me to the hospital. Sometimes she would have to call an ambulance. Most of the time, because we didn't have a car, we would take the bus to Denver General. During those frequent visits to the emergency room, I felt uneasy about my frail condition. The smallest incidents could affect my stomach, and I would vomit if I became too emotionally upset. The doctors gave me shots to treat the meningitis. I don't remember the injections being too painful, but we did have to wait for ages in the hospital lobby. One of my earliest memories of being in the ER was when the police brought in a shackled woman. I remember she looked like Lena Horne. She must have been a "lady of the night," and seeing her in irons upset me so much, I started vomiting.

My illnesses lingered until I was nine or ten, when the spells became fewer and less severe as I got older and stronger. Up until then I was bound to catch the flu once a year, and when I caught the flu, it caught me! I would get so deathly ill that my shoes would be too big by the time I got well again.

Elizabeth worked as a domestic, cleaning and ironing for the household of Denver oil tycoon Marvin Davis and his wife, Barbara. My mother also worked for Ms. Peggy Crane, a member of another prominent wealthy family in the city. We moved around a lot in Northeast Denver. I remember one time I kept a count: Between the first grade and high school, my mother, sister, and I moved more than fifteen times before Mom bought a house of her own for $9,500 on Pontiac Street, near the old Stapleton Airport.

My mother later adopted Eddie's last name, Bailey. Eddie stayed with us off and on, and my sister and I went through our early lives confused as to whether or not my father and mother were ever legally married. Turns out they weren't.

African American migration made a significant impact on areas like Colorado. Many African Americans, especially those who had been living in the South after the Civil War, began to spread around the country, particularly after the American Industrial Revolution of the late nineteenth and early twentieth centuries. The African American population shifted to the urbanized Midwest, the North, and the West Coast. Blacks left rural sharecropper lives and migrated to city industrial centers like Detroit and transportation hubs like Denver and Chicago. (More than 60 percent of

African American migrants to Colorado ended up in Denver, not counting the black men who became cowboys, working the range and the ranches throughout western states like Colorado and Texas.)

Black families like the Crosslands came to the Denver area to work for the railroad. Throughout 1914 and 1915, during the First World War, black workers filled the labor void created by the cut-off of cheap European immigration into American urban centers. Even black women could get jobs for two to five dollars a day by filling positions in meatpacking houses in Chicago or automobile factories in Detroit.

Improved health care and better jobs were also offered in states like Colorado, as opposed to the squalor in Deep South states like Alabama and Mississippi. Racial violence against African Americans, which occurred in cities like East St. Louis and Chicago from 1917 to 1919, confined blacks to certain neighborhoods. Denver was a small city at that time—and even smaller in terms of its black population.

The African American community in Denver remained fairly concentrated compared to those in other big cities in the United States. In 1957, when I was in the first grade, my sister and I were the only black children in our grammar school. Later, once we moved to Park Hill in the northeast section of the city, I attended a mixed primary school called Columbine Elementary (not to be confused with the Colorado suburban school of the same name that was the site of the 1999 student massacre). At the time the city had one black junior high school, Cole Junior High; and one black high school, Manual High School.

The most popular social gathering point for African Americans in Denver was the Five Points neighborhood, where five streets converged in the northeast corner of the city and formed a vital central community. By the 1890s a viable black middle class had arisen there. The area was home to many churches and black businesses, restaurants, drugstores, saloons, newspaper offices, barber shops, doctors' and lawyers' offices, and other establishments. Every Sunday after worship, if a person had a car, he would drive down to Welton Street in the Five Points and make sure he got a primo parking spot, because the district was a mob scene every Sunday afternoon. After church you could hardly get through the area because of the number of people sitting in their cars, watching the world go by, or parading around wearing their Sunday best, cruising and just hanging out. It was a family affair, and after the sun went down, the kids would go back home while their parents returned and partied for a few more hours.

A lot of the men who lived in the Five Points worked for the railroads. Some were Pullman porters; others were in the military. Schoolteachers, preachers, shopkeepers, businessmen, and other elders and respected members of the black community congregated in this small sector of commerce. There were at least a dozen bars, nightclubs, and restaurants, and most people patronized all of them. As a result, everybody knew everybody else's business; so once you gained a reputation, they knew about you.

During the *I Love Lucy* decade of the 1950s, families in Denver, generally speaking, had a very simple set of moral values—especially regarding fatherless children like me. In the neighborhoods where I grew up, people would think nothing of asking me, "Philip James, where are your mom and dad?" Unless your mother was a widow (or possibly divorced), some families wouldn't let you play with their kids if you came from a "broken" home.

I was raised mostly around women. As a kid, I had lots and lots of "aunties," although they weren't real aunts by blood. Elizabeth's friends were people much like her—single women who liked to drink, dance, entertain boyfriends and have a good time, and tip a few on the weekends.

One of my earliest childhood memories, a vivid recollection that's indelibly etched in my psyche, involves my mother and Eddie Bailey. At the time I hadn't started kindergarten, so I must have been about three years old. There was constant emotional turmoil in their relationship, and as I later found out, it was mostly because Eddie was wavering as to whether or not he would leave his other family for ours.

It was a cold, wintry night during a bad blizzard, and my sister and I were huddled in the backseat of the car. At the time, Eddie Bailey was finishing up another hitch in the air force and was stationed at a nearby military base in the city. In those days black airmen lived in segregated shacks. He had just been stationed north to Idaho, and had made the major commitment to leave his first family and take us there with him.

I recall my mother screaming hysterically at my father, telling him that she was not about to uproot her children to Idaho to live in some military tenement and freeze to death. As a result, Eddie completely lost it and got out of the car to grab a crowbar from the trunk. My mother locked the door and wouldn't let him back inside. My father stood outside in the frigid air, screaming and waving the crowbar. After this fight, Eddie Bailey left for Idaho, and their relationship ended.

I recall another incident when one of my mother's boyfriends came over to the house late one night, cut up from an encounter at a card game. Back then, you could easily get cut or robbed while gambling. A guy would make fifty bucks and want to double or triple his cash by shooting craps in the back room of a pool hall. If you played around with the wrong guy, he'd rob your stash or take you out with a knife. My mom didn't take up with too many rowdy men. In fact, this guy was a pretty nice fellow, though a bit country, like me.

You never quite knew what you were getting, psychologically or otherwise, with my mother. She displayed a wide range of moods, ranging from loving to extremely short-tempered. Beverly and I had grown used to our mom's erratic behavior. She had two sides to her personality. One was the sentimental, loving side; the other was governed by a very unstable disposition, which meant she could lash out at any time. Looking back, I suspect that she might have been manic-depressive, or bipolar. One minute she'd sob and cry, and the next, she'd be tender and affectionate, smothering us children with kisses and hugs.

I was very close to my mother as a child. Sometimes when "Bevvy" and our friends would get into mischief or throw rocks, I would be the one to break ranks and tell when my mom wanted to know who had misbehaved. Then my mom would hug me affectionately and tell me what a good boy I was.

But Elizabeth was rough on my sister. When I was twelve years old, she threw a pan of hot water at Beverly. Maybe she saw a lot of herself in her daughter. The two would argue furiously, and Mom would call Beverly a bitch and a whore. Later, my sister got pregnant and had a child at the age of fifteen.

In the midst of the volatility, we did our best to cope with everything that came our way. Unlike my sister, I didn't suffer abject abuse from my mother—verbal or physical—although as kids, we both received vigorous whippings. By today's standards, these were whippings that would have resulted in a parent's drawing heat from a child-protective agency. But as was common practice among traditional African American families at the time, I often had to go outside to the tree in the yard and select my own switch. On more than a few occasions, I would go off to school sporting some serious welts.

My mother encouraged us to speak our minds, and we felt free to voice our opinions or feelings. She had a bizarre sense of humor and displayed a strange way of parenting. Mom said some very cruel things to me and my sister—and I wonder if she realized it at the time. Once, when Beverly and I were getting on my mother's nerves, she threatened to put us up for adoption! We had a "play" auntie who had adopted a boy—he was a few years older than us—so we had heard firsthand scary stories from him describing what it was like to live in foster homes and to be on your own.

My mother didn't know when to let up. "All right, you kids!

Pack up your stuff because you're both moving out! The adoption people are on their way to come get you," she once threatened, and Beverley and I ran outside to the swing set, crying our eyes out. I made a solemn promise to my sister that day: "I'll come and find you." Foolishly, my mother didn't come out and tell us that she was kidding.

Another time, when I was very young, my mother warned me that if I didn't finish my dinner, I would die of leukemia. Once again, she didn't take back the comment, so I believed her. That night I sat in my bedroom, terrified, sobbing and thinking that I was mortally ill. We were going to a Catholic church at the time, so I recited the Lord's Prayer over and over until a strange spiritual presence settled in the room, giving me assurance that there was a God out there looking over me.

We didn't live in any tenements or in rundown apartments and only spent a brief period in the Denver projects when I was very small. On occasion, though, when times were tough, we'd move in with my grandpa Crossland until Elizabeth could get back on her feet again. My mother had a fierce common sense ethic. She called it "mother wit." Elizabeth would say, "That person may be smart, but they don't have no damn mother wit." My mother had acute common sense. As a result, her employers loved her, and the Davis and Crane children would often confide in her, almost as if she were family. Elizabeth could talk to anybody, and despite her hot temper and shortcomings raising us, she was a very gregarious person to socialize with.

While my mother worked for the Davis and Crane households, there were many times that Beverly and I would have to stay at home by ourselves—especially when Elizabeth's employers were out of town. My sister would have to take care of me on her own—and she was only a year older. At other times, when the Cranes went out of town or on vacation, Mom would take my sister and me to work with her. Bringing us along was as much about showing us how the "other half" lived as it was for her maintaining peace of mind, knowing that we weren't stuck at home by ourselves. During that time, I picked up a childhood phobia—a fear of abandonment—after being left home alone too long.

I did have a distant friendship with a man my mother was married to from the time I was nine years old until I was seventeen. Robert James Combs was a short-order cook and chef for the railroad who loved to play the saxophone but who had forsaken a career in music in order to help provide for our family. I don't think my mother loved Robert but had married him in order to survive. I never had a single in-depth conversation with the man. It wasn't that Robert was mean. On the contrary, he was a taciturn and remote fellow. At home at night—when he wasn't drunk—he would walk through the door, sit down, nod at me, and routinely ask, "How ya doin'?" We had so little to say to each other, only once did he raise his voice at me.

"Did you hear what your mother said?"

I was so shocked to hear his unexpected outburst that I wet myself. His deep male voice scared the hell out of me! I remember one time he showed me and my sister how to slice vegetables without cutting ourselves. Apart from that, there wasn't a bonding moment between us. Robert was a goofy guy. Although he was a professional cook, he didn't prepare a single meal for me or my sister at home. Many years later, he came to visit me in Southern California and nearly drowned in my swimming pool—in the shallow end, in only three feet of water! Robert James Combs was not the sharpest guy in terms of either intellect or charisma.

Robert tolerated my mother's violent moods, never raising a hand to her, even when the pressure of her tumultuous behavior got to be too much. One night he came home late, a little tipsy, carrying a set of bongo drums and a small puppy under his arm. And then the shouting began. In an outburst of rage, my mother pulled out a carving knife and slashed at Robert and threw him out of the house.

Outside on the porch, Robert angrily hurled our metal milk box through the front window, smashing it to pieces. In retaliation Mom, wearing her most stylish pointy shoes, dropkicked Robert's new puppy through the shattered window. Amid the screaming and cursing, my sister and I hid beneath the covers in my bedroom, petrified with fear. We had heard their fighting before, but never this loud and intense. Next we heard the sirens of an ambulance, and then the police arrived. As Robert was taken to the hospital, I surveyed the damage to our tiny home, which was littered with busted furniture, broken glass, and trails of blood on the floor. Miraculously my mother wasn't carted off to jail that night.

When Nicky, my aunt's husband, left for work on the railroad, a guy named Banks, used to sneak in through the back door to secietly visit my Aunt Mae. Banks turned out to be a pretty pleasant guy. We would go out walking whenever he came over.

But as I watched Robert passively submitting to my mother's fierce temper, I also watched him forgo his musical dreams. That had a lasting and profound effect on me. Unlike my sax-playing stepdad, I vowed that one day I would realize my own musical dreams, and before long I would seek success as a professional musician with the ultimate aspiration of becoming a shining star.

2

"BAILEY, GET OFF THE FIELD!"

There were childhood incidents and memories that made a huge impression on me in my quest to become a musician. At the age of six I wanted to play saxophone, like my stepfather, but my mother was afraid that blowing a horn would aggravate my respiratory issues.

During the summer my mother would send me to Kansas City to visit Aunt Alice in nearby Leavenworth, Kansas. One day my auntie took me to a parade near the town square of Leavenworth. I was so small at the time that I couldn't see anything from the sidewalk. I was this tiny kid stuck in a sea of legs and humanity, looking out from among a forest of people twice my size.

But I could hear and feel a tremendous thundering force of rhythmic sound.

When I ran out of the crowd to get a better look, I saw a glittering marching band strutting down the avenue in flawless formation, wearing brightly colored matching uniforms. It was a full band and drum corps, and the awesome power of its beat put the zap on my head. I could feel the full range of percussive impact—particularly the bass drum and the snares—in my chest. My whole body reverberated. I felt as if my heart were going to thump out of my body.

Back home in Denver my mother had a small area of the front yard cordoned off with chicken wire to keep the hens that laid our eggs from running off. The perimeter of the chicken wire was held up by small wooden poles that were a little fatter than regular drumsticks. I pulled a couple of the sticks out of the ground, grabbed a trash can, turned it over, and made my first attempt at playing the drums. I banged nonstop so hard and heavy on my makeshift drum that eventually my mother surrendered and bought me a real drum.

During that time my mother took Beverly and me down to the dog races with her. Toward one end of the grounds was an orchestra that performed as the dogs raced around and around the track. My mother would sit us kids up in front of the band to keep us occupied and out of trouble while she and her friends gambled and drank. She could place me in one spot and didn't have to worry about my straying, because I was going nowhere! It must have been a thirty-piece orchestra, and I was transfixed watching the conductor.

My mother had a friend named Erlene Love whose young daughter, Phyllis, was about the same age as me. Erlene's live-in boyfriend played upright bass in a jazz quartet. When we visited them we found loads of jazz records lying on the living room floor. Whenever the adults would play those records, I would lie quietly on the floor, absorbing the sounds of classic jazz and bebop. I found out later that most of the LPs in the collection were from the Blue Note Records catalog, so I was able to listen to topflight artists like the young Tony Williams, Joe Henderson on tenor saxophone, and Philly Joe Jones on drums. Listening to jazz made me feel like I was flying.

Because it was the 1950s, the jazz that was popular with my mother and her friends included the music of Lionel Hampton, Duke Ellington, Morgana King, Nancy Wilson, Ella Fitzgerald, and Sarah Vaughan. Whenever they were in party mode, the women would listen to the more popular R&B sounds like Little Richard's as well as the blues. After I became acquainted with jazz, my mother married my stepfather, Robert, the ex-saxophone player, who had his own jazz record collection that he also played around the house.

My mother would occasionally take me out to a club in Colorado Springs where her nephew was gigging. He played the alto sax, and there was another horn in that ensemble, a tenor sax. I remember their slick routines up on the bandstand. One night when he opened up the case, I got to see his horn up close. It was this gleaming, shiny instrument lying in a smooth bed of purple velvet. How regal it looked! That night I went home, bent a curtain rod into the shape of a saxophone, and took a broken clothespin and stuck it into the end of the curtain rod for my reed and mouthpiece. I found one of my mom's suitcases and put padding inside for my "horn." Then I walked around the house playing "professional musician" going to a gig with his horn case.

Soon the performing bug bit me. There was something called a "show wagon" that came around to different parts of the city in Denver every summer. It was a traveling stage, and they would audition young people, and if you were good enough, you could perform at different shows at parks, recreation halls, and other venues. One year I got up the nerve to audition. I was in the fourth grade. I rehearsed the song I had to learn, but when I got up to sing it, my voice wouldn't work—not a sound came out of my mouth. It was a humiliating experience. About a year later, after we moved to East Denver, I auditioned again with a friend of mine named Philip Buckman. This time "the two Philips" passed the audition, entered the talent contest, and actually won a prize. That was the beginning of my winning talent competitions; I discovered that I was a pretty good vocalist.

From the time I was in grade school, everywhere I went, you didn't see me without a pair of drumsticks in my hand. I'd walk down Columbine Street, twirling my sticks. I first joined the school band in the fourth grade, where, by the time I was ten, I had learned to read music properly. Later I played the drums in the junior high school band, and I made it to the All-State Band.

Luckily I'd come up through one of the best school systems in the country. Denver was an ideal place for music education! We were taught about the entire family of instruments—brass, woodwinds, strings, percussion—and how they sounded (I could tell the difference between a tuba and a sousaphone, a tenor and a baritone saxophone, a glockenspiel and a xylophone) and harmonized together, like an oboe with a clarinet or French horns with trombones. We also learned about different styles of music, including Native American, and they even brought in the Air Force Band to play for the schoolchildren.

As a preteen, I played the snare drum, but once I joined the high school orchestra I began to play other percussion instruments like the bells, tympani, glockenspiel, and marimba. I took part in various musical ensembles, including vocal madrigals and brass, string, and woodwind groups. I had the chance to see and hear music on a firsthand basis and got a deep education. The funny thing was, at the time, it didn't feel like I was getting educated.

I had developed a sixth sense when it came to learning how to play a new musical instrument. In junior high school I walked into stage band and noticed they didn't have a bass player. So I picked up the bass fiddle and joined in. The teacher, Mr. Richards, asked me, "Philip, do you play bass?" He was amazed when I told him I had never played before. I was simply goofing around, but somehow it fit, and playing it made perfect sense to me. It turned out that Mr. Richards, sent me to a bass teacher who was a principal bassist in the Denver Symphony Orchestra. After calling my mother, he arranged for me to receive private lessons. The school loaned me a bass to keep in my house! To get to my lessons I would climb onto the bus carrying my gigantic bull fiddle.

My aspiration in high school was to play in the symphony and become a professional percussionist. I was a huge fan of drummer Harvey Mason when he was a young session man. I gazed in awe at the magnificent CTI Records four-color gatefold albums that he'd drummed on. (CTI, short for Creed Taylor Incorporated, was the mastermind of jazz producer Creed Taylor, who had also helmed Impulse! Records in 1960.) I studied the pictures and credits of his recording dates. I knew when Harvey played marimba on this record or tympani on that one.

I'd march to school playing my drums as loud as I could. I played constantly through middle school and high school. I was in the concert band, stage band, marching band, and drum corps, and also joined the choir. Plus I had my garage bands on the side where I played drums, sang, or did both.

After years of winning talent contests and putting bands together, I bought my first drum set for fifty dollars. It had that customary glittering silver metalflake finish. It came with a cymbal, snare, tom, and bass drum. We lived on Madison Street at the time, so I must have been in junior high or middle school. Getting my own set of drums was quite a major deal. I could either form or join bands. The drums were also a way that my mother disciplined me as I got older. When I grew too big for her to whip me, or if I didn't do what I was told, she'd say I couldn't play at such-and-such a gig on a Friday night. If she told me I'd have to miss the gig, I'd break down crying, explaining that she was hurting everybody else in the band. But she didn't care; it was her only effective form of discipline.

I was *not* a great athlete in school. In fact, I was hopeless. I had one unlucky incident on the baseball team, which I'd joined only because I liked the way their uniforms looked. But the first time I tried to field a ground ball, the ball shot up my arm and hit me right in the throat. I couldn't breathe for a while, and that was the end of my baseball career, over and done with.

Another time I decided that since I could run pretty fast with the football, I would try out for tight end. I lined up on the end and ran out for a pass. I was quickly tackled and got the wind knocked out of me. As I lay there stretched out on the grass, the coach yelled, "Bailey! Get off the field!"

Finally, I tried out for basketball at Denver's Red Shield Center. I was so scared they were going to put me in the game that I nearly peed my pants. I was sitting on the bench and the coach looked over at me and shouted, "Okay, Bailey, you're in!"

I was so nervous that when someone passed me the ball, I dribbled as fast as I could until I noticed that nobody was guarding me. Turns out I had dribbled toward the wrong basket!

I held a lot of jobs as a kid. Coming from a single mom's household, if I wanted extra money, I had to work. My days started early—cutting grass, delivering papers, doing odd jobs. At fourteen I washed dishes at a Walgreen's café. Then I worked at the Denver airport. Those jobs helped me to see only what I did *not* want to pursue as a career. Going to work with my mom and watching her toil away as a domestic inspired me to do whatever was necessary in order to become a proficient professional musician. As a result, I practiced hard and worked my butt off, the final reward being that I could do something creative with my life.

Every week I sang in the church choir with my longtime friend Steve Dyson. Dyson and I had both gone to Columbine Elementary School and later held jobs together at the high school. "Dice" and I would show up in the morning and again in the evening to clean up around the school. One day Dyson noticed a milk truck parked with its doors open, revealing bottles and bottles of chocolate milk.

"Go get the milk," Dyson ordered me.

I did precisely what Dice told me and put the milk in my car. But instead of just grabbing two or three bottles, I nabbed a whole crate. When I got home and pulled into the driveway, my mother spotted both me and my illicit cargo.

"Philip, where did this milk come from?"

"Dyson and I found it. It must have just fallen off the milk truck."

"Philip James, did you steal this milk?"

"Dyson told me to grab it."

"Take that milk back!" my mom screamed at me, and I did. It

only proved one thing: that I was more frightened of my mother's wrath than I was of getting caught stealing.

Otherwise, I was a well-behaved adolescent. My sister's first husband was what you might call a gangbanger, though on a much less serious level. He was put in reform school and later on was sent to jail. His kind of lawless behavior scared the bejesus out of me. Getting in trouble with the cops wasn't anything I needed to pursue. I remember a fourth-grade teacher at Gilpin Elementary School named Mr. Davis, who told me that I was not going to amount to a hill of beans. Now I wonder, why would someone tell a kid that? Yet for some reason, those memories stick in your mind as you grow older, waiting for the day when you can prove them wrong.

Music gave me self-esteem, a way to live and a destiny that sheltered me from being fatherless and having to move all the time and deal with family instability. Unfortunately, my sister didn't develop the same safeguards and ambitions to help her out as she grew up.

While I wasn't rebellious, I did have a cocky attitude, which drove my mother crazy. By the ninth grade, when the music teachers at school saw that I had musical promise, I thought I was pretty hotdog. One day I sassed a teacher. We had a night rehearsal for a big year-end concert recital, and I lived about twelve blocks from the school. The teacher had warned everyone in the band to be on time at six-thirty. When he caught me arriving a few minutes late, he locked the door on me. I was so angry that I picked up a rock and shattered the window. That little stunt ended up getting me expelled. After my mom went down to the school to see the principal, she was far from sympathetic to my side.

"You know what?" she told the principal in her typically stern, colorful way, "If he thinks his shit don't stink, then don't let him play in the recital either."

Because of my mom and my attitude, I missed the recital. In retrospect it was the best lesson I could have learned . . . and one I never had to learn again. It was the lesson of arrogance. Boy, did I get set straight. The band had worked so hard, and here I was, one of the primary performers in both the band and the choir, missing the biggest gig of the year. It was crushing; I was devastated. But I learned.

Interestingly, Beverly and I have developed entirely different outlooks about being raised by a single parent. I never pined to have a dad around or felt sorry that I was a fatherless child. Nor did I feel a void or that there was something radically missing in my life, like male companionship. Maybe it was because I was a confident young man. Later on, after I gained more life experience, I saw that there was something missing in my own life, pieces which, had they been in place, could possibly have enabled me to make some wiser choices and do some things a little better and smarter. (I'll elaborate on that later.) All in all, though, I wasn't too shook up about it.

That was not the case with my poor sister. She harbored a lot of regret and carries baggage about our early life to this day. She not only suffered from not having a father around, but she often took the brunt of my mother's brokenness, too. Even today, she's working through it.

That's why I emphasize that the circumstances of your birth must *never* determine who you are or rule your destiny: what you are to become. Nor should they determine the significance of what you're striving to accomplish in life or how you plan to contribute to the world . . . to become that shining star!

That's why I send tiny messages out to my Twitter and Facebook fans. I call them "Shining Stars"—they contain little, positive messages about what's on my mind or in my heart. I started out in life as a "miracle baby." First, I could have been aborted. Second, I could have died from early illnesses. Third, based on the circumstances of my upbringing, I could have become a nonachiever—not to be confused with being a lazy underachiever. A nonachiever is a detriment to society instead of a credit to the world.

Fortunately my mother had that "mother wit" of common sense to help me through. She possessed a good barometer for reading people, a talent that I picked up from her. I consider myself a quick judge of good and bad character. From around the corner, I can sense people who are trouble. If we're lucky, we can inherit positive attributes from our parents that can set us in the right direction. Conversely, we can pick up their negative traits, which can put us on the wrong path. And believe me, I've had my fair share of situations where I found myself traveling down that particular path.

3

SOMEBODY SAY AMEN!

Between the ages of fourteen and sixteen, I sang in a large gospel choir called the Echoes of Youth. It was composed of fifty or sixty voices and was an impressive and powerful vocal entity. We traveled from Denver to Los Angeles to perform during the Watts riots in August 1965. Echoes of Youth was a fantastic experience for a young singer like me, an opportunity to hang around a congregation of amazing vocalists and musicians. Some were more talented than I was, and some were accomplished bandleaders and multi-instrumentalists. Their virtuosity gave me something to strive for and compete against. I found that what I lacked in ability, compared with some, I made up for in initiative.

As a budding high school musician, I practiced and practiced to get my shot at becoming a professional. Soon, instead of washing dishes and doing yardwork, I began playing the drums at casuals with various Top 40 cover bands. The first time I was paid a few dollars for playing a gig, I was blown away.

"You can get *paid* for playing music?"

Before I could even legally drink alcohol, I was playing several sets a night in bars and nightclubs all over Denver. Among music circles they used to say that it didn't matter how old you were, whether you were black or white, handsome or ugly, skinny or fat . . . as long as you had the chops and could jam on your instrument or sing well, there was a place for you if you wanted to work in the clubs in Denver.

As a young player, at fifteen and sixteen years old, I led a double life. I would perform at the school proms and the talent shows during the daytime. I also played sock hops in an old warehouse converted to a teenage canteen called the Jackson Center. In the evenings I would play five sets a night through the week in the good-time bars and nightclubs in Five Points. There were also a couple of after-hours joints that I would play on the weekends—the Voters Club and a place called Protocrat's. An ex–basketball player named Wayne Hightower opened a swinging place called 23rd Street East and ran it with his brother. It would later prove to be a very important music venue for me in the Denver area.

Soon I moved from behind the drums and percussion to become a spotlighted lead singer. I formed a local doo-wop harmony band called the Soul Brothers. Clarence Dale Hinton sang with me in the group along with another vocalist, Winston Ford (now deceased). Dale was a funny and clever kid, a year younger than me. He was a fantastic singer with a great ear, and became a positive influence in developing my musical tastes.

Another one of my groups was called the Dynamics. Then I played in an R&B / Top 40–flavored band called the Mystic Moods. Those early shows mainly consisted of my singing R&B cover tunes. My bandmate Dale Hinton would come out and do a James Brown–inspired number, which included throwing off his shirt, much as the Godfather of Soul did with his cape on his famous 1964 T.A.M.I. show appearance. I would follow Dale and sing a sweet doo-wop love ballad called "Rainbow," made popular by Gene Chandler. That became my signature tune, and it drove the ladies crazy. I loved to sing the hits by The Temptations, Dionne Warwick, and The Supremes and mimic the falsetto of the Tempts' lead vocalist, Eddie Kendricks.

Throughout my early days I met interesting and talented musicians in Denver, particularly a boyhood friend, Larry Dunn. Larry was two years younger than me, so I was like a big brother to him. Larry started out playing organ and keyboards and became very proficient at re-creating the latest hit sounds from the radio. He could pick up on horn parts from different records, which he would then re-create on whatever keyboard he was playing.

Larry was born in Denver. His mother was Italian and his father was black. When they were married in 1950, they had to get hitched in Mexico because it was illegal in Colorado for a white and black couple to legally marry. As a child prodigy, Larry learned to play Beatles songs on the guitar, took piano lessons, and played the baritone horn and trombone in the school orchestra. As a preteen, Larry never had to be told by his mom to practice; rather, she had to make him stop and go to bed. His first love soon became the organ, and he worshipped at the altar of jazz virtuoso organist Jimmy Smith. Larry learned the great Jimmy Smith organ jams like "The Sermon" and "The Champ" on the Hammond B-3 by playing Smith's albums at 16 rpms on his turntable so he could imitate the soulful licks and solos.

Larry and I started playing together in the clubs when I was seventeen and he was fifteen. Larry had just gotten permission from his mother to play the over-21 clubs with his band. In the beginning we would show up to club gigs wearing fake mustaches to make ourselves look older. Then we realized that the owners didn't care if we were underage.

One night we shared the bill with both of our bands. Larry played covers like "Grazing in the Grass" by Hugh Masekela while my band, the Mystic Moods, featured our three frontline singers in seamless harmony. Larry dug us when I sang a sweet, simmering version of a Curtis Mayfield and the Impressions tune called "Moonlight Shadows." Soon we ended up merging his band of players with my three singers and starting up a brand-new group. One night the veteran R&B group The Whispers came through Denver and saw us play. They were amazed at how young and talented we were. Later when Young-Holt Unlimited, fresh from their 1968 smash hit "Soulful Strut," came into town and caught one of our shows, they were knocked out, too.

Larry and I played every different genre of music, from rock to jazz to R&B to doo-wop to oldies to Top 40, and everything in between. We performed up and down Colorado together and played in many "groovy" cities and resort towns such as Vail, Aspen, Breckenridge, Fort Collins, Greeley, Boulder, all the way west to Grand Junction. Many of our audiences were predominantly white. The farther away we played from the Five Points district, the more rock and Top 40 material we added to our repertoire. At that time one of my favorite groups was Grand Funk Railroad, the hard-rock power trio from Detroit.

Larry and I explored different styles of music as we regurgitated everything we heard on the radio—from pop bands like Three Dog Night, Santana, and Rare Earth to the hard-core blues bands from Chess Records in Chicago. We also dug some of the R&B doo-wop singing groups, though I was especially influenced in 1969 by the psychedelic soul of The Temptations during their "Ball of Confusion" / "Papa Was a Rollin' Stone" Norman Whitfield period. Larry and I also played in a lot of jazz/rock/R&B bands that featured horn sections mimicking Blood, Sweat & Tears and Chicago Transit Authority. By 1970 I had moved toward the more organic singer-songwriter sounds of Carole King and James Taylor.

We regularly played the partying college town of Boulder at a club called the Hornbook and packed the joint every night. The owners loved us. We served up everything from James Brown to "Jumpin' Jack Flash" by The Rolling Stones, as the drunken white crowds stood up on the small round tables and went crazy as we wailed onstage. The Hornbook burned down in 1972 following a sensational two-year run.

As a working, traveling musician, I had to learn early how to keep an audience engaged and how to pack the room in order to satisfy the club owners who smiled as we kept their cash registers ringing throughout the night. I never had problems holding an audience's attention—and don't to this day! Whether we were playing for a few hundred or a few thousand people, we tailored the intimacy of each performance to whoever hired us to entertain. I learned a lot playing to tough audiences in those Rocky Mountain taverns and clubs.

Although I was making a decent living as a musician while in my teens, I was country at heart. What I loved most about playing music in Denver was that I didn't have to deal with the whole racial challenge. The fortunate thing was—and I realize this doesn't apply to a lot of urban black musicians—Colorado taught me how to deal with people as just, well, people. And that's how I relate to audiences today; I don't trip on anyone's color or race.

Even though my mom worked as a domestic housekeeper, she didn't come home complaining about racial oppression. She didn't speak with disdain about white folks as devils. And she never planted those notions in my head. She taught me about good and bad people—of every skin color. Again, I fully realize this may not reflect other people's racial experiences in the United States. Maybe I was the lucky one. I didn't suffer the indignity of being profiled and harassed by the police. By the same token, because I wasn't the lawless type, I wasn't hassled by "the man" to any great extent.

The one thing I most regret in life is not having grown up in a larger, more traditional household. Today, when I look at my children and grandkids, I see the broad network of support they enjoy from having a mother and father, brothers and sisters, grandmothers and grandfathers plus cousins, uncles, nieces, and nephews encouraging them to accomplish their goals in life. I didn't get the kind of encouragement, attention, or personal sustenance I needed, having only a mother and a sister. While my mother nurtured me in terms of achieving success, most of the time she wasn't able to attend my shows or live performances. She was too busy working, putting food on our table. As a result, we rarely shared the glory of my early musical achievements.

My early life as a professional musician threw me headfirst into the adult world, and my sexuality came alive. I wasted little time: I fraternized with the older female customers who often hung around in the bars after shows, to the point where my friends began to call me out on my "slutty" behavior. I once got sexually involved with a tall, thin older woman my friends jokingly called Sergeant Sam. There was also a white woman whom I had eyes for and used to see on the side. I found it strange: While the giddy junior high and high school girls I went to school with eyed the cute athletic boys on the football and basketball teams, I was ensconced in the clubs, hanging out and getting it on with horny, freewheeling older women. Although I was part of the public-school social scene at Cole Junior High and Manual High, I wasn't the type of flashy, colorful dresser that most of the girls were interested in. The cute, curly-headed schoolgirls I fancied wouldn't pay attention to me because, in their eyes, I was too skinny and dark-skinned, and I dressed down in shades of black and brown.

Looking back, playing around with older women wasn't the most ideal situation for me, especially as a young teenager just getting initiated into the world of sex and intimacy. Playing in bars and nightclubs, *I* was the one who was ripe for the picking, not the women. I learned later that during a young person's sexual awakening, there needs to be a high level of emotional maturity and intelligence that precedes intimacy and physical attraction.

I guess most guys would say, "Wow! You lucky dog! What's wrong with all that female action?" But when a young man starts thinking, as they say, with the little head instead of the big one, problems eventually appear on the horizon. Scoring women at such a young age, I was giving up the power of my sexuality—and not the other way around! (Later on, I would write one of my very best songs, "Reasons," which tackled that very subject.)

As I would learn, my lack of sexual maturity created an emotional imbalance that was difficult—but not impossible—to repair later on in life. I found that sexuality plays such an inestimably strong part in establishing our identities and decision-making processes that you can lose your ability early in life to love and to sustain a proper relationship. Then, without realizing that you're broken, you live out your "brokenness" over and over again in every relationship that follows. (More on that later.)

When I think about the circumstances of my conception, I have to wonder, what were my parents thinking? Were they chasing the sexual act without the relationship? There was a lot of collateral brokenness, pain, regret, guilt, and shame there that would be passed on to me and to my sister.

I grew up with my mother and sister, and I did have plenty of close female friends. I thought I understood women simply because I was around them so much. I would listen to them talk and foolishly think that I understood them!

What I should have learned as a young man but didn't, was that the sexual act is a demonstration of love and relationship. Instead I'd be chasing the thrill of the sexual act, mistaking it for true love and a meaningful relationship, when it's neither. Later on I would come to understand that once you act out sexually before establishing a loving relationship, you end up chasing your tail for a very long time.

Now, somebody say amen!

4

THE FREE SPIRIT

I met my first wife, Janet Don Hooks, way back in the fourth grade when I first played the snare drum in the color guard that brought out the flag at Columbine Elementary School. Janet was a year behind me. I threw newspapers on her block during the winter. She and her sister would run out of the house and empty my papers onto the ground in the snow. We weren't boyfriend and girlfriend at the time, but we both went to the same church and shared the same teachers in school. My mother was acquainted with Janet's mother and father, and Janet and my mother and sister would play a little bingo-type game at our house for pennies and nickels. When my mother worked late, Janet and I would have parties at my house. We ditched school together, much to the ire of Janet's parents. One night when my mother was out of town, we took the car out during one of our party runs and broke the key inside the ignition. Later we had to scramble to fix it before my mother got home and threw a fit.

Janet liked to be different. She cut and styled my locks and braided my hair. We were good "hanging out" buddies because Janet wasn't possessive about my fraternizing with the various women I saw in the clubs at night. Later on, when I was in high school, she began dating a handsome saxophone player named John, who was in the school band. I remember telling John to back off because I really liked her and that we were now more than just buddies. So she and I started seeing each other, and soon we had a serious relationship going while I was a senior and Janet was in the eleventh grade.

In 1968 Janet became more outspoken than most of the high school girls I knew. What got me interested in her as a girlfriend was her big Afro and her nice round booty ass. She was one of the first girls in school to wear her hair in a big proud Afro. Janet spoke her mind and followed me and my music instead of hanging out with the usual high school crowd. Janet watched me play tympani and other percussion instruments in the large All-State orchestras and sing in various gospel choirs.

Janet loved to head down to the nightclubs and hang around with me when I played. She was also a good seamstress and sewed crushed-velvet stage costumes for me to perform in. At the end of the night, after the last set, she would help me break down my equipment and load up my car. Janet and Larry Dunn were my two closest pals at the time. We were "the three stair steps": me the senior in high school, Janet a junior, and Larry the sophomore.

The year Janet graduated from high school, I got her pregnant. Her mom didn't like the fact that I was a working musician, and hated that Janet and I were so close. One day she took me aside and said, "Philip, you either have to marry Janet or stay away from her." In my heart I felt I owed it to Janet because she had been loyal to me. So I asked her father for her hand in marriage, and he approved.

I was initially attracted to Janet's free spirit. She was into going out to the clubs at night, sneaking out and misbehaving along with me and the other musicians. She had a bohemian streak about her, though neither she nor I knew at the time what the heck that word meant. She was content in her role as my high school girlfriend, and in having the fella that the other nightclub girls coveted. Yet she also longed one day to be married, have children, and live in a big house with a nice white picket fence out front, just like any traditional young woman at that time.

Janet and I were wed on June 19, 1970—Juneteenth, which was also Larry Dunn's birthday. (Juneteenth is also known as Freedom

Day, an American holiday celebrated by African Americans in more than forty states, commemorating the abolition of slavery in Texas in 1865.) I was nineteen when we tied the marriage knot. I admit that I married Janet with only halfhearted intentions of being faithful. Why? Because fidelity and faithfulness were not major components of my upbringing, and weren't the norm where I grew up. My mother had several men, and most of her girlfriends enjoyed numerous casual relationships with guys, too. By nineteen, I was already well initiated into casual sex.

The year after I graduated from high school I was accepted to Metropolitan State College to study classical music. I started classes there in the fall of 1969 while moonlighting as a musician. At one point I tried to contact my father, Eddie Bailey, to see if he could help me qualify for student financial aid based on the fact that he had served so long in the military, but my attempts to reunite and communicate with him were unsuccessful.

Janet graduated from high school on June 12, 1970—the week before we were married—and received a scholarship to attend the University of Colorado in Boulder. When she showed up that summer to register for fall classes, they placed her in the married family housing section. As a result, I spent more and more time at her school in Boulder until I briefly transferred there to start my second year of college. During that time my band, the Mystic Moods, played a slew of dates at the Hornbook, as we booked more gigs outside of Denver in order to be close to the Boulder area.

But Janet and I lasted less than one year at the University of Colorado. I left college after four semesters; I realized I no longer had ambitions to become a full-time classical musician. Although I loved classical music, I didn't see myself playing it exclusively. Soon I was offered a job to play in Kansas City, Kansas, at a brand-new nightclub called the Fifty-Yard Line—so named because the owner was a former NFL star who had played with the Kansas City Chiefs. My good buddy Larry had recently married his girlfriend, Debbie, so the four of us decided to relocate to Kansas City together.

Our time away from Colorado would last only about a year. We moved back to the Denver area in 1970 after Janet's uncle hired us to work at his cleaning service, which renovated old houses and turned them into office spaces. We took the job because it would allow us to work around my busy music schedule.

My last band in Colorado was a mixed group called Friends & Love. We had originally called ourselves Electric Black and performed mostly cover material but when we changed our name to Friends & Love, we played less R&B and added more of a contemporary Sly Stone/rock/pop feel to our repertoire. Friends & Love was a large ensemble with three frontline vocalists, including me on vocals and percussion. The other singers were Carl Carwell and Winston Ford. Larry played organ alongside a smoking rhythm section, and we later hired two white guys to play saxophone and guitar. In addition to R&B and jazz, we were influenced by the acid rock of the day as well as by progressive black musicians like bluesman Taj Mahal and contemporary jazz singer and poet Gil Scott-Heron. While I didn't consider myself to be the leader of Friends & Love, I was in charge of making sure the band rehearsed often. Janet liked it that I could put an interesting spin on our song arrangements so that they wouldn't sound like the original recordings, but more like our own material.

Although we had three lead singers, we didn't follow the model of The Four Tops or The Temptations, singing and dancing in front of the group. We were more like Three Dog Night or Sly and the Family Stone, incorporating different lead vocalists within the group. This would prove to be a very important distinction that would later result in my participation in a whole new style of the contemporary live-band experience.

Happy couple that we were, Janet and I became the proverbial Colorado hippies, roaming the state in our VW bus with our bed in the back. It was the counterculture era, and songs like "Psychedelic

Shack" and "Cloud Nine" were all over the airwaves. Like a lot of other young people in 1969, we experimented with drugs. Back in the more innocent, pre–Charles Manson flower-children days, you could trust people. There were parts of Denver where makeshift communes and minicommunities thrived and where hip folks could congregate and hang out. We lived, learned, and carried on. It was an extremely idealistic time in my life. Oddly, many of those former free-spirited hippie types have gone on to become some of the most conservative and rigid people you could ever meet.

I must admit, my hippie days were the most flowery and wonderful days of my life. Natural food, good weed, fine mescaline . . . and acid, occasionally. We didn't smoke a lot of weed because at the time we didn't have enough money to spend on marijuana. Instead, we would place a dose of mescaline on our tongues. I had learned about mescaline and magic mushrooms from an interesting horn player I met in Denver, a guy named Andrew Woolfolk, who was a year older than me.

Before John Denver sang "Rocky Mountain High" and "Take Me Home, Country Roads" on the radio, Janet and I drove our VW up to Boulder early in the morning and journeyed into the mountains. We would watch the sun come up—an extraordinary experience on mescaline. We went up there many times, and during one sunrise Janet began to weep so hysterically that I thought she might be bum tripping.

"What happened?" I asked her. "What's the matter?"

"I can see."

"See what?

Turns out that she had just gotten a proper pair of eyeglasses, and when she saw the sunrise clearly for the first time on mescaline, it was so beautiful and powerful that she broke down in tears.

Janet and I enjoyed a very carefree relationship. Together we were vagabonds, moving easily from one situation to another with a minimum amount of planning, hassle, or commitment. We would book tickets for a holiday train trip into the Rocky Mountains through a travel company called Jack and Jill. Instead of skiing, we would drop acid and marvel at the mountainous vistas in the country, and I would fish. Janet and I made love in the open air, one of our favorite romantic pastimes.

We also had magical times at the music festivals, breathing the clean mountain air. At one outdoor concert in Washington Park, Jimi Hendrix and Buddy Miles jumped up onstage and serenaded the crowd. It was a timeless period of unparalleled optimism, featuring amazing musical heroes and icons like Jimi and Buddy.

So, would I recommend drug use to anyone? No, especially not today. The open-mindedness of the bygone days of the late 1960s was a sign of the times we lived in, and by the grace of God I made it through okay experimenting with natural substances. Luckily neither Janet, myself, nor anyone I knew suffered any bum trips or went crazy. The late 1960s was a unique era, a completely different, innocent environment, especially when compared to the current use and abuse of corporate pharmaceuticals like cocaine, methamphetamine, Oxycontin, Ritalin, and powerful medicinal marijuana.

I won't lie to you: I enjoyed getting high and experimenting with drugs. Once, though, I did a show high and thought that I was something else onstage! It felt great performing stoned—that is, until I heard a tape of the show. I sounded awful! So I decided enough of that, forget the illusions. My music was far too important, particularly when it came down to the quality of the music as opposed to the quality of the high.

God watched over me during that crazy countercultural era! For instance, one day as I was driving on the freeway, I slowed down to make a turn in the center median to reverse direction. I was struck at high speed by a dump truck that was also attempting to make the same U-turn in the middle of the interstate. The collision seemed to take place in slow motion, and I was catapulted out of my funky VW bus headfirst. Flying through the air, I landed hard on the ground. The impact of the crash knocked the shoes right off my feet. At first I thought my legs were broken. In a state of adrenaline delirium, I got up and ran for the roadside and saw that the VW was totaled—completely demolished. The ambulance and the police came to take me to the hospital. I suffered one lone scar. They put my foot in a cast, but once I got home, I took the cast off and climbed into the bathtub.

A week later there was a similar accident on the same stretch of freeway involving similar vehicles, except that everybody involved was killed instantly. When I went down to inspect my totaled Volkswagen bus, I thought about how I'd been spared and how I'd cheated death by surviving the crash. I didn't see my survival as an act of happenstance. I felt as if God had a plan for me.

My new domestic life with Janet progressed quickly. At twenty years old and soon to be a father, I had a three-story house with a basement and big front and back yards. I was now a provider. Working "normal" jobs in the real world had only reminded me how much harder I would now have to work in order to accomplish my creative goals and dreams as a musician.

I hadn't become a working musician simply to accumulate worldly possessions. To me it wasn't about delusions of grandeur or the glitz and the glamour. My equation for success meant honoring the purity of the music while trying to imitate the sounds I constantly heard bouncing around in my head!

5

THE MOST INTERESTING MAN IN THE WORLD

The most influential music person I met in Denver was a man named Perry Jones. To me, Perry was the most interesting man in the world. He had everything going for him. He had a life full of experience, including service in the war in Vietnam and a stint as a radio deejay. He was fashion forward and a real ladies' man. He sported a giant Afro and carried himself like a male model. He was a mover and a shaker. And like me, Perry played the drums.

Raised in Des Moines, Iowa, Perry listened to Wolfman Jack and was hosting teen sock hops at thirteen. One Christmas night when the Viet Cong had mercilessly bombed Perry's battalion's compound in Southeast Asia, the USO canceled the holiday party. In response Perry staged his own music show for the troops. Coming home from Vietnam, Perry left Des Moines and resettled in Denver and soon became "psychedelicized." He would later describe himself as a "Rocky-Mountain-hippie-meets-Superfly."

Perry got turned on to hard-rock music and underground radio and worked with famed Colorado music promoter the late Barry Fey, helping Fey stage concerts featuring leading acts like Joe Cocker and Country Joe & the Fish. With the advent of FM underground rock stations—most notably free-form, highly rated KFML in Denver—Perry deejayed progressive music ranging from

Tom Rush to King Crimson to Muddy Waters. Six years after the 1964 Civil Rights Act, Perry saw the 1970s as highly charged and revolutionary. He watched in awe as R&B music transformed itself from the traditional music of the chitlin' circuit to the psychedelic hybrids of rock and soul.

By 1970 Funkadelic had trumped the sounds of Jimi Hendrix and Sly Stone with a farther-out blend of blues, funk, and psychedelia. Even earlier, regional labels such as Chess Records had been pushing the envelope with ambitious bands like the Rotary Connection, a group decades ahead of its time, which featured an amazing five-and-a-half-octave lead vocalist named Minnie Riperton and a master arranger named Charles Stepney. Rotary Connection was just one band we loved that experimented with innovative and progressive arrangements of rock, soul, and jazz and that were hallucinogenic and "out."

One night in 1970 Perry visited the 23rd Street East nightclub and saw a fantastic band tearing it up on the bandstand. It was Friends & Love. Jones loved our sound and saw our potential. Because of our mutual interest in mixing divergent styles of music, he and I struck up a fast friendship. Perry instantly became a mentor to me and the other members of the band, especially Larry Dunn.

After Perry first saw us play onstage, he pulled me aside and said, "You guys are great. One day you're gonna make somebody a whole lot of money."

Then he began his critique.

"But the next thing you need to do is change your act!"

Perry advised me to step out a little. Play the congas and percussion while you sing! He had just seen an incredible show at Mammoth Gardens in Denver featuring a band called Eric Burdon and War. Their hit "Spill the Wine" had crossed over big-time from underground radio to Top 40 audiences. Although Burdon was best known as the white front man of the legendary British

Invasion band The Animals, his latest conceptual band, War, featured a nearly all-black lineup that included one other white member besides Burdon, Lee Oskar on harmonica. War was quite revolutionary for its time. Perry saw us in that same vein.

Another touchstone band that put the zap on Perry's head was Santana. Led by the San Francisco Mission District–based guitarist Carlos Santana, Santana was immensely popular in Denver, combining hard-driving rock and roll with Latin percussion and rhythms and a strong sensibility of the blues.

Perry was the first truly professional record promotion guy I had met. He worked out of Denver for Transcontinental Distributing, a regional record distributor responsible for promoting singles and albums to local AM and FM radio stations. Perry also serviced retail outlets throughout Colorado; Utah; parts of Nebraska and Kansas; and Phoenix, Arizona. He'd walk into the local radio stations and record stores with a box full of the latest LP and single releases from Transcontinental's product lines, which included Warner Brothers, United Artists, Liberty, Mercury, and Roulette. Perry soon became the conduit that turned me on to brand-new, happening music. I would hang out at his apartment and sort through the two hundred singles and one hundred album titles he received each week.

Perry deeply influenced my constant thirst for new sounds. We would listen to important new artists like Joni Mitchell and Crosby, Stills & Nash as well as more obscure ones like Baby Huey from Chicago. James "Baby Huey" Ramey led a rollicking band called Baby Huey and the Babysitters. He recorded for Curtis Mayfield's Curtom Records, where pianist-arranger Donny Hathaway served as his arranger. Baby Huey weighed between 350 and 400 pounds—which is how he got his name, from the cartoon character. Huey later died of a heart attack resulting from his heavy intravenous drug use.

Meanwhile, Friends & Love, buoyed by Perry's enthusiasm,

became one of the most popular bands in and around the Colorado area. We frequently played Denver's top two clubs, the 23rd Street East and the Shapes. For the time being, I was happy with the band's regional success and my ability to make a decent living for myself, Janet, and our baby that was on the way.

6

NEW HORIZONS

Change was heavy in the air for me and my friend Perry Jones in 1970. Earl Wolf, Perry's boss at Transcontinental Distributing, had alerted him that that he might be in the running for a very interesting position in the music industry. At the recommendation of Earl and a few other people, Warner Brothers Records contacted Perry and flew him down to Puerto Rico to interview him for a new promotional position that was opening up at the label. Perry was ecstatic; this could be his dream job.

Much to his delight, Perry was interviewed by two legendary Warner Brothers record executives, label president Mo Ostin and executive vice president Joe Smith. Warner Brothers and its sister label, Reprise Records (started by Frank Sinatra), were quite well known for being a progressive record label group that was also very artist friendly. In 1967 Ostin had attended the fabled Monterey Pop Festival and signed The Jimi Hendrix Experience to Reprise. Warner Brothers also had given two of its top artists, Peter, Paul and Mary and the Grateful Dead, unprecedented full artistic control over the music they recorded and released on the label.

Headquartered in Burbank, California, instead of New York City or Los Angeles, Warner Brothers was a major creative juggernaut in the record business. During the time Perry was interviewed, it was in the process of expanding its empire to become Warner Communications, adding two more legendary labels, Elektra Records, founded by folk maverick Jac Holzman, and the R&B beacon Atlantic Records, to its conglomerate roster.

In the fall of 1970 Perry was offered the chance to be the first black national music promotion director in the history of Warner Brothers Records. (His official position was "national promotion director for special marketing," and for unknown reasons, Warner chose not to include the word "black" in his job title.) What a break! The label had elected to expand its promotions-executive roster to incorporate a full-time staffer like Perry, who would help develop African American acts signed to Warner. These acts included the soul-funk outfit Charles Wright and the Watts 103rd Street Rhythm Band, the progressive and eclectic ensemble Earth, Wind & Fire, and a few new signings, including a gospel-flavored group called The Stovall Sisters and the esteemed jazz pianist Herbie Hancock, who was entering an exciting phase of experimenting with electronic instruments à la Miles Davis's *Bitches Brew.*

Warner had made the financial commitment to ramp up a new black promotion department partly at the behest of ex-NFL football great and actor Jim Brown. In addition to starring in movies on the Warner film lot, Brown had an eye to start managing music acts. He had advised Warner Brothers that starting a black music department would be in their best interests if they had aspirations to expand their black-audience horizons and blossom into a full-service, full-format label similar to the large East Coast entities like Columbia and RCA.

Perry phoned me, excited about his new job. He quickly relocated, moving from his apartment in Denver into a sunny duplex in the Hollywood–Los Angeles area on Crescent Heights Boulevard. It was an unbelievable turn of events. Perry had hit the big time, and I was genuinely pleased for him. If anybody could handle such a groundbreaking position, it was Perry.

Of course, Perry wasn't shy about extending a special invitation to me, his dear and loyal friend. "Philip," he said, "if you would ever feel like coming out to Los Angeles, just give me a call."

I could hear the wheels turning in Perry's head as we spoke. He was a man of ideas.

Perry began his job training with Warner Brothers when Ostin and Smith sent him to New York City to spend a few weeks with the crack promotional squad at Atlantic Records. Atlantic was arguably the most successful R&B label in history, with superstars like Aretha Franklin and Wilson Pickett recording under its famed banner. Atlantic label executive Ahmet Ertegun, like Ostin and Smith, had already moved the famed R&B and jazz imprint toward mass-appeal rock success by signing Led Zeppelin and Crosby, Stills & Nash in 1969. Atlantic and Ahmet were also in the process of stealing The Rolling Stones from stodgy London Records.

When Perry later reported to work at Warner's Burbank offices, he was introduced to Maurice White, bandleader of Earth, Wind & Fire, and the two hit it off immediately. Perry later visited Maurice's apartment so they could more fully discuss the concept that White envisioned for his band, and what promotional efforts they could undertake together to break them nationally. Maurice believed that music had a positive, life-affirming power that could change the world. He also believed that our bodies are sacred temples and that music, like a proper diet and lifestyle, could raise people's consciousness a few notches and elevate their personal goals. Music could have a cleansing effect on its listeners, and could be more than just background noise against which to party or get high. The two had a very long, philosophical, and productive talk as Maurice spelled out his musical vision in grand detail, describing how he hoped to transcend the genre of R&B and create a blend of other musical forms that encompassed jazz, blues, and rhythms from around the world. Face-to-face, Perry was mesmerized by Maurice's extensive and persuasive ideas, which borrowed from many religious and global truth-seeking sources. While listening to Maurice elucidate his lofty ambitions for Earth, Wind & Fire, Perry's love for hippie, free-form rock and new kinds of soul music came flooding back into his psyche.

7

"REESE" AND VERDINE JR.

Maurice White is ten years older than I am. In terms of life wisdom and experience, a ten-year difference is a significant amount of time, almost a generation.

Maurice White was born December 19, 1941, in Memphis, Tennessee. He grew up very poor in the projects on the south side of Memphis. Like me, he became obsessed with the drums as a kid and played in the drum and bugle corps. His mother, Edna, had left Memphis to start a new life in Chicago and married Dr. Verdine Adams Sr., a podiatrist. Maurice remained in Memphis and was raised by his grandmother. Every year Edna would send for young Maurice, and he would journey from Memphis to visit his extended Chicago family, which included young Verdine Jr. and Maurice's half-brother Freddie. All three stepbrothers became passionate about music at an early age.

Although they were technically half-brothers, Verdine Jr. looked up to Maurice as a full-blooded older brother. While the ten-year difference in their ages would have made it likely that the pair would find separate paths socially, such was not the case with Maurice and Verdine. Throughout his childhood Verdine, built tall and slim like Maurice, preferred the company of older people to kids his age. The two were close, and Verdine undoubtedly viewed Reese—Verdine's nickname for his older brother—as the ultimate hipster and all-around cool guy. On the other side of the coin,

Maurice was an astute listener and observer of the young. Reese respected Verdine, and the two communicated freely with each other and exchanged ideas about the one thing they truly had in common—namely, their mutual devotion to music. The synergistic relationship between the two would later play a key role in the evolution, formation, and reaffirmation of Earth, Wind & Fire.

Shortly after graduating from high school, Maurice left Memphis in 1960 at the age of nineteen and moved in permanently with his mother and stepfather in Chicago to begin a new life in Illinois. Chicago at that time was a de facto segregated city. African Americans lived in one area; Asians in another; and Italians, Jewish, and Polish residents occupied their own sections of town. People very rarely crossed from one neighborhood to another. For the first ten years the Adams family lived in a housing project. Then with the advent of the 1960s civil rights movement, activists like Dr. Martin Luther King Jr. targeted Chicago as one of the prime battlegrounds for their fair-housing campaigns. At the time, Dr. King worked with a young Chicago community activist named Jesse Jackson to help African Americans secure home loans in their neighborhoods. As a direct result of those efforts, Verdine Adams and his family moved to the South Shore area of Chicago. Because Dr. Adams (called Pops around the house) practiced medicine, his family was upper middle class or "bourgey" (short for bourgeois), as Verdine likes to describe them.

Once settled in the Windy City, Maurice proved to be an extremely talented drummer and was able to secure session work with Chess Records. Founded by Polish immigrants Leonard and Philip Chess in 1950, Chess was possibly the most respected record company in the city. Although other pop and R&B labels like Mercury and Brunswick were also headquartered in Chicago, Chess, along with its subsidiary imprints Cadet and Concept, as well as Chess Studios, was respected for its innovations, particularly in the fields of blues, rock and roll, jazz, and R&B. Chess enjoyed worldwide respect, especially among top British Invasion rock and roll groups like The Rolling Stones.

Maurice served as a session drummer for many prestigious Chess artists, including singers Etta James and Betty Everett and vocal group the Dells, plus blues legends Muddy Waters and Buddy Guy, and played on such timeless Chess jukebox classics as "Rescue Me" by Fontella Bass and Billy Stewart's modern pop renditions of "My Guy" and "Summertime." Maurice's time at Chess also taught him music production and the ins and outs of the music business.

Verdine watched with awe at how well his brother progressed as a hired-gun studio musician. Maurice had that charisma, that confidence, that *thing*. To Verdine, Maurice was as slick, urbane, and worldly as a Miles Davis or Sam Cooke. In a comparatively short time, he had the world on a string, and there was no limit to what he could accomplish as a musician.

A Chess session that took place on Monday could be mastered, pressed, and ready to go out to radio and retail by Friday. Every week Maurice would bring home the next hot batch of new 45s and acetates, white-label copies marked "demonstration record only, not for sale." Verdine would proudly play them on the family record player. What a thrill! As youngsters, Verdine and Freddie visited their sophisticated brother when he worked in the studio, which fueled their ambition to one day become professional musicians themselves. While Dr. Adams had hoped to see his namesake attend medical school, young Verdine was already gravitating toward a career in music.

In 1962 Maurice left the family home in South Shore to share a place with a young saxophonist named Don Myrick, whom he had met in the studio. He and Myrick joined a few other of their studio comrades to form a band called the Jazzmen, which included trombonist Louis Satterfield and pianist Jack DeJohnette, who would later make his mark as one of the jazz world's premier drummers. The Jazzmen played a lot of gigs around town, and the Adamses would regularly go out to watch them perform in the clubs. Although Verdine and Freddie were too young to frequent nightclubs, Maurice shared photos of the gigs with his younger brothers.

During that time the Jazzmen won a notable competition at a large Chicago musical gathering called the Harvest Moon Festival.

In 1966, at the age of twenty-five, Maurice hit the big time when he joined the Ramsey Lewis Trio. Lewis was a very popular jazz pianist on Chess's Cadet label, and had scored his first major national crossover hit in 1965 with the timeless party anthem "The In Crowd." Maurice replaced drummer Isaac "Redd" Holt, who had departed along with the trio's bassist Eldee Young to form the soul-funk ensemble Young-Holt Unlimited, which went on to record "Soulful Strut," a giant instrumental hit in 1968.

At fifteen, Verdine watched his older brother play live under the stars with the Lewis trio at the Ravinia Pavilion in Highland Park. Maurice was a heavy, powerful drummer, adding subtle theatrical elements to Ramsey's live sets. At the end of a performance, each member might exit the stage individually, one after another during the final number.

Maurice would remain with the Ramsey Lewis Trio for three highly productive years. Ramsey was a great role model for young Reese. Lewis did things with a lot of class and style, and he taught Maurice the art of stage production and leadership and advised him to keep his standards high. Maurice toured the world and recorded nine LPs with the Lewis trio. One of those albums, *Another Voyage* (1969), included a two-minute piece called "Uhuru," which featured Maurice performing on a small handheld instrument called the *kalimba*, or African thumb piano, which Reese found in a Chicago drum store.

During his tenure with Ramsey, Maurice lived the good life in a fancy Chicago penthouse. Verdine would often visit his brother's pad on Maurice's rare days off. The product of a new era, Maurice had become quite worldly and wise at a young age. Jazz success had given him the opportunity and confidence to spread his wings and conceptualize future musical ideas that he might want to pursue. Contemporary music was expanding its borders—especially in genres like jazz, progressive rock, and R&B. In addition to local musicians like Louis Satterfield and Don Myrick, Maurice worked with skilled studio arrangers like Tom ("Tom Tom 84") Washington and the highly talented producer-arranger Charles Stepney. All of these contacts would prove highly valuable to Maurice in the future.

During this time Verdine began seriously taking bass lessons after having messed around with the instrument for about a year. Maurice introduced his younger brother to a veteran Chicago bassist named Bill Terry, who played in a jazz style similar to that of the late Scott LaFaro of Bill Evans Trio fame. Maurice and Terry presented Verdine with an amazing gift that would forever change his life: his own acoustic bass! Just as when my old music teacher Mr. Richards did it for me, having an upright bass was a stone luxury for Verdine, who could now practice nonstop at home without the hassle of being a skinny kid schlepping the bulky instrument back and forth on the Chicago Transit Authority. As he worked toward mastering the instrument, Verdine took lessons with Maurice's old studio pal Louis Satterfield. Maurice also arranged for Verdine to study with an acclaimed classical musician named Radi Lah, bassist with the Chicago Symphony Orchestra. With Lah's classical tutelage and Satterfield's slammin' R&B and jazz approaches, Verdine became completely immersed in "the bottom line." On Sundays Verdine would head over to Louis Satterfield's house, where "Sat" would teach Verdine how to swing while reading studio charts.

Along with his jazz and classical studies, Verdine was deeply influenced by the pop and R&B hits he heard on the radio. It wasn't long before he glided over to the electric bass, which proved to be an easy transition. The electric bass opened new doors for him, and like me, the teenager began to audition to play in bar bands. In the summer of 1967, at the age of sixteen, he took his funky red bass on the bus up to Chicago's North Side to buy himself a shiny new Fender Telecaster bass. Because Verdine didn't have enough money for a case, the music store salesman stuffed the Telecaster into a paper bag and sent him on his way. Verdine's new axe made quite a statement.

It was white and pristine—and nobody his age had one! Only the pros—like Satterfield himself—dared to play a flash white Telecaster. A year later Verdine bought an Ampeg B-15 amp—again, the same set-up Satterfield played on his record dates. In order to raise money for more lessons and make back the $160 he spent on the Ampeg, Verdine helped his dad during the summer, working as a hospital orderly. By his junior year in high school, he was musically on fire. Thanks to Reese and his older brother's influential friends, with access to great teachers and top professional gear, he was ready to roll.

Verdine and I were on a parallel trajectory. In order to spotlight his hot new gear, Verdine played at local high school talent shows, just as I had. On the weekends—also like me—he played Top 40 and R&B bar band gigs. When he became first-chair bassist in Illinois's All-American High School Orchestra, he excitedly informed Satterfield, who was quick to put him back in his place.

"First chair?" was Louis's lukewarm response. "That still means y'all are playing the same bass parts, ain't it?"

Carmen Dragon, who conducted the Hollywood Bowl Orchestra, came to Chicago as guest conductor of the All-American High School Orchestra. He arrived wearing an expensive camel hair coat and matching scarf, a fashion statement that impressed Verdine immeasurably. During rehearsals, the student players, including Verdine, were extremely nervous playing in front of the maestro. Dragon spoke fondly of his young son, Daryl, who at the time was playing in rock bands in California and cutting sessions in Los Angeles with The Beach Boys. Daryl went on to become the "Captain" of Captain & Tennille with his wife, Toni Tennille. Years later, when Verdine and Daryl met, he reminded Dragon that as a teenager, he had played in an orchestra that Daryl's father had guest-conducted.

In April 1970 Maurice White took a major gamble: He gave Ramsey Lewis notice that he was leaving the trio. It was a very risky—borderline insane!—move at the time, especially with the wide success Reese had enjoyed being Ramsey's well-paid sideman. But throughout Maurice's time with the Lewis trio, he had been carefully mapping out on paper and in his head a concept for a new kind of musical adventure. When Maurice explained to Ramsey that he was leaving to put together a larger, more experimental pop ensemble, Ramsey calmly told him to "take an aspirin and go back to bed." But Reese didn't go back to bed. He hung up his jazz shoes and with two studio keyboardists, Wade Flemons and Don Whitehead, formed a group that wrote songs and commercials in the Chicago area. Chess's Cadet arranger Charles Stepney, impressed with Maurice's new songs and catchy commercial spots, dubbed him with another unlikely nickname, "Rooney," as in "Rooney Tunes," a play on the cartoon series Looney Tunes. Soon Maurice's trio scored a recording deal with Capitol Records and cut two singles under the name the Salty Peppers. One of their songs, "La La Time" became a midchart hit in the Midwest, while their second single, "Uh Huh Yeah," completely stalled, causing them to lose their label deal as quickly as they'd scored it.

Undaunted, Maurice had a much bigger concept in mind. He planned to expand his group to eight pieces, change its name, and rather than keep headquarters in Chicago, he would relocate to Los Angeles! Reese's concept called for the formation of a unique and limitless-potential band that could cross over numerous genres of music, much like what we were experimenting with in Denver with my group, Friends & Love.

While Verdine feared that his brother was treading on dangerous professional ground, Edna and Verdine Sr. were upset that their son would leave such a cushy gig with Ramsey. They dug Ramsey; he was successful, and Reese was doing great just playing drums in the trio. To start a new band—with eight pieces!—and leave Ramsey, who was a big name with not one but two pop hit records (the second was "Wade in the Water") was unfathomable!

Yet Maurice saw things differently. He realized that Lewis's credibility had taken a serious hit with the hip New York jazz players because of his crossover success. And as popular and well respected as Chess Records was during that time, it was limited in its ability to sell records and break and develop acts, compared to the larger East Coast–based labels like Columbia, Decca, and RCA or West Coast labels like Capitol and Warner Brothers. Chicago would always take a backseat in the music business. When Verdine went to a free summer concert in Chicago's Grant Park with the late, great rock and soul singer Baby Huey, he was amazed to realize how Huey had failed to become a big star outside the Midwest. Meanwhile, another act on the same bill, Sly Stone, recording for CBS-owned Epic Records, would soon explode into an across-the-board crossover star. Who knew?

As Maurice prepared to leave for the West Coast, the unthinkable happened: He called Verdine and invited him to come to California with him! At the time, Verdine had safe and firm plans to stay where he was and—like me, in Colorado—to enjoy being a big fish in a smaller pond. He was also on track to study classical music in Chicago. He had already been awarded a full-ride, four-year scholarship to attend music conservatory, along with an inside track to becoming a premier session player in the Windy City. With Maurice heading west, Verdine had had stars in his eyes to become the next Lou Satterfield.

When Verdine announced to his mother and father at the family dinner table that he was going to California with Maurice, they laughed as if he were telling the joke of the evening. Looking back, even Verdine didn't realize the magnitude of his decision. Moving to California with Reese was a monumental step, and as scary for him as my blindly leaving Denver for LA would be for me. By splitting Chicago, Verdine was turning his back on some potentially lucrative opportunities.

Reese's and now Verdine's announcements rocked the Adams household to its core. Up until then nobody had left the family nest, much less young Verdine, the gawky, skinny, nineteen-year-old with buck teeth and pimples, weighing in at "a buck-o-five." In the end Pops Adams, the family patriarch, gave the boys his heartfelt blessing, and by 1970 the brothers were on their way to greener Southern California pastures to navigate the uncharted musical horizons of Hollywood. Upon leaving the family in Chicago, Verdine (and later Freddie) made the symbolic gesture of familial solidarity toward his older brother by adopting the White surname. Maurice and Verdine White were on the road to make their bones in sunny Southern California.

8

CITY SLICKER, COUNTRY BOY, AND A YELLOW KAZOO

Maurice had formed Earth, Wind & Fire in Chicago in 1969, with Verdine on bass and Wade Flemons and Don Whitehead, the two keyboardists from the Salty Peppers. He added singer Sherry Scott and a Chicago percussionist who called himself Yackov Ben Israel. Yackov Ben Israel's real name was Phillard Williams, but the band nicknamed him "Fee Fee." He was one of the first dudes the Whites had met who wore an earring—a Star of David.

The auditions continued in Los Angeles, where Maurice and Verdine hired a guitarist from Southern California named Michael Beal and added a horn section with Chester Washington on woodwinds, trumpet player Leslie Drayton, and trombonist Alex Thomas. True to Reese's expanded dreams and schemes, the band had swelled to a ten-piece group! With so large a lineup, the group was quite raw in terms of defining its roots and its musical direction. Would it borrow from jazz, soul, R&B, rock, blues, or all of the above? Maurice dubbed the band "Earth, Wind & Fire," based on his astrological sign, Sagittarius, which had elements of fire and the "seasonal qualities" of earth and air (i.e., wind)—whatever that meant!

Upon arriving in Los Angeles in 1970, Maurice scored a major coup for his fledgling band. After being introduced by a mutual friend to Jim Brown, Brown had agreed to become Earth, Wind & Fire's first manager. Jim was one cool customer and had set up an organization in Los Angeles called BBC, short for Brown, Bloch and Coby, featuring Brown along with talent rep Paul Bloch and entertainment lawyer Richard Coby. BBC managed the slick R&B pop group Friends of Distinction, which recorded for RCA. BBC had also intervened on behalf of heavyweight boxing champion Muhammad Ali after Ali had refused conscription into the army in 1967. The sports powers-that-be had called on Brown and the BBC organization to meet with Ali. Brown enlisted an envoy of African American dignitaries to try to help resolve the deadlocked problem. Afterward Ali fought his draft-evasion charges and government prosecution all the way through the appeals process.

During the explosive late 1960s, the American people had become bitterly divided over the United States' involvement in the Vietnam War. Many publicly challenged Ali's personal integrity and accused him of being a draft dodger. Four years later, after being stripped of his boxing titles and licenses, Ali was exonerated by the Supreme Court. Resuming his boxing career, Ali later went on to become the World Heavyweight Champion three times in a row.

In June 1970 the Whites were invited to attend a Hollywood party at Jim Brown's house. Reese scowled when Verdine put on his finest suit, one he had worn in high school the year before. It was decidedly unhip, so Maurice took his gangly younger brother down to a Hollywood Boulevard boutique and bought him some bell-bottom pants, a pair of sandals, and a big floppy hippie vest. As the pair approached Jim Brown's house on Sunset Plaza Drive, Verdine was jet-lagged from his Chicago flight.

Brown opened the door and greeted the musicians. He said, "Welcome to the family, young man," to Verdine, who felt both intimidated and impressed to be in the company of the football legend.

It was as if the brothers had stepped onto the TV set of Chicago's

Playboy After Dark! Reese and Verdine surveyed the room, which was filled with famous celebrities, including movie star Richard Roundtree of *Shaft* and the Temptations' lead vocalist Eddie Kendricks. Verdine immediately knew that he had made the right decision to move to Los Angeles, and that this was the beginning of an unbelievable musical journey.

Maurice and Verdine took up temporary digs at the famous Landmark Motor Hotel at 7047 Franklin Avenue in Hollywood. Rock musicians like Jim Morrison, Janis Joplin, and Alice Cooper regularly stayed there, and five months later, in October 1970, Joplin would die from an accidental overdose of heroin in room 105.

Jim Brown and BBC soon arranged a record deal with Warner Brothers Records for Earth, Wind & Fire. Joe Smith, the label president and an ex–disc jockey out of Boston, was an astute record exec. He was not afraid to dabble in and experiment with new forms of contemporary music and he signed EWF to a multirelease deal. The label arranged for Earth, Wind & Fire to conduct its early rehearsals on the Warner Brothers film lot in Burbank. It wasn't a glamorous setting; the place resembled a large, empty barn. But the band dutifully set up its gear, and its self-titled debut album was released in late 1970. It sold a respectable twenty to thirty thousand units, not bad for a debut record from an unknown and untested eclectic ensemble. The album was produced by a Warner Brothers staff producer named Joe Wissert, who had previously worked with the pop band The Turtles and would go on to mine platinum sales with Boz Scaggs. The EWF debut featured a vocally rich tune called "Love Is Life," weaving the seamless group singing of Maurice, Sherry, Don, and Wade with a full-blown horn section. The song sparked a modest progressive underground-radio following that would help boost the band onto the college circuit.

In 1971, prior to cutting their second album for Warner Brothers, Maurice and the band were chosen to compose the original soundtrack music for Melvin Van Peebles's indie movie *Sweet*

Sweetback's Baadasssss Song, today considered a classic. The underfinanced, much maligned underdog film became a box office smash after counterculture figures like Huey P. Newton and his Black Panther Party embraced it and urged their black brothers and sisters to do the same. Maurice, ever the persuasive and gregarious type, became friends with the eccentric Van Peebles when the director enlisted him for the project. One day when Reese had to fly to Houston for a business trip, he dispatched Verdine to spend the day with Van Peebles. Verdine drove from Hollywood to Pasadena with him to visit Van Peebles's father. During the visit, Melvin pulled out a yellow kazoo.

"This is going to be the theme of the movie," he announced, before blowing a few notes.

The original lineup from the first EWF album performed the *Sweet Sweetback's Baadasssss Song* soundtrack on a Paramount Studios soundstage on Santa Monica Boulevard. Maurice sat behind the drums and Verdine played bass as the band improvised its way through a free-form score in front of a giant movie screen, watching key scenes and playing along live. The entire soundtrack was cut in three days. Verdine recalls that an engineer at the Paramount Studios session was Brian Bruderlin, actor James Brolin's brother.

Reese cued the band through the various themes and changes from behind the drum set, suggesting, "Try this here, try that there." On one ballad Verdine flubbed the bass part with a few bad notes, but there was no time for second takes, punch-ins, edits, changes, or overdubs. The sessions were hit-and-miss, and there was little budget to woodshed the soundtrack, which was later released on Stax Records. (For the record, Earth, Wind & Fire was the first African American band to write, perform, and score a movie soundtrack.)

Earth, Wind & Fire's second album, *The Need of Love,* released in November 1971, was smoother and less raw than its first. Maurice's drumming was exemplary, particularly on a solo from a tune called "Energy," which had a free-jazz, electric Miles Davis /*Bitches Brew* feel to it. During the sessions noted R&B and disco singer Jean Carne was living in the same apartment building as Maurice and Verdine. Her first husband, Doug, played organ on the record and Jean sang background vocals. (Reverend Ike, the audacious storefront preacher-turned-television-evangelist, lived just above the White brothers in the same complex.)

In the space of a year and a half in Los Angeles, EWF had recorded two albums and a movie soundtrack, and Verdine hadn't yet turned twenty-one. It was a priceless learning experience for the young bassist, who was quick to adapt to a generously creative studio environment. Cutting the first two EWF records was a far richer experience than he would have had as a traditional session bass player. These weren't like the usual three-hour record dates back in the old Chess Studio days. Maurice and Verdine were ensconced in the studio for weeks at a time. "Fire" would experiment for ten hours a day, allowing Maurice to perfect his concept of the band along the way.

The original Warner Brothers Earth, Wind & Fire lineup was much more Afrocentric than most rock or R&B bands at the time, with earthy jazz overtones and a psychedelic bent. They weren't exactly a commercial entity. While Maurice and the group weren't necessarily militant, they did have the appearance of being so. Chicago had a strong community-activist vibe. At the time African Americans in large American cities were embracing their blackness and reaching back to their indigenous African roots in dress and style. Maurice did his part by introducing the *kalimba*. The early Earth, Wind & Fire lineup was commercial only in the sense that it wasn't as jazzy as the Ramsey Lewis Trio.

One of Perry Jones's first priorities as national promotion man for black music at Warner Brothers was Earth, Wind & Fire. Perry's initial goal was to break EWF by organizing an ambitious national airplay promotion campaign that would focus on top R&B stations throughout the country. Although this was prior to the days of format-specific marketing and radio airplay within the music industry, Perry had an idea: He would request that Warner Brothers ship copies of Earth Wind & Fire's albums directly to black-owned record stores, as opposed to having them purchase the titles from the one-stop wholesale outlets, where black retailers traditionally purchased their stock with cash.

Perry's next move was to introduce the band to a lineup of top black radio programmers on a regional basis. Perry and Maurice's early game plan was to arrange a minitour of radio stations across the Northeast. Their first stop was a performance to be staged at the Gaslight Theater in New York City, sponsored by WBLS and hosted by deejay extraordinaire Frankie Crocker. As a result of that successful showcase, the traveling EWF road show continued. Perry reached out to more deejays and programmers, such as Georgie Woods and Jimmy Bishop at WUS in Philadelphia, and set up a small network of promotional appearances through various influential radio stations. The venues were primarily meet-and-greets, followed by short live sets held in nightclubs where the deejays had their own personal connections. At other times Perry would help set up stage events at local hotel ballrooms where Earth, Wind & Fire would play live for a crowd of lucky radio listeners. After an appearance in Philly, the band moved on to a club in Boston, and then to a meet-and-greet show in Chicago staged through E. Rodney Jones, one of the founding fathers of black radio in the Windy City. Other stopovers included Detroit, Miami, Memphis, and Houston.

Perry and EWF's minitour was arranged on a shoestring budget. Jones placed plane tickets and per diem expenses on his credit card through a sympathetic publicity department at Warner. He regularly put in money from his own pocket, while Maurice used his funds as well to keep the band afloat. Verdine contributed his unemployment benefits to help support the campaign on the road.

Since EWF was a departure from the current crop of traditional top R&B stars (like Aretha Franklin and Al Green), Perry's efforts were often met with resistance and skepticism from some of the sales executives back at the label. Because the concept of an adjunct black promotion department was new to Warner Brothers Records, not everybody on the promotional staff was as gung ho as Perry.

As the tour wound down and it was time to head back to Los Angeles, Perry arranged for one final show to be held in his old stomping grounds of Denver. Since it was a homecoming of sorts, he called in a few favors and phoned a friend who worked at the Hilton Hotel there. He told his pal that he and the band were on their way back to the West Coast and needed a quick venue in order to stage a stopover show in the Mile-High City.

"I'll get you a room to play," Perry's friend told him. Next, Perry reached out to a radio personality called Dr. Daddy-O from KDKO, a Denver R&B station.

Perry then phoned me. It had been a while since I had seen him, and he told me he was stopping in Denver for a few days and had made arrangements for my band, Friends & Love, to open a special showcase appearance and help draw a crowd to Earth, Wind & Fire's Denver promotional premiere event. Wow, too cool!

On June 23, 1971, Earth, Wind & Fire—billed on an orange engraved invitation as "Warner Brothers' Hottest New Rock Group"—appeared on a Wednesday night at the Hilton Hotel Empire Room before an audience of more than a hundred people who had paid $2.50 to see both bands play.

That night Perry introduced me to the band. The first time I laid eyes on Maurice White, he smelled of coconut oil. We were riding down the elevator together with Perry and Larry Dunn just before the show. Reese was dressed in a pair of white bell-bottom pants, a skintight satiny body shirt, and a sequined cowboy hat. I, on the other hand, was wearing my high-water pants and a dark shirt. When we shook hands, Maurice was the smooth city slicker, and I was the country hick.

When I heard Earth, Wind & Fire for the first time live that night in Denver I was impressed with two things: I loved the introduction of the *kalimba*, because I had never heard anything like it before; second, I loved watching Verdine play the bass. With his frenetic energy, he literally ran all over the stage. EWF in June 1971 was far different from anything I had seen or heard from any group, black or white. Compared to horn bands like Blood, Sweat & Tears, which were so popular at the time, EWF's ensemble sound had a unique aura. Their jazzy musical changes and colors were different from anything else being played on the radio.

We had heard, thanks to Perry, advance white-label copies of Earth, Wind & Fire's records months prior to their coming to Denver, so we had already embraced their music. In fact, Friends & Love had covered a couple of their tunes in some of our own live sets. In the beginning we had no idea what Earth Wind & Fire looked like. Once the albums hit the stores, we were surprised to find that they were an African American group!

The show at the Hilton went down very well, even though Dr. Daddy-O didn't show up to introduce the bands. Afterward Friends & Love did a special after-hours set at our usual haunt, 23rd Street East, and sitting in the club and digging the scene were Maurice and Verdine White. It had been a great night of music, and I had just made what I had hoped to be a very opportune musical connection.

It was great seeing Perry again, and meeting Maurice and Verdine. We all seemed to have so much in common musically. I had taken Janet with me to see *Sweet Sweetback's Baadasssss Song*, and we both thought it was special, even though the music sounded "out" to the two of us at the time.

After the showcase in Denver, Friends & Love took up another residence at the Hornbook in Boulder. Meanwhile, I had sensed the shifting winds of change in my own life. I felt as if my musical career were heading toward a crossroads. In spite of the regional success of Friends & Love, I'd come to the conclusion that very few major record labels and artists and repertoire (A&R) men would travel to Denver to scout and sign a band like ours unless we were a country-and-western act.

In addition, it was getting more and more difficult to run our Friends & Love rehearsals. Some band members had become complacent. Perry had previously warned me that I would be in danger of becoming a "local yokel" in the clubs, the big fish in a small pond only until the next new kid came along. But I sure wasn't aspiring to that, and neither was my longtime friend Larry Dunn. Yet the other band members were more interested in meeting women and partying hard than expanding and exploring the band's sound. They didn't share the dedication I felt to improving. We were making money, but that wasn't good enough for me. I was coming at it from another place. I had already played the best regional venues with the best local musicians. I needed more.

While Perry was toiling away on the road with his new job with Warner, I was feeling more and more musically and professionally trapped. Aside from visiting my family or getting the occasional out-of-state club gigs in Kansas City, I'd hardly been outside Colorado. That fact bothered me, too. Now, through my association with Perry, I realized I couldn't become a successful recording artist and also remain in Denver.

It was during the summer of 1971, not long after the Hilton show, that I came home one night and announced to Janet, who was seven months pregnant, "I can't deal with this anymore. Let's go to California. What do you think?"

I had made up my mind. We were moving to Los Angeles. It turned out that Janet, too, had dreams of one day moving out west. So I made the call, phoning Perry to tell him the news.

"That's it! We're coming out to California."

We stuffed my congas and all of our belongings into some duffel bags that Janet and I had bought down at the pawnshop. A couple of my friends were also heading west, so I loaded my stuff into their van, and we hit the road. Because Janet was pregnant, we made arrangements for her to join me a few weeks after she had had our child and I was settled in with Perry.

As I sat in the van on the way to Los Angeles, my head was spinning. *I was going to Los Angeles. This is where they make it happen; this is where it's done.* I thought long and hard about becoming a new father and putting my musical career on the line by going to the West Coast. Heading over Donner Pass and across the California border was a major milestone. I was about to pursue my dream of becoming a shining star in Hollywood.

9

STARS AND STRIPES HIPPIE SHIRT

I landed in Southern California in the summer of 1971 and crashed at Perry Jones's duplex on Crescent Heights Boulevard, which he also shared with William "Hop" Johnson, a friend of Perry's and Maurice's, who lived in the upstairs part of the building. Perry was living the swinging bachelor's life, having separated from his wife, Jean, after joining Warner Brothers Records. He drove around the city in his kelly green Triumph TR6. His new girlfriend was an exotic hottie—a mixture of Filipino and African American. She had a beautiful sister who sometimes tagged along, and Perry would bring them both around to Hollywood parties.

Perry's house was a bit of a scene, with starving musicians dropping by and taking advantage of his Warner Brothers expense account and his swimming pool. We would have parties and silly jam sessions, parading around the house while banging on various drums, toys, and percussion instruments. As I had during my childhood, I lay sprawled out across the living room floor, listening in awe to the sheer volume of new music flowing into the house, checking out every record Perry brought home. One of my favorites was the new album by Joni Mitchell, *Blue*. Joni was much more than a folksinger. Her songs were extremely poetic and personal, and also very musically complex.

Whenever various radio programmers came to California, they would stop over to see Perry. You never knew who would be there.

I got to meet Patti LaBelle, one of my favorite singers, when Perry invited her over for a lobster dinner. I was thrilled, and Patti was a real nice lady. Little Richard showed up at Perry's pad, too. He had recorded a song called "Dew Drop Inn"—which he did all the time. Fresh off the Rock & Roll Revival circuit, Richard had recently resurrected his career after recording a new album with Reprise called *The Rill Thing*. He returned to the soul and Top 40 charts with a hot, contemporary-sounding hit called "Freedom Blues." Another frequent visitor was the illustrious Sly Stone. At the time Sly and the Family Stone was one of the hottest bands in the world. There were rumors that Sly wanted to leave Epic Records and would possibly sign with another label.

One night Sly showed up at Perry's carrying a mysterious-looking violin case, which he would take with him into the bathroom—for hours. Turns out there was no Stradivarius inside, just a cache of recreational drugs—baggies of sticky Columbian pot, quaaludes, hashish, hallucinogens of every description, and plenty of pills to get Sly back up once he came crashing down. Not only were the drugs plentiful and part of the landscape, they were pure and uncut. There was also a hefty supply of Sly's latest favorite pastime: powder cocaine. At one point, he brought over animal tranquilizer, which he offered to share. I passed because I liked to stay in control.

While admittedly I partook of Sly's stash, by the grace of God I didn't indulge to the point of being captivated or controlled by drugs. Music mattered too much to me. It was my personal calling, the thing that had brought me to Los Angeles. I was in awe of Sly's success, but I was more of a starstruck fan than a follower of his bad habits. One day Perry asked me to drive Sly's then wife, Debbie, down from the Hollywood Hills to the Burbank airport so she could catch a plane to San Francisco. She ended up staying with Carlos Santana and later married him after splitting up with Sly.

A television personality named Harold Dow also stayed at Perry's and later went on to become a network news anchor in New York City. The Crescent Heights house was a way station for people on their way up. It represented a beautiful and unique time in my life, when Perry and Hop embraced a young person like me and provided a roof and shared their food, drugs, and contacts.

I was lucky to have a mentor and a friend like Perry looking after me. Just as Maurice had done with Verdine, Perry took me out to a boutique and bought me some new clothes—a stars and stripes hippie shirt and some groovy velvet bell-bottom pants—so I could fit in with his hipster crowd. He was a free-spirited guy, a holdover from the Swinging Sixties. All the other smooth city-slicker R&B label promotion guys on the circuit would laugh when they ran into Perry the Happy Hippie, with his huge trademark Afro, tie-dyed jeans, riding boots, and handmade flowered shirts. While R&B radio program directors typically wore flashy suits, sported diamond rings, and played poker and drank like fish with the other label promotion fellas, Perry was the "hippie postman." He could light up a room with his bag of goodies, which he kept next to the LPs and singles he was promoting inside an old leather U.S. Post Office mailbag.

With payola in full bloom, many unethical record labels were not above buying radio station personnel vacations, washing machines, and refrigerators in return for getting their records charted higher on the radio station's playlist. Perry had a different method. He would book himself into three- or four-star hotels and hold court. Then he'd break out the goodies from his mailbag and create his own swinging hospitality suite. It was his way of leapfrogging the competing R&B labels. Perry would play the music and let the good times roll. He always traveled with a state-of-the-art thirty-five-pound Sony reel-to-reel tape deck with monster speakers so the jocks could convene in his hotel room and enjoy a little taste of music—and other things—and listen to the latest hit songs, including, for example, Van Morrison's single "Domino," which Perry helped cross over to some of the larger R&B markets. As an experienced promo guy, Perry knew where to draw the line between getting too wasted on the road and keeping professionally cool.

I had been to the West Coast once before moving to LA. Yet many musicians from the Midwest felt an almost magnetic pull to migrate there. The farthest I had lived from Colorado was Kansas City. I thought I would have been more intimidated, because my mother had instilled so much fear into my sister and me when we were kids. Anytime we left the house, she would warn us, "Now, don't go here," or, "Don't go there. Something bad might happen. Be careful!" But coming to Los Angeles was like going to Disneyland for the very first time. Sitting up in the Hollywood Hills at night, looking down at the spectacular skyline with its twinkling lights, I was starstruck. At first I was afraid to drive on the LA freeways. I didn't know my way around and I was driving someone else's car. I remember finally pulling over one day, looking at myself in the mirror, and having a stiff conversation with myself:

Look, either you are going to get over this or you should take the 10 Freeway and get on back to Colorado. You cannot live in fear. Either you're going to ride the freeway to your destination or return to Denver!

At the time, I wasn't a record company–savvy person, so I didn't know what was going on in the record industry. I was too focused on developing my talent. The advantage of being twenty years old and at life's crossroads is that we don't know any better, and as we get older and become more aware of the challenges facing us from within and from without, they can paralyze us. Looking back, if I had known how difficult it would be to make it as a professional musician in Southern California, logically I might have never left Denver.

When I rolled into town, Perry hatched a plan to put some money in my pocket. Warner had just signed and recorded a new act, The Stovall Sisters, on Reprise Records. Lillian, Netta, and Joyce Stovall, from Oakland, California, were the background singers on Norman Greenbaum's immortal hit on Reprise, "Spirit in the Sky," and on their own sang gospel rock—contemporary Christian music well before its time—with a liturgical message that wasn't too overt. The label had rented them a house up in the Hollywood Hills that had once been leased to the Jackson family. Back then, record companies would sign budding acts like the Stovalls and give them both artistic and practical support, like leasing a house, paying the bills, and lending them cars. All of a sudden their lifestyle spiraled up from the Oakland flatlands to the luxury of the Hollywood Hills. How well they had been treated showed me exactly how record companies operated during that time. As a hired gun, I saw how the benefits were being dispensed, and it looked like a pretty sweet deal to me.

Though Perry was constantly on the road, he hooked me up with the Stovall Sisters to help them put a band together for an imminent tour. At first the Stovalls were looking for just a percussionist, but Perry figured I could act as musical director, too. I had learned all their songs and sang them while rehearsing the material with the band. My job was to whip the musicians and the singers into shape and get them ready for their first Los Angeles gig at the noted R&B nightclub Maverick's Flat on South Crenshaw Boulevard. While the famous Sunset Strip music venues like the Whiskey a Go Go and the Troubadour hosted mostly white rock and folk acts, successful black acts like Ike and Tina Turner, the Temptations, the Fifth Dimension, and Marvin Gaye played their gigs over at Maverick's Flat.

Once I landed the Stovall gig, I phoned Janet with the good news, and we made arrangements for her to join me in a few weeks. The first gig I played in Los Angeles at Maverick's Flat with The Stovall Sisters was on September 10, 1971, the day our first son, Sir, was born in Denver. The Stovalls realized I could also sing, so they gave me a number to perform before they came out.

In the end The Stovall Sisters act didn't get off the ground. They released their record with a lot of artistic muscle flexing, but failing to score a hit record put a severe dent in their plans, and the act broke up at the end of 1971. My time spent with The Stovall Sisters wasn't completely fruitless, though. As luck would have it, checking me out in the audience as both a percussionist and a singer the night my son was born was Verdine White! He would later report back to Reese about seeing this young singer and percussionist whom EWF had played with in Denver the previous June. After that show I went and visited Verdine at the Landmark Hotel. It was the first time we had seen each other since the Denver EWF show, and we got along well.

Once The Stovall Sisters gig fizzled, I had a huge decision to make: Was I going to go back to Colorado with my tail between my legs, or would we stick it out in Hollywood? I thought about sending Sir and Janet, who had only recently arrived in LA, back to Denver until I figured out what to do next. Bummer! At the time, we had just moved out of Perry's place and into another apartment on Gramercy Place. But now I was in a bit of a bind. I had lost my gig, and the rent was due, and I didn't have it. I figured Janet and I were going to have to move again. Times were tough, and we were already living off McDonald's and oatmeal. My short-term plan was to share a new place with a friend for a brief time. I got ready to move our stuff, which was only our personal belongings and whatever we were sleeping on.

It's funny how grace works, because an interesting chain of events would soon occur involving both Maurice and Perry during the holiday break between Christmas and New Year's.

As 1971 was winding down, Perry was making progress with the new black music division on the Warner lot in Burbank. Maurice had gone into the studio with Earth, Wind & Fire after their summer minitour and emerged with their second album, *The Need of Love*. Perry was also making headway on the progressive-radio front. A few more underground FM rock programmers had jumped on the Earth, Wind & Fire bandwagon. Two highly influential jocks dug the band—Electric Larry from WBCN in Boston and a legendary free-form-rock programmer named Bill Ashford from

KFML in Denver. But not long after I lost my gig with the Stovalls, trouble was brewing on the label's executive horizon for both Perry and Maurice. Perry got into an intense disagreement with someone in the Warner Brothers sales department over the label's support of EWF. According to Perry, the disagreement turned into a heated argument that produced some ugly racial insults.

"I don't like black acts," the Warner staffer angrily told Perry. "In fact, I don't like niggers, period."

Perry was devastated by what he had heard. Like me, he wasn't accustomed to such heavy racial confrontations. He was born and raised in Des Moines, Iowa—hardly an inner-city stronghold! The verbal exchange caused him to break out in tears in his office, and Mo Ostin took him aside and tried to console him. Mo admitted that those kinds of racist incidents were a part of life and that Perry would have to rise above them. But despite having Ostin's support, Perry could feel the ground shifting beneath his feet.

With the November 1971 release of *The Need of Love,* it seemed like smooth sailing for EWF. Maurice was pleased with the inroads Perry was making at the label. The new album had attracted a loyal group of stations that were playing the record, and sales were higher than those of the debut album. Then, during the week between Christmas and New Year's—a traditional closing-down time for the music business—Perry received a frantic call from Maurice.

"I just had to cut my group loose!" was the story an exasperated Maurice first told Perry. "We're having major problems. The guys weren't getting it, anyway. I was hearing something different than they were. Now it looks like it's just me and Verdine. What can we do?"

Actually, Reese's group had just walked out on him on the heels of the new record's release! He had gone as far musically as he could with that lineup. The band members had gotten into an explosive disagreement, the issue being Maurice's strict control of the group. They ceremoniously exited, leaving the White brothers holding the bag. Perry, realizing that Maurice would have to start from scratch and reconfigure his group, tried to reassure his friend. Maurice had a fresh direction for EWF, but he had the wrong set of musicians to execute that vision. As Perry was urging him to find the right players to help his ideas come to fruition, he flashed on the Denver showcase at which Friends & Love had shared the bill and opened for Earth, Wind & Fire at the Hilton. He then put two and two together, remembering that my gig with the Stovall Sisters had also run its course.

"Maurice, don't worry," Perry assured him. "You remember Friends & Love, that little group I had open for us when I steered you guys to Denver?"

"Yeah . . . those young kids," Maurice replied pensively.

"Man, I'm telling you, the guy you need from that band is Philip Bailey. He's perfect for you. He can sing falsetto like Eddie Kendricks at Motown. But way past that, he's also a fantastic percussionist and a great drummer, just like you! And he's been practicing, and he's only gotten better since then. Plus I can get that hot organ player from the band, Larry Dunn. He's young, but he can play his ass off! And speaking of Larry, there's a whole bandful of talent just sitting there waiting in Denver."

Maurice paused to consider and then said, "Can you get Philip over here? I like his range."

"No problem," Perry said.

10

OPEN VESSELS

I didn't come to California to become a singer, although I knew I had the gift to both sing and play. I was still studying with a percussionist, because that was my main focus. Besides playing the congas and the drums, my teacher instructed me on marimbas, vibes, xylophone, and tympani. My original goal in coming to Los Angeles had been to become a percussionist and do recording sessions like my drummer hero, Harvey Mason.

Out of the Stovall gig, I auditioned for different people, including Latin percussionist Willie Bobo. I played congas with Willie at a gig in Hollywood at the famous jazz club Shelly's Manne-Hole, and lasted only one night. I got fired because I didn't know the fundamentals of Latin-style percussion. (I'd describe myself as more of a ghetto-style conga player.) After I was sacked, I approached Willie humbly and asked, "Is there any way, sir, I could come down and you could point out some tips for me?"

"Son," Willie replied drily, "this ain't no school."

So I called up some guys who actually played Latin percussion and got them to come over and jam with me. There was also a crew of Hispanic percussionists who played in the park, so I took my drums down there in the afternoon and played along. Later, I got the chance to play with drummer Sheila E. and other Latino greats when we toured with Santana, and I picked up some additional Latin nuances. Even then, nothing was conclusive. The Latin musicians would debate among themselves the merits of Afro-Cuban versus Latin rhythms. They would even disagree on which beats the clave belonged.

In January 1972, after I lost my music-director gig, I was living on Gramercy Place. I had sent Janet and Sir back to Denver temporarily and decided to stay on in Los Angeles and see what I could find. Whatever happened would happen; I would cast my fate to the wind.

Then, on a Sunday afternoon—and in dire financial straits—I was getting ready to move in with a friend when Maurice and Verdine dropped by.

Prior to meeting with me, Maurice had asked Verdine whether they should consider hiring me or my former bandmate Carl Carwell from Friends & Love. Having seen me in Denver, Maurice was impressed with my voice and was drawn to my vocal range and my ability to interpret a song. "Definitely Philip," Verdine replied. "He's a good guy who I think could handle things for the long haul. He sings, plays congas and a little piano and harmonica." Verdine preferred to play alongside musicians his own age, whereas with the previous lineup, Maurice was more comfortable working with more experienced players who could jump right in and think on their feet.

Once we all took our seats, Maurice did most of the talking and got straight to the point. "We're looking to reform our band and we're wondering if you want to join."

Maurice and Verdine explained to me that they were restructuring Earth, Wind & Fire. I couldn't figure out from what they told me whether the other members had left or were kicked out. I heard that the heart of the disagreement was the understanding as to who actually comprised Earth, Wind & Fire, who "owned" it, and who called the musical shots. If EWF was Maurice, the rest of the members no longer wanted to continue building equity in an entity they didn't have a share of.

The early version of Earth, Wind & Fire hadn't performed live much for two reasons: First, there weren't that many places for a progressive black band to play; and second, the band wasn't attracting a wide range of music fans. They were a bit scary to white people, and young black listeners didn't especially relate to their music, either. Older black listeners simply weren't on board. Instead, early EWF appealed to a fringe group of Afrocentric blacks who tended to be more educated, holistically minded, and politically aware.

I thought about Maurice's offer to join, and although I was excited that something so opportune was coming my way in my time of extreme need, I wasn't just going to say yes to Maurice and Verdine automatically. I wanted to make sure Earth, Wind & Fire would be the right gig for me. My experience with previous bands, particularly Friends & Love and the Stovalls, gave me pause; I didn't need to relive the frustrations of dealing with a band that wasn't one hundred percent serious, or wasn't performing for the right reasons. That's what had driven me out of Colorado.

But in the end you feel a calling that is so profound that it doesn't have to make sense to other people. It's a calling you can't resist. That's what happened with Maurice, Verdine, and me. The more we discussed it, the more it seemed to me, intuitively, that EWF was the real deal. I felt as if I were being guided in this situation. Then my idealism took over. I thought about it and said, "I'll do it on one condition. . . ."

"What's that?" they asked.

"I want to be in the best band in the whole world."

Maurice smiled. "You're in." And that was it, right there. Done. I was a little stunned. Although they had checked me out onstage on at least three occasions—at the Denver Holiday Inn, 23rd Street East, and Maverick's Flat—I didn't sing a single note or audition on my instruments for Maurice.

Once I was officially in, I joined in the audition process to recruit the other members of the band. They listened halfheartedly to a couple of musicians, until I reminded Maurice, "Listen. I've got a keyboard player in Denver that you will love."

"Get him out here," Maurice responded automatically.

Soon after I had left Denver, when Friends & Love split up, Larry Dunn began playing Hammond B-3 in another bar band. His new group had just opened for War at a gig in Colorado when I reached him. I told him that I had put in the good word for him and that Maurice White had purchased a ticket for him to fly out to LA and meet with him and audition. I said to Larry on the phone, jokingly, "I told Maurice that you could *really* play and that you were a nice guy, even though you didn't have a lot of experience."

"Don't tell people that!" he snapped back. Larry was only nineteen when he got his invitation to join EWF. When he arrived in California, Verdine picked up him up at the airport, driving Maurice's green van. As they turned onto Century Boulevard and headed toward the Hollywood Hills, Verdine began his impression of Mr. Magoo at the wheel. Larry cringed as Verdine jerked the steering wheel and made a quick turn, speeding past the turning lane and careening into oncoming traffic to a chorus of horn-honking drivers forced to swerve around him.

"Perfect," Larry muttered under his breath as he sank farther down into the passenger seat. "First time in LA, and I get creamed in a car accident."

Because Larry was being flown out, and the White brothers had already heard him play the organ at 23rd Street East the year before, he felt fairly poised and confident. He had memorized all of the tunes from the first two EWF albums on Warner, and by the time he and Verdine made it up to the Hollywood Hills (in one piece), Maurice had hooked up an electric piano for the audition. Verdine and Larry then played through a couple of tunes from the EWF albums. Afterward Larry segued into a taste of the Herbie Hancock tune "Maiden Voyage." The tryout was brief, and Larry was hired.

A young drummer from Los Angeles named Ralph Johnson was also auditioned. Although he was a big Beatles fan and listened to

The Byrds on the "boss jock" Top 40 stations KHJ and KRLA, Ralph mainly played professionally within LA's R&B and jazz circles. At the time the EWF guitar chair was held down by Michael Beal, the lone surviving member from the first two Warner albums. Beal and Johnson were friends who had played together in bands at Maverick's Flat. Johnson got the call about the EWF audition through Beal after having spent ten weeks in Japan playing with an LA band. Although he realized that EWF was bubbling far under the Billboard Hot 100, Ralph had been intrigued by their first two records as well as by the prospect of playing for a band that already had a record deal in place.

Ralph's tryout was conducted at Beal's house in the Baldwin Hills area of Los Angeles. Beal's father was a dentist who owned a nice place in Leimert Park. Verdine had already seen Ralph play onstage at Maverick's Flat, just as Ralph had seen me there playing congas with the Stovalls. Ralph set up his drums, Beal and Verdine plugged in, and the three began to jam, playing through a few numbers as a guitar power trio. Neither Maurice nor I was on hand for the audition. Maurice, waiting to hear back from his brother, trusted Verdine's opinion implicitly. He realized that Verdine was the one who was going to have to play with the new drummer. Verdine gave Ralph an immediate thumbs-up.

Prior to finding Ralph, Maurice had auditioned a woodwind player named Ronnie Laws, the younger brother of famed jazz flautist Hubert Laws. Ronnie, like his older brother, was a very gifted and jazzy musician. Larry and I were both excited to have Ronnie in the band, mostly because we were such huge fans of Hubert's CTI records, and we especially loved Quincy Jones's 1969 release *Walking In Space,* which featured Hubert on flute. Back in Denver, Larry and had I listened to that record over and over again!

When I first joined EWF, I messed around with a lot of different instruments—including guitar, harmonica, and drums. (Maurice had asked at my audition if I played piano, and though I couldn't,

I wasn't going to tell him no. As soon as I sat down and tried to pick out a few chords and lines, he saw right away that I wasn't really a piano player, and that's when I recommended Larry.) The reason I wasn't originally hired to be a lead singer was because in the early stages of the group nobody knew exactly what our roles were going to be. The band was evolving. I knew I could sing and play percussion, while Maurice didn't know how much drumming he was going to do. Would he sing from behind the drums or venture out in front? EWF was a work in progress, and as we began writing songs together, Maurice's and my roles as vocalists became more defined. In the early days no one in the band could interpret, cowrite, and shape our songs better than Maurice and me. We developed a nonverbal synergy, and I was better able to grasp the Concept without the two of us doing a whole lot of talking about it. Once the new songs surfaced, our roles quickly solidified. Maurice looked to me to become a co–lead singer; he would sing lead on certain songs while I'd take that role on others.

Maurice had already forged a signature vocal style on songs like "I Think About Loving You" from *The Need to Love* album. After I accepted my new role as a singer in EWF, I asked myself, *Who's the hottest modern singer making the most impact? Sly Stone!* I already had knee-high boots just like Sly's that I wore onstage, even though they killed my feet, nearly bringing me to tears.

Still, I asked myself, *Whom should I emulate?* It dawned on me: *How about being* me? *If I can just be true to myself, nobody can beat me at my game.* It came to me as divine inspiration: I would become the best me that I could be, and discover my own human potential. Finally, I didn't have to wear those boots anymore, and after my epiphany I threw them away.

By the summer of 1972 the EWF lineup was starting to gel. We had a female vocalist named Helena for a quick moment until we found out that Jessica Cleaves was available since she'd left Friends of Distinction. Jessica used to drop by to visit Maurice and Verdine after they moved into a house on North Westmoreland and

Fountain Avenue in Hollywood. We loved her, and I was elated when she accepted Maurice's offer to join the group.

Then came the period when we did a few warm-up gigs performing the material from the first two Warner albums. One early Earth, Wind & Fire appearance was in the Oakland East Bay area with another group on the bill, The Sisters Love, an act Sly Stone was developing. I remember the crowd yelling back at us, "Bring back The Sisters Love!" It was at that show that guitarist Michael Beal decided to pack it in. He couldn't hang any longer with the new lineup and lost hope. After he left, finding the right guitar player would prove to be a long search. In the meantime Maurice chose a young session player, Roland Bautista, to replace Beal. Unlike Michael, Roland was much more of a rock-style guitar player.

Later that summer it was reported in the music press that Earth, Wind & Fire had reorganized and that Maurice White had gotten himself seven "whiz kids" to take over from the previous older, more established band members. The new lineup was set: Maurice White, myself, Verdine White, Larry Dunn, Ralph Johnson, Jessica Cleaves, Roland Bautista, and Ronnie Laws. With all of us in our early twenties, we were pretty green on the national scene, rookies full of energy and optimism with no opposition to Maurice's steering the ship and defining the group's new musical direction. Maurice now had everything he needed in terms of raw talent to proceed without pushback or opposition. We were in the "vessel" together, crafting a new, exciting sound and direction. With our combined talents, we crossed several stylistic boundaries of music, including R&B, rock, jazz, fusion, and pop.

Make no mistake, Earth, Wind & Fire was definitely Maurice's vision, even though it wasn't quite clear at that point what the final vision would evolve into. For my own part, I was prepared to go along for the ride and give the new group enough time to take shape and gain traction. Don't think that we weren't looking at the popularity of Sly and the Family Stone or War—as well as forerunners like James Brown—while we were trying to find our way.

When I first joined the band, there wasn't a specific stylistic road map for us to follow. EWF was a unique assortment of genres and musical personalities. Vocally, Maurice and I were both heavily inspired by Sérgio Mendes and Brasil '66. Brasil '66 was composed of four men and two women, with Sérgio playing piano and arranging the music. We both liked that Mendes sound: that high- to low-octave, singular-voice sound where the melody is sung in a high register with multiple voices, then sung in the lower register with more voices. It comes off sounding very airy, cool, and breathy. Their tunes were tight, catchy, and seamless, with vocal arrangements of contemporary hits and standards that featured mixed world rhythms like Brazilian samba and jazz changes with a positive bounce. We listened carefully to early albums like *Herb Alpert Presents Sérgio Mendes & Brasil '66* and *Equinox*. Mendes later recorded hit covers of The Beatles' "Fool on the Hill" and Dusty Springfield's "The Look of Love." When you analyze our songs in the context of high-and low-octave blend, there's a lot of Brasil '66 shining through!

Originally I was vocally trained as a baritone, but I could also sing falsetto. I didn't really know I had a falsetto until a voice teacher heard me singing in that register in a nightclub one night and explained exactly what a falsetto was. I loved female vocalists, so I was imitating Dionne Warwick, one of my main influences. I loved her sound as well as the songwriting of Burt Bacharach and Hal David. I sang a lot of Dionne's material in the clubs, and Nancy Wilson's songs, too. I loved imitating the great singers I heard on the radio and on the records my mother and her friends played in Denver, which is how I unknowingly developed my falsetto. I was singing to match the key of the original recordings.

Maurice also had that high-to low-octave vocal blend going on, which became more pronounced when I joined the band. To Maurice's surprise, he also could sing in a great falsetto, so we could come up with our Sérgio Mendes–style harmonies when we arranged the vocals. I'm a natural baritone, and since Maurice was, too, when we sang up and down the scale together, we soon developed a unique and natural style that would become our Earth, Wind & Fire signature vocal sound.

Early on, the band members were feeling one another's musical chops. I played percussion and sang in a high voice, my great falsetto. Ralph Johnson was an "in-the-pocket"–style drummer, and Verdine and Ralph, as a rhythm section, hit it off instantly. Larry's keyboard chords were richer than those found in your standard pop and blues progressions. Roland Bautista played his rock-style chords bathed in lots of guitar effects.

We checked one another out. Who had what to offer? Who brought what to the table? I felt the constant ebb and flow of energy as our talents and strengths meshed. Even with a ten-year "generation gap" between Maurice and the rest of the new lineup, Maurice embraced our youthfulness while we respected his leadership and street-oriented experience. There was something about our youth that was contagious, and the new lineup gave Maurice a burst of energy and inspiration in ways he never imagined or anticipated. We were open vessels, and Maurice melded our exuberance with his worldliness.

11

MAURICE AND THE WHIZ KIDS

Maurice led his new band of rookies not by intimidation but by example. Case in point, he turned us on to eating nutritiously as a group. We started going to health food stores together, places like Johnny Weismuller's American Natural Foods on Hollywood Boulevard. In the 1970s health food stores were esoteric little mom-and-pops, nothing like today's conglomerate food chains such as Whole Foods. I remember the first time Maurice made us fresh vegetable soup. I got a serious vegetable high! My whole body went crazy with energy. Campbell's soup didn't do that for me! Because Maurice had been around the world, he taught us how to eat with chopsticks and got us to try different kinds of cuisines. The first time I tasted organic food—a tuna sandwich stacked with lots and lots of sprouts on nine-grain bread—I thought, *Damn, this is good . . . and different!* It was a long way from smothered pork chops and my mama's cooking. Under Maurice's guidance, everyday life was a learning experience. It was a time of discovery.

If Maurice were an animal, he would be a cat, innately highly aware of movement and of everything around him. Maurice doesn't necessarily gravitate toward groups of people or cliques. More of a one-on-one person, he's not the gregarious type who hangs out a lot. In social situations, he's likely to pull away.

Maurice is a sponge for information; he doesn't accept things at face value. He looks deeper into the soul and adopts a humanitarian point of view. Early on, Maurice felt empathy for the suffering and plight of humanity. Through his extensive travels he had experienced the pain and indignity of racism, segregation, and violence. That's why he created a new kind of band; his music would be a healing balm for the ills of society.

In his earlier days in Chicago, Maurice drank alcohol. I'd seen pictures of him with the Ramsey Lewis Trio before he stopped drinking, and he was noticeably heavier. Ramsey once told me that when Maurice played with him, he was very soft-spoken, almost to a whisper. Then, as he adopted his new awareness through proper diet and meditation, operating more from an Eastern philosophical standpoint than from a traditional Western Judeo-Christian one, Maurice became the slim and trim guy we all recognize.

Maurice also turned us on to self-help books like Napoleon Hill's *The Master Key to Riches* and *Think and Grow Rich,* as well as *Psycho-Cybernetics: A New Way to Get More Living Out of Life* by Dr. Maxwell Maltz, which deals with self-image psychology. EWF's message was to bring the people to a higher consciousness.

We might as well have been in college, it was such a hands-on educational journey. Maurice would sit with me at his house on North Westmoreland and Fountain Avenue and talk about his favorite subjects. He wanted to produce music that had a universal appeal. At the time, he felt that music was geared too much toward very specific groups, and he wanted to create something that sounded new but was familiar across the board.

Maurice believed that music should be a positive force in people's lives and help them rise in personal stature. When he explained such lofty ideas as maintaining the dignity of music, we band members were at first too young to know what that meant. Most of us just wanted to be in a group that was smokin' hot.

Yet under Maurice's guidance Earth, Wind & Fire did come to signal a new era in music. While Sly and the Family Stone achieved fame by wanting to take us higher, Maurice was operating on a different level of "family." He wanted to take the listener to a higher plane of consciousness, not to a higher altered state. His philosophical approach was more universal than personal or family-oriented. While Sly fried his brain on drugs, Maurice didn't; he wanted EWF to embark on an earthly, holistic path. It wasn't about re-creating a psychedelic experience, or indulgence in drugs; Reese's musical idea was grounded in love, personal power, spirituality, and lifting the consciousness of humanity.

Maurice studied Eastern philosophy and was profoundly touched by its reverence for the arts, and he was distressed that that dignity and respect had been abandoned by the artists and musicians in Western society who were high on drugs and lived to party. Maurice felt that such errant lifestyles tarnished the level of esteem in which musicians had once been held. While playing in Chicago, he saw firsthand how drug and alcohol abuse took its toll; jazz legends shooting heroin; blues masters passed out on booze. I had never actually witnessed that kind of decadence. I had only seen the Billie Holiday movie, *Lady Sings the Blues,* and when anybody mentioned heroin, I thought of Ray Charles.

Drug dealers and the drug culture were an inescapable part of the landscape of show business, and I had seen a little of it in the bars and clubs. As a band EWF didn't embrace that kind of behavior. Maurice did not indulge, and he wasn't going to put up with anyone who did. As a result, drug abuse wasn't something we were tempted by. By the grace of God, my own single-mindedness for the music had enabled me to escape that scenario, whereas many other bands and artists convinced themselves that they could handle hard drugs without paying the consequences—which was not the case.

Our mission was to tell people, "Hey, you're naturally high, and you can maintain that natural high by discovering who you are—by opening your third eye." We weren't just saying it, we were living it. Within our entourage were people who were into holistic medicines and herbs. Later, as we toured around the country, be it

DC, Philly, or Los Angeles, that crowd became a part of our fan base. Instead of drug dealers and druggies hanging around the band, we had folks bringing us teas, juices, and herbs, the opposite of drugs and toxicity. We were forging a natural path. My body responded to the wholesome natural organic foods, while my mind was opened by the recommended readings. And Maurice was the catalyst for all that. What we discovered through him is what we sang about.

After moving out of Perry's place, Janet and Sir returned to Los Angeles and we shared an apartment on Blackwelder Street with Larry Dunn and his wife, Debbie. They lived in one room, while Janet, Sir, and I shared another. Perry's on-again, off-again wife, Jean, lived in the same building. Our coffee table/dining room table was one of those giant telephone-cable spools. Although we had a high chair and a crib for Sir, the rest of us slept on waterbeds—not the expensive ones on pedestals, but the funky ones with the hardwood frames resting on the floor. As Sir ran from Larry's room to our room, I was afraid my new son would fall down and bust his head.

EWF also rented a house in the Hollywood Hills, where we rehearsed, and conducted interviews and meetings. I don't recall who paid for that house—it might have been the record company–but Leonard Smith, our road manager and Maurice's right-hand man, lived there for a while. That's where we mapped out our future. While Maurice was our conceptual leader, a collaborative spirit also existed. Maurice wasn't like Stevie Wonder, who was a total package, self-contained through his singular vision, talent, and ability. To a great extent, Earth, Wind & Fire's vision was a group collaboration.

Because we wanted EWF to be about more than just the music, we interviewed a stage director from Las Vegas to see if he could help us put together our live show. In Maurice's view there had to be rhyme and reason to our onstage visual presentation, and he had drawn a series of preliminary sketches to illustrate his ideas. During our first meetings he had shown me the drawings. He had sketched the eight members and how he envisioned Earth, Wind & Fire would appear onstage. The chemistry between Maurice and his seven whiz kids enabled him to take what he had on paper and make it into a reality onstage and in the studio.

When I first joined the band, Janet had painted the set of congas that I brought out from Denver. They were black, and I had three of them, so Janet painted an *E* on one, a *W* on the second, and an *F* on the third. In the early days each member of EWF was responsible for figuring out his or her wardrobe. Of course we had no money by way of a clothing allowance; that would come much later. So when it came time to fashion my own look in the band, I knew two things: We weren't going to wear matching doo-wop suits or outfits, and we weren't going onstage dressed like a rock and roll band in T-shirts and jeans. Janet and I cruised through Hollywood's thrift shops and used-clothing boutiques looking for stage clothes and finally came up with the idea for me to wear tie-dyed thermal underwear and long socks!

There was an army surplus store near Studio Instrument Rental (SIR) off Santa Monica Boulevard and Vine Street that sold thermal long johns that we dyed various bright colors. Then I would throw on a loose, hippie-type shirt and over that a vest, too. Later Janet found a shop that sold striped socks and colored leg warmers of the kind that professional dancers wore. Finally, Perry's wife, Jean, knitted the band those groovy woolly crocheted caps, the same kind she made for Sly Stone to wear on his album covers. In the very beginning, for us there were no African prints, robes, or exotic attire. It was just us funky do-it-yourself folks being ourselves.

Maurice and I connected seamlessly on the artistic side, and I could comprehend his ideas and musical direction without his having to overly clarify. Not having to explain everything in minute detail is an important asset in artistic collaboration. Out of everybody in the band, it was Verdine and me, and sometimes Larry, who could best transpose what was going on in Maurice's head. What I needed to learn was how best to present my own ideas to him so that I could contribute on a higher level.

What I had quickly come to love about being in California was that everything was so open. Ideas were open; the music was open. Places like New York and Chicago were cool and hip, but tight, cliquish, and insular. You had to wait to get your shot, whereas in Los Angeles something was going on every night. You could hang out at clubs and parties and network (before they called it that). Everybody in the room was hip. If a person wasn't somebody, then he was on his way to becoming somebody.

You never knew who you might run into. Singer-drummer Buddy Miles might be sitting next to you. One night Verdine met Jimi Hendrix, who showed up unexpectedly at a party. Although he was venerated as a rock god, Jimi sat down next to Verdine without any pretension and asked, "Whath' up, brother?" (Jimi spoke with a lisp.)

We'd head over to Shelly's Manne-Hole, the jazz club on North Cahuenga Boulevard in Hollywood. Verdine told me about the time he went to see Cannonball Adderley all four nights of his gig there! Cannonball had some seasoned New York veterans in his group: Roy McCurdy on drums, Joe Zawinul on piano, and Walter Booker on bass. Verdine, young and wide-eyed, approached Booker and told him that he played in a new group called Earth, Wind & Fire. Booker burst out laughing—he thought it was a big joke.

By 1972 black exploitation films—called "blaxploitation" movies—were happening big-time on the screen. EWF, by having recorded the soundtrack for *Sweet Sweetback's Baadasssss Song,* helped set the pace in the marketing of a new kind of motion picture to black audiences. With the success of *Sweetback,* and later *Shaft* and *Superfly,* plus dramas like *Sounder,* Hollywood realized that African Americans were a viable audience willing to support black cinema. Each of those films had a musical connection via hit soundtrack albums: *Sweetback* to EWF, *Shaft* to Isaac Hayes, *Superfly* to Curtis Mayfield, and *Sounder* to Taj Mahal.

Black music was not just finding a broader audience, it was expanding its horizons. When Marvin Gaye's Motown masterpiece, *What's Going On,* was released in 1971, Maurice and Verdine were living at the Landmark Motel. Upon first hearing the album, Verdine nudged his brother. "One day, Reese, we'll be able to cut a record like that . . ."

Maurice looked over at his brother, shook his head, and answered wearily, "We're not ready yet. We haven't lived long enough. Not ready yet."

12

THE IMAGINARY LOCK AND KEY

When the new youthful lineup of Earth, Wind & Fire arrived on the Warner Brothers film lot in Burbank to continue rehearsals, the band encountered a huge set of teeth sitting there, left over from a Pepsodent toothpaste commercial shoot previously held on the sound stage. Larry Dunn, our resident smart-aleck keyboardist, saw it as an omen for our new musical mission. He climbed up on top of the seven-foot pearly whites and proclaimed, "This band is going to be gigantic."

During the 1950s and 1960s, not as many African Americans populated the studio session circuit in Los Angeles as they did at places like Chess Studios in Chicago. Top LA session cats like the Wrecking Crew, who were regularly employed by Phil Spector and other Southern California producers, included pianists Leon Russell, Jack Nitzsche, Don Randi, and Larry Knechtel, bassist Carol Kaye, drummer Hal Blaine, singer Sonny Bono, and saxophonist Steve Douglas. While the Wrecking Crew was primarily white males (the exception being drummer Earl Palmer), change was in the air. In 1972 Berry Gordy moved his Motown Records operations to Los Angeles but briefly maintained its stable of predominately black session musicians, nicknamed the Funk Brothers—a group that included the legendary bassist James Jamerson and pianists Earl Van Dyke and Joe Hunter—in Detroit. Would Maurice be the one to bust open the doors for more African Americans working alongside the top white studio players in Los Angeles?

The original lineup of EWF had logged studio time with Warner staff producer Joe Wissert. Wissert was a supportive figure for the band, and worked in the studio mostly in a supervisory role, giving Maurice and Verdine plenty of hours and the leeway to hone their skills on both sides of the glass. Joe was more like an executive producer, as it became clear that nobody could produce EWF but Maurice. He knew what he wanted and had the foresight and vision to bring it about. Nobody could tell him otherwise.

One day Maurice confided to Wissert that he wanted to find a new manager to replace Jim Brown's BBC organization. Wissert recommended that Maurice speak with an East Coast music industry transplant named Robert Cavallo and his partner, Joe Ruffalo. At the time, Bob Cavallo represented one of Warner's most progressive, up-and-coming rock bands, Little Feat, originally a four-piece led by Southern California guitarist and singer Lowell George. George and Little Feat were label favorites, and Warner Brothers had high hopes for them.

Bob Cavallo got his start in the entertainment business in the early 1960s in Washington, DC, running a legendary nightclub in nearby Georgetown called the Cellar Door. At that time he met two talented folkies named John Sebastian and Zal Yanovsky, who were headquartered in New York's Greenwich Village along with their production partner, Erik Jacobsen. Cavallo became involved with Jacobsen in the creation of a fantastic folk-rock band called The Lovin' Spoonful. When the band entered the studio in 1965 to record their timeless debut hit, "Do You Believe in Magic", Cavallo found that he hadn't the temperament and patience for the studio recording environment. So Bob and Erik made arrangements for Jacobsen to take over the recording and production duties while Cavallo and Erik would comanage the band.

When it came time to shop the band, nearly every major label slammed the door in The Lovin' Spoonful's faces. Cavallo ultimately signed the group with Kama Sutra, a subsidiary label of MGM Records. By 1965 The Lovin' Spoonful had become a household name and enjoyed a long string of hits. "Do You Believe in Magic" became a monster Top 40 smash, and the band was one of the first American rock bands to balance quality musicianship with expert songwriting skills that would rival the work of Sebastian's Greenwich Village buddy Bob Dylan. In 1966 the band recorded a masterpiece album entitled *Hums of The Lovin' Spoonful.* Counting double-sided Top 40 hits like "Nashville Cats" and "Full Measure," the Lovin' Spoonful mined more than a dozen hit songs throughout their short but fruitful career.

After the Spoonful hit it big, Cavallo relocated from Washington to New York City. When the affable John Sebastian left the Spoonful in 1968, Cavallo took him over as a client and brought him to Warner Brothers as a solo artist. Sebastian's career flourished after his appearance at Woodstock and in the subsequent acclaimed 1970 documentary on the festival. Later Cavallo relocated to the West Coast and settled in the Los Angeles area of Tarzana in the San Fernando Valley.

Shortly after Wissert's conversation with Maurice, Joe met with Cavallo to tell him about EWF's desire for new management. Wissert made arrangements for Cavallo to see the group perform live, just before the first lineup made its final exit. Cavallo listened to the original band's set and later told Wissert that he was unimpressed with the band's heavy jazz fusion leanings and lack of commercial potential.

Wissert asked Cavallo for a personal favor. Would he speak with Jim Brown anyway on Maurice's behalf about BBC's no longer representing EWF? The next day Cavallo sat face-to-face over lunch with the imposing former football star, unsure whether or not he would draw Brown's ire by broaching the subject. Bob decided to tackle the matter (so to speak) with brutal honesty.

"Jim," Cavallo said to the ex-Cleveland Browns running back, "I don't want to rain on your parade, but I don't think Earth, Wind & Fire are going to make you a lot of money."

Instead of reacting angrily, Brown appreciated and respected Cavallo's honesty. During their discussion he dropped his guard and told Cavallo that he was willing to amicably part with the group and grant Maurice's wish to leave BBC management. In addition, Brown wouldn't demand a huge payout. The matter was seemingly settled. Then Cavallo received a call from Maurice asking if the two could meet over lunch to discuss EWF. Having just broken up the first lineup, Maurice wished to persuade Cavallo to represent a new version of the group and to discuss with him his ideas and ambitions.

"What's your plan?" Cavallo asked Maurice candidly.

Just as he would with me and the other newly recruited members, Maurice laid out his lofty plans for a new and improved Earth, Wind & Fire. In an attempt to recruit Cavallo to his cause, Maurice explained the Concept. According to Cavallo's recollections, Maurice laid out an articulate explanation of the band's universalistic goals, of how he wanted to inspire greater musical messages of hope and optimism and span many influences and genres. Maurice envisioned a fifty-fifty, multiracial lineup. The performances would be highly spontaneous. He explained that if the band members were moved to dance, there would be no planned choreography as in the old-school R&B vocal groups and doo-wop bands. They would be dancing onstage strictly for the moment. As Maurice described his vision, Cavallo felt drawn to his unbridled enthusiasm but gave him two important pieces of advice, having seen the original lineup play live and feeling lukewarm about their future. Unlike his frank dealings with Jim Brown, Cavallo framed his comments with upbeat optimism.

"Maurice, this is a fantastic idea, but you need to pursue things from a different angle. There are so many talented and unknown kids out there, that's what you should draw from." Because Maurice's vision was pure, idealistic, and almost wholesome, Cavallo pictured the journeyman jazz drummer surrounded onstage by a troupe of fresh-faced young musicians. "If you could enlist some younger players in their early twenties to join the group, I believe you could have a major success on your hands."

The two men shook hands and parted ways after their luncheon discussion, and weeks later, after Cavallo assumed the EWF matter was closed, he received a surprise follow-up phone call from Maurice.

"I took your advice, Bob."

"Really?"

"Yes, I have a whole new group of whiz kids. Wanna see?"

"Sure," said Cavallo, who was admittedly taken aback that someone as driven and self-confident as Maurice had taken his advice so literally.

"Let's meet at SIR, Studio Instrument Rental. I'll have the group there ready for you to see."

Cavallo, admittedly intrigued but not knowing what to expect, brought along his partner, Joe Ruffalo. We took the stage and performed a short set for the two men. It was a full dress rehearsal designed to impress potential management. A lot of the material we had rehearsed would appear on our next album.

We were on a mission, and we wanted to blow these guys away. As young players desperate for a break, we didn't feel the least bit awkward or anxious about auditioning for a tiny audience of two. We gave it all we had, as if we were performing for several thousand. Cavallo and Ruffalo witnessed Maurice's bright new lineup, funky homemade long-john wardrobes and all, plus a fiery and exciting vocal front line that included Maurice, Jessica Cleaves, and me. After the last song, Maurice approached his two guests.

"Well, what do you think?"

Cavallo was speechless. It was a far cry from what he'd seen weeks earlier on the concert stage. Rather than try to play it cool, Cavallo instead made a rather grand gesture to illustrate how blown away he was by what he and Ruffalo had just witnessed: He walked over to the SIR rehearsal room door and "locked" an imaginary lock, placing the imaginary key in his pocket, as if to say, "No one is leaving this room until we've signed a deal!"

"That was fantastic! This band is remarkable," Cavallo jubilantly told the band. Maurice smiled with delight. Cavallo and Ruffalo had fully grasped the Concept.

13

WILL I HEAR THEM FROM MY DRESSING ROOM?

Following our gangbusters audition with Cavallo-Ruffalo, Maurice made arrangements to meet up with Bob Cavallo to finalize management discussions for Earth, Wind & Fire. He brought the whole band along in his green van to Bob's Tarzana home, with all eight members ready to put their signatures on a contract! Cavallo cordially met with us all and then sent the entourage home. He made arrangements to meet with Maurice individually for a one-on-one sit-down at a later time. After Cavallo had seen the new, improved model of EWF, the two men were on an equal footing, and each had something that the other wanted. Maurice could bring the band fresh representation, while Cavallo could add a potentially hot act to his burgeoning lineup.

Cavallo asked Maurice one more time, "What's your plan?" and Reese laid out his hopes and aspirations.

"Bob," Maurice insisted, "I'll sign with you on two conditions. First, you'll have to get me off the Warner label, and second, you'll have to sign me up with a major record company that is going to pay me."

In other words, Cavallo surmised, reading between the lines, Maurice wanted to be on a large East Coast–based, traditional full-service label so that the group could get the specialized attention it required. Maurice wanted to steer clear of the traditional R&B

labels, like Berry Gordy's Motown or Stax or Chess, that might pigeonhole the group and limit its potential mass appeal, or worse, not pay its members fairly.

"I know exactly where we should go," Cavallo replied confidently. The two men laid out their plans, and Bob set to work. His first order of business was to visit Warner Brothers and work out a release from the Burbank record company. Cavallo sat down with label executive Joe Smith, an old friend with whom he had a good working relationship through Little Feat.

"I'm managing Earth, Wind & Fire now," Cavallo announced.

Smith was stunned. "Jesus, Bob, why?" he asked.

"No, no," Cavallo continued, "they're really good."

Smith paused. "But . . . they're so . . . militant."

It was an innocent comment, a sign of the times, and Cavallo just smiled at the remark. Sitting across the table from a macho ex–football player like Jim Brown might be enough to scare or intimidate anyone, but EWF's message was anything but militant. At that point it became obvious to Cavallo that Maurice had not showcased the new lineup to Warner. Smith was basing his judgment on the older personnel and the first two albums, or he probably wouldn't have considered letting the group go.

Cavallo continued to play his cards close to the vest and asked, "Joe, what can I do to get them off the label?"

Smith explained to Cavallo that, although the group's sales were modest, EWF was still in development and the label was roughly forty thousand dollars in the hole. As a result, Smith would require an "override," extra financial compensation in order to spring the group from the Warner roster.

With Joe Smith's assurance that EWF could leave Warner with a forty-grand-plus buyout—not exactly chicken feed to someone like me—Cavallo set out to implement part two of his grand plan. Cavallo-Ruffalo had their sights set on New York–based Columbia Records as a new home for Earth, Wind & Fire. Cavallo was sure that label president Clive Davis would be as enthusiastic as Bob had been when he first saw us play at SIR. The next logical step was to set up another private showcase at Sunset Sound, just like the one Cavallo and Ruffalo had attended.

Clive Davis was (and still is) one of the most charismatic record executives on the music industry scene. He took a stodgy New York–based corporate entity known for releasing middle-of-the-road records to a much higher (and diverse) creative plane by attracting and signing top contemporary talent. A Harvard-educated lawyer, Davis had joined Columbia at the age of twenty-eight as a general counsel for the label. He rose through the ranks quickly and in 1966 became both vice president and general manager of Columbia. By 1967, when the label went through a massive creative reorganization, Davis became president, replacing longtime executive Goddard Lieberson.

Davis boldly pushed Columbia Records beyond its super-square image as a label primarily known for Broadway musical soundtracks, *Sing Along with Mitch* (Mitch Miller) albums, and MOR crooners like Robert Goulet and Johnny Mathis, and put it on a fast and hip track, concentrating on signing exploding countercultural rock acts like Santana and Janis Joplin and her band, Big Brother and the Holding Company. He had also taken on an African American gospel/folk-rock act from Los Angeles called the Chambers Brothers, whose groundbreaking album *The Time Has Come* enjoyed phenomenal sales and wide airplay across both Top 40 outlets and underground FM radio. Davis helped diversify the appeal of jazz icon Miles Davis toward a younger audience by introducing him to the rock press, and competed with Warner/Reprise head-on by inking progressive artists like Laura Nyro; Blood, Sweat & Tears; a young singer-songwriter named Bruce Springsteen; and a fresh new horn ensemble called Chicago Transit Authority. It was clear that getting Clive Davis on board with Earth Wind & Fire would be the keystone of our success.

In the summer of 1972 Maurice excitedly called a band meeting to inform us that Cavallo had made arrangements for Clive

Davis to fly out to Los Angeles to see us perform. He was pleased with the fast-track progress his new management team was making. At the time, I was operating strictly on the creative level and wasn't involved in any of the talks regarding management and business decisions or label strategies. It was Maurice's responsibility to get us a record deal.

We set our sights high by aiming for Clive. Columbia Records believed in artist development, and their support would be unprecedented for us. Plus, they had the patience and resources to hang on for the long haul with a unique band like ours. I pictured the band progressing gradually through a series of albums: At first we'd sell a respectable 50,000 copies. After that, through tour support and gaining a fan base, we might progress to 100,000 or 200,000 in sales. Soon after, we would sell 500,000 units to score our first gold record, and after that, zoom our way to the top with platinum million-selling status and superstardom. Hey! As a twenty-one-year-old transplanted country bumpkin from Colorado, I was entitled to dream. The brass ring was within reach. and I had already come a long way from playing Top 40 songs in Denver bars.

I don't remember much about the Sunset Sound showcase gig, other than that the room was smoking hot and we were in full dress-rehearsal mode again. We wore our stage costumes and had planned a short thirty-minute set of material, which we performed in a blur. I recall Clive Davis walking in with a couple of his Columbia lieutenants in tow.

Verdine leaned over to Maurice and asked him, "Which one is Clive?"

Maurice pointed him out. "The cat in the white Gucci loafers."

After our brief performance Clive approached Bob and said, "I don't want to be coy, but I think that I like them a lot. We will be talking."

A few days after the Columbia showcase, Maurice announced with a big smile on his face that Clive was very interested in signing the band. Davis had the foresight to take a chance on us, partly because of the huge crossover success Sly Stone already had had for CBS. We had the same edge as well as the same crossover potential. But EWF was a different kind of band than Sly and the Family Stone. We shared a universal message of joy in our songs, and I'm sure that Clive saw us as a logical progression from the music Sly was producing.

Davis and Columbia were also willing to buy out the Warner contract, but first he needed to see us play a live gig in New York City so that his staff could see us perform in a proper concert environment. Although Davis had the power—and the inclination—to sign us to Columbia, it was important for him to include his promotion executives and A&R group in the decision. Our next hurdle was to find a show in New York City that we could attach ourselves to as quickly as possible. It would be difficult to book us into a club in Manhattan since we were primarily a West Coast talent without an East Coast audience. (Even when Perry Jones was taking the band around the Northeast, he had trouble setting up paid East Coast nightclub gigs.) How could we make this happen?

Cavallo finally came up with a crazy idea, but pulling it off would be like a miracle. He contacted one of his other music clients, singer-songwriter John Sebastian, the former leader of The Lovin' Spoonful, who was scheduled to headline a concert at the Philharmonic Hall in New York City. (Philharmonic Hall is now called Avery Fisher Hall and is part of the Lincoln Center for the Performing Arts complex.) Built in 1962, it featured state-of-the art acoustics and was a perfect venue for a folk-rock act like Sebastian. The seating capacity was about twenty-five hundred, just right for us, large yet intimate enough for Columbia to check out our act.

The problem was, John Sebastian had no problem selling out the Philharmonic Hall on his own. Frankly, he didn't need an opening act, especially since the show was billed as "An Evening with John Sebastian."

Cavallo called Sebastian anyway. "John, I need a favor from you."

"What is it, Bob?"

"I have this hot new band I'm representing, and I gotta have Clive Davis see them in New York."

"What kind of band are they?"

"Uh, uh, eight black folks. But when Clive sees them play, he's gonna want them on Columbia. Can you help me out, John?"

Sebastian, an easygoing fellow, was willing to help. "Will I hear them from my dressing room?" John asked, hoping for a little peace before going onstage.

"No," Cavallo said, biting his tongue.

"Well, make sure I don't hear anything."

God bless John Sebastian. He gave us our all-important, much-needed break, and it was a safe bet that he could hear every note we played that night from his headliner's dressing room.

Along with an audience scratching their heads at the sight of a dancing, all-black eight-piece power ensemble opening for a laid-back singer-songwriter like Sebastian, Clive and his entourage attended the show, as promised. Cavallo and Clive sat about halfway down on the left aisle of the Philharmonic Hall. After about two songs, Clive leaned over to Cavallo.

"This is great! We have a deal."

I remember that, as the band was heading back to the hotel, one of the promotion men from Columbia approached Maurice, Verdine, and me and said, "The man is looking for you."

The three of us looked at one another. We thought he was talking about the police, and soon our walk turned into a slow trot, which then turned into a jog.

"No, no, no!" the promo guy said, running after us, "I'm talking about 'the man' man. Clive Davis is the man."

We visited Clive at the label headquarters at the CBS Building at 51 West Fifty-second Street, nicknamed Black Rock. We couldn't just go up in the elevator but had to check in through security downstairs. Later the label invited us to see the band Chicago (forced by the actual Chicago Transit Authority to shorten its name) play at Madison Square Garden and offered us tickets to see any other CBS artists we wanted to. It was a different culture and atmosphere from Warner Brothers.

The tricky part of this whole wacky scenario was that Cavallo had to be extremely low-key in his dealings until the contracts with Columbia were signed. He didn't want word to reach Joe Smith and Warner that their archrival Columbia had put in a bid to sign Earth, Wind & Fire out from under them. In fairness, Warner Brothers at the time was a victim of its own arrogance. John Sebastian and EWF were both Warner artists, and had there been a halfway astute Warner contingent present that night at Philharmonic Hall, or even a single Warner A&R or promotion person in the audience to check out the new band that Maurice had assembled, we would not have been granted our release!

Instead, we kept cool and were out the door at Warner a few weeks later. Cavallo bought out the EWF contract with money supplied by Clive Davis and Columbia, and after Maurice signed the new recording contract, we were set to enter the studio and begin work on our first album for Clive, which was to be entitled *Last Days and Time*. Everybody was stoked.

But there was a twist: When Earth, Wind & Fire moved from Warner Brothers to Columbia, a pivotal business decision was made between Cavallo-Ruffalo and Maurice White that would deeply affect the course of the band for years to come. Back when Maurice drove the entire band out to Tarzana to meet our new manager and sign individual contracts, Cavallo had taken him aside and held him off. He convinced Maurice in a subsequent meeting that he shouldn't let the entire band own anything. He advised Maurice that he alone should own the production, the publishing, and the name and should retain total leadership and control. His logic was that if eight band members each had a voice in the band's direction, nothing would get done properly, and the project would lose focus and fail. Cavallo felt Earth, Wind & Fire needed one person to call the shots—preferably someone whom management trusted—and since it was Maurice's concept from the start, he should be the man in charge. A separate compensation plan would then take care of the other members of the group. Once a year, Cavallo suggested, Maurice and management would get together and distribute money among the band members according to how important each was to the group as a whole. That money would come from a percentage of the profits. Unbeknownst to me, I was to be a key man in Earth, Wind & Fire, so I would receive one of the larger annual shares. Although I did not know that at the time, I still felt the need to enrich my role in the band and become more indispensable.

Maurice took his managers' advice, convinced that, although we had just scored a major coup in getting EWF signed by Clive Davis to Columbia Records, the road to fame and fortune was fraught with fallen stars, ruined plans, and broken dreams. In Maurice's mind, we had a hell of a long way to go in order for us to become shining stars.

14

NOT A FUNK BAND

In its infancy the second incarnation of Earth, Wind & Fire enjoyed an early underground college buzz, as the group maintained a pocket of fans in the Washington, DC; Philly; and Baltimore areas from its Warner Brothers days. College crowds were more adventurous, and because the first EWF lineup was Afrocentric, our early student audiences were more African American than mixed or white. During my first EWF tours, I experienced my own brand of culture shock. I had grown up playing in places like Aspen and Vail, so when I got to larger cities like Philly and DC with Maurice and the guys, I was stunned. Whoa! My playing experiences had been with audiences that had been predominantly white, mixed at best, and I was comfortable with that dynamic. Now all these people looked like me, and there was a whole bunch of them. I had never seen so many black folks in my life! I felt as if I were in Africa.

Once we got on the road, we grew up. We started wearing goatees and got hipper. Traveling the country and visiting those colleges, we got a feel for what America was about. Then we found ourselves, too. Back in 1972, in order to get exposure to the circuit of college audiences and student venues—eschewing the traditional R&B chitlin' circuit—there was an audition convention of sorts held every year in Cincinnati where bands would be invited to perform. When we had played that gathering, we were placed on a showcase bill with the progressive jazz ensemble Weather Report and power drummer Billy Cobham's latest fusion band. Subsequently we scored a few college gigs with Weather Report. At the time jazz fusion was becoming very popular on the concert circuit as well as in smaller halls and nightclubs. Being jazz-influenced ourselves, we were okay doing those kinds of shows, as we could stretch out and develop our chops onstage. At the time, that was right down Maurice's alley, he being a drummer at heart.

We played a particularly memorable gig at Temple University in Philadelphia that year, performing material we had learned from the first two albums. We were getting through to the students, partly because they could relate to our youthfulness and partly because they were looking for something fresh. We also owed our early ascent to loyal college radio stations like WHUR-FM at Howard University in Washington, DC. WHUR broadcast a jazzy format, and it was one of the first stations to get behind our records. By the time we headed down to Howard University to play, we already had a following in DC, a mostly African American crowd that was hip to our music. It was my idea to add some rearranged cover tunes like Bread's "Make It with You" and Pete Seeger's "Where Have All the Flowers Gone," two songs I sang live in Denver with Friends & Love. In addition we performed a couple of Sly Stone tunes.

From a purely stylistic standpoint, Earth, Wind & Fire was a commercial fusion group, as opposed to a funk band like Cameo or the Ohio Players. By musical definition, funk groups weren't running through the cycle of fourths in a tune, like we were. James Brown–influenced funksters like Parliament-Funkadelic, George Clinton, and Bootsy Collins didn't use bebop horn licks on top of Afro-Cuban rhythms like we did. EWF had a unique collection of cultural and world influences. Also, Larry on keyboards was playing big "spread" chords and extended jazz chords instead of basic pop and rock triads which, in combination with Maurice's exotic concept of rhythm and ear for creative melodies and my multioctave vocals, thoroughly broadened our sound. Plus there was an unmistakable gospel influence that Maurice and I both had acquired from growing up in the church and singing in the choir.

I use the term "fusion" for just what it means: all different kinds of music combined. I'm talking about a fusion of genres, world sounds of different musicality. Whatever you hear in EWF's music, from gospel to classical, we made a commercial yet original, entity.

During the recording of *Last Days and Time,* we had Ronnie Laws on woodwinds and Roland Bautista on guitar. Yet we were in transition as far as the roles of guitar and horns were concerned. Roland was very rhythmic, but had more of a rock feel in his phrasing, while Ronnie was definitely a straight-ahead jazz horn player. Reese hired Joe Wissert to return as producer, and he and Maurice laced ribbons of big-band-style horn arrangements throughout the record. The album included our melodic covers of "Make It with You" and "Where Have All the Flowers Gone" but wasn't without a sense of humor, featuring a couple of twenty-three-second snippets like "Interlude #1," a short burst of squawking free-jazz saxophone à la Albert Ayler, or "Interlude #2," a piano spoof of Thelonious Monk meets pianist Bent Fabric's 1962 novelty hit "Alley Cat." The album's high point is "Power," the instrumental jam we created in the studio that brought the house down at the Uptown Theatre.

What was interesting about the artwork of *Last Days and Time* was that it leaned heavily on the transitional schematic drawings that Maurice first showed me when he was recruiting me and the others to join EWF. To Maurice's delight, Columbia hired Mati Klarwein, the artist who painted the illustrations for the famed Miles Davis *Bitches Brew* cover, to create the gatefold artwork for *Last Days and Time.*

To me it was still all about the music. As I sought to forge my own musical identity, I made a conscious decision for the time being *not* to listen to one artist I dearly loved: Stevie Wonder. So deep was my admiration for him that I was sure that if I listened to him too much, his styles would rub off on me and I would end up perceived as a pale imitation.

In the studio, the vocal sound of EWF was finding its way through the combination of two primary voices. Jessica Cleaves was playing less and less of a role with the band. As Maurice wrote the bulk of the material, he and I worked closely in tandem on the vocal arrangements. Once we saw that the other guys in the band weren't accomplished singers, and since I was in charge of making sure the live background vocals were up to par, soon it became easier for Maurice and me to sing most of the vocal parts ourselves and double-track everything in the studio. We didn't realize that by splitting the vocals between the two of us we were developing a key element of the EWF sound. We weren't out to consciously exclude the other members. Rather than recording umpteen takes with people who couldn't stay in tune or execute the proper phrasings, Maurice and I could sing the parts together instinctively.

The way that we injected variety into the overdubbed vocal parts was to approach them with different attitudes. One version might be noticeably edgy, while another would be sexier, more breathy. We would then merge these multitracks of the various "attitudes" to create a single unified vocal sound. The two of us were very much in synch throughout the process of creating our intricate vocal arrangements. Maurice and I were forging a strong bond creatively, partly because we both came from similar family backgrounds in which there was a limited strong male presence. Yet our bonding wasn't that of close buddies; it remained one of mentor and student.

Although we made steady career progress with a Columbia recording contract, a new album, and the support of an aggressive management team, we encountered a few rough patches along the way. We hit a major bump on the road in our relationship with Perry Jones.

At the end of 1972, after we'd left Warner, Perry also departed from the label. He ended up staying at Maurice's house on North Westmoreland for nearly four months. Gone with Perry's Warner gig were his generous expense account, the promo goodies, and the pretty girls who hung around him. While crashing at Maurice and Verdine's pad, Perry was under the impression that he would have an opportunity to take the reins and manage EWF. But then along came Bob Cavallo and Joe Ruffalo, followed by Leonard "Bafa" Smith, who joined the team from Jim Brown's BBC group. He served as Maurice's right-hand man and called himself the "general manager" of EWF. Leonard was a big, strapping, handsome bald dude, Maurice's jack of all trades. On the road he was both a manager and a babysitter for us younger band members. Most of us came from small cities and hadn't done a whole lot of traveling. Leonard was a very macho dude with a deep, booming voice who would introduce our live shows.

It sounds crazy, but it was Leonard who taught me how to write my first check. When I found a new apartment, I had to pay the first and last months' rent, so I filled out the lease agreement and handed Bafa the check. He looked over everything and then said, "Come over here," and showed me the proper way to write a check. Before that I didn't even have a checkbook.

In many respects I grew up within EWF—on a personal, manly level—from the most basic stuff like check writing to wearing deodorant and colognes to dressing fashionably, and all of that formative stuff. Most of us had gone from Mama and living at home straight to EWF, without a period in between in which we could become self-sufficient, independent men.

Given the management presence of Cavallo and Bafa, things soon grew awkward between Perry Jones and the rest of the group. Because he was so close to Maurice and to me, Perry was perceived by Cavallo-Ruffalo and Leonard as a threat and a distraction. Having Perry around caused tension within the ranks, until at the end of the year he left Southern California and returned to Denver.

I felt bad seeing Perry go, since he had done so much as a friend, and hoped that one day our paths would cross again.

The biggest challenge in the band's infancy was touring, as our bookings were very touch and go. In the early days we experienced many false starts and failed attempts at putting the new lineup on the road. Maurice would spread the word: "We got this gig. Meet at the airport at such-and-such a time." Then I'd show up and get a call from Leonard on the white courtesy phone.

"Didn't happen. We're not gonna do it. Come on back."

I have to say, to Maurice's credit, he never let himself appear down-and-out in front of the band. He was positive about bad news and saw it as a means for something good to happen for us. He was a great example for a twenty-one-year-old like me. Tenacious about the Concept, he was tested on every front, and could have said at any time, "Man, I can't do this. I have too many guys depending on me." Instead he would tell us, "Okay, we'll hang in there. It only means there's something better for us on the horizon." It's tough holding up an entire organization during those tough times.

Also, Maurice was so particular about making sure that we were ready to be seen live that his perfectionism delayed our ability to earn money on the road. In the very beginning he wouldn't take certain gigs because he thought doing so would destroy our mystique. He used to say, "The same people who paid ten dollars to see you in a club ain't gonna pay fifteen dollars to see you at the Forum." He would avoid the smaller places and instead kept the band busy rehearsing. That, in turn, made it hard to keep food on the table to feed my family and pay the rent. With the mounting pressure of supporting a wife and son, I often had to think about whether I should take another job on the side or change professions altogether.

At one point I was feeling so discouraged that I began looking through the job opportunities section in the newspaper. When Hop Johnson caught me scanning the want ads, he took a no-holds-barred approach. In his eyes, Earth Wind & Fire demanded nothing less than *total* dedication.

"Philip, either you're going to be a musician or not," he said, snatching the newspaper out of my hand. "If you're going to be a musician, then go back in and practice. If not, then sell your damned congas!"

This was exactly what I needed to hear. Hop's challenge made me want to commit to the band even more. I learned that even though times were lean and scary, and despite the unfulfilled promises of shows and tours, I needed to hang in there and believe in the Concept.

Things would soon change after Earth, Wind & Fire played the monumental gig at the Uptown Theatre, the 2,000-seater in Philly where we shared the bill with New Birth and The Manhattans. It was one of the most exciting shows we had done. People weren't expecting to see us on the floor when the curtain opened. At first we were loudly booed and heckled by the crowd, but we won them over. We finished our set with the crowd up on its feet.

In preparation for our first album on Columbia, we were invited to play a special showcase at the CBS convention in London. We were scheduled to perform a brief set in front of not only the executives from the label but also their entire sales department, branch offices, promotional divisions, and A&R staff. Columbia spent a fortune flying in employees from all over the world. The CBS national conventions were a big deal, and a chance to unveil the newest acts and releases for the coming year in a party atmosphere. The label put us up in a posh hotel in London called Grosvenor House, where we celebrated Verdine's twenty-first birthday.

We shared the bill at the convention with another new, much-heralded label act, Azteca, a Latin rock spin-off group fronted by ex-Santana percussionists, brothers Pete and Coke Escovedo. Azteca had full bars set up in their hotel rooms, and they took full advantage of them. As for us, true to Maurice's influence, we stayed clearheaded and ready to rumble.

When we broke into our "Power" jam and then "Make It with You," the CBS contingent went crazy. Unfortunately for Azteca, their set was flat. They even got smashed on the airplane coming back. Once again, taking the high, wholesome road and the clean-living approach that Maurice espoused worked to our advantage.

Released in April 1972, *Last Days and Time* sold a respectable 40,000 units and stuck around on the Billboard charts for twenty-five weeks. The first time I heard myself on the radio was when Larry and I, along with our families, were living in our tiny apartment on Blackwelder Street. When "Where Have All the Flowers Gone" came on the air, Larry and I were euphoric.

"That's us! That's us!" We were jumping up and down, going crazy. Larry and I both came from modest backgrounds, but here we were, struggling and trying to make it. And now we had a chance. We felt that the band was on a nice, solid trajectory, and that our first Columbia record was the start of a fruitful relationship with the label, though not the end of the dues-paying era needed to kick the band—and the Concept—into full gear.

15

THE STATION WAGON TOURS

Soon it was time to tweak the Earth, Wind & Fire lineup again. Horn player Ronnie Laws was on his way out of the band. He had ambitions to pursue a solo career like his older brother, Hubert, so I stepped in to recommend Andrew Woolfolk, who had played with me in Denver. Andrew was a versatile horn player and could play flute as well as tenor and soprano saxophone. Just as I had done with Larry Dunn, I remember excitedly phoning Andrew, who at that time was studying with the famous bebop saxophonist Joe Henderson in New York, to tell him that we had an opening in the group. (I had invited him to the gig we did in New York when we opened for John Sebastian while Ronnie was still in the band.) A short time later, Andrew auditioned and succeeded Ronnie.

The next adjustment was to change guitar players. Roland Bautista was a great axe man and an able studio session player, but he didn't quite have the commercial sound Maurice had in mind for the band. We needed to beef up our guitar section rhythmically. When Roland left the band, somebody from New Birth told us about a killer young guitarist in Kentucky named Johnny Graham, who was a funky and bluesy player. We sent him a plane ticket to Los Angeles without having heard him play a note.

Maurice told me about another guitarist he had met named Al McKay. Al had played with Charles Wright and the Watts 103rd

Street Rhythm Band, the other R&B group that Warner had on its label alongside EWF in 1970. Bill Cosby supposedly helped form the band, but soon after McKay joined he could see that it wasn't going to live up to its potential. Maurice had first met Al in a music club in Seattle called the Black and Tan. At the time Maurice was still working with Ramsey Lewis, and Al was on tour with the Watts 103rd. Like me, Al was also a drummer, which gave him something in common with Maurice as well when the two first met. They exchanged phone numbers, and when Maurice relocated to LA, he kept in touch with Al. Jessica Cleaves, who went to high school with Al, highly recommended him.

Soon after they met, Al received a call from Maurice to audition for the first version of EWF, but Al had by then begun working with Isaac Hayes and couldn't fully commit to playing with the band. Al later got a job with Stax Records working as a musical contractor with various artists on the label once they hit the road on tour. The second time Maurice called Al to audition, now to replace Roland, Al showed up at the rehearsal hall in Hollywood, which was surrounded by mirrors and looked more like a dance studio than a rehearsal hall. Al plugged in and jammed with the entire band, which had just added Woolfolk on saxophone. I was in attendance, along with Larry, Verdine, Ralph, Maurice, Andrew, and Jessica. Johnny Graham also auditioned that day.

I remembered seeing McKay play live at the Whiskey a Go Go, and was well aware of his badass musical style. I liked Al's playing, and I thought that he could light a fire under the band rhythmically and become an integral part of our sound. In addition to gigging with Isaac Hayes, he had also played with Ike Turner and Sammy Davis Jr. During the audition McKay sensed that we had something special going on and was simpatico with the other band members.

Once Maurice hired him, McKay warned us that his gig with Stax as a music contractor might interfere with our schedule. One weekend when we had a gig in San Francisco, Al couldn't make the show because of a conflicting date that he couldn't break. This pissed us off big time, and Maurice was so upset that he fired Al from the band. Subsequently we hired Johnny Graham as Al's replacement. Although Maurice and I agreed that Johnny was great, there was something missing without Al in the band. In November 1972 Maurice decided to bury the hatchet, and invited Al to drop by his house and join us, the band, for Thanksgiving dinner. After that, the band would proceed with two hot guitar players, Johnny and Al.

Al was the consummate funk rhythm player with his James Brown–style chicken scratchin' licks, while Johnny came from the meaty, bluesier Albert King style of guitar playing. Johnny was the hotter soloist. His solos burned because of his secret technique: He used light strings and tuned them down a half step. Whenever he bent a string, it would push his leads into the stratosphere. Al made no bones about being an R&B funk guitar player, even when we tried to turn him on to the heavy jazz fusion players that Larry, Andrew, and I loved to listen to. We played him Chick Corea and Miles Davis, some of which he liked, most of which he didn't.

When Al first joined the band, we were fairly jazz-oriented and acted like jazz musicians onstage, with nobody dancing or smiling very much. At first Johnny and Al played on the same side of the stage and began competing against each other at shows, each guy turning up the volume more and more. It bothered me whenever the band played too loud, so we moved Al to the other side of the stage, next to Verdine. In addition to Al's chunky guitar rhythms, it was he who got the band moving around a lot more onstage. McKay liked to dance and play, and the more Al and Verdine strutted their stuff, the more the rest of us joined in. Pretty soon we had our own dance steps, moving and grooving with a different energy. Bringing in Al and Johnny definitely made us a slicker live band.

Having Al on board also brought a more commercial and radio-friendly structure to our sound. Because Maurice came from a recording background with Chess, and he and Al were older, both had similar concepts of tonal structure and how it could be used to put down a groove and make it simple. Whatever Al laid on top of Larry's fancy jazz chords gave our material more bounce. Instead of closing our eyes and digging our music, we'd want to move around and dance to Al's lines.

Al played a fat Gibson L-5 hollow body box guitar from the days when he gigged with Sammy Davis Jr. He also had a sweet Gibson red 345 double cutaway that was a gift from Isaac Hayes, which provided a thicker and fuller sound. With EWF, Al also played a Fender Telecaster and a Gibson Les Paul Custom.

Once we began recording *Head to the Sky* in early 1973, I gave Maurice a song with lyrics I had written called "Evil." It became my first piece to appear on an EWF album. Previously I had brought different songs to him, and on occasion Maurice would listen intently and then rub his nose with the palm of his hand and say, "Yeah . . . pretty nice little idea . . . you gotta break that down, though."

" 'Pretty nice little idea'?"

I could have interpreted his critique as a backhanded compliment, and if I had been as supersensitive as some of the other guys were about Maurice's comments, then I might have felt intimidated about bringing him more material in the future. But I wasn't. Maurice was brilliant at taking a song's central idea and improving it by putting his stamp on it. I looked at it this way: No matter what songs I brought Maurice, even if he looked at them as just "pretty good little ideas," I would at least have learned what he wanted, and I knew I was going to get better at the submission process. Reese's criticisms only added to my determination. As a result I ended up being the cowriter on many other EWF hits, once we connected creatively.

Maurice decided to open *Head to the Sky* with "Evil," and it became another college radio favorite. With a funky duo of guitars, we began stretching out our songs with layers of my falsetto vocals. "Zanzibar" was an experimental thirteen-minute-long tour

With my sister Beverly at our home in Denver in 1954.

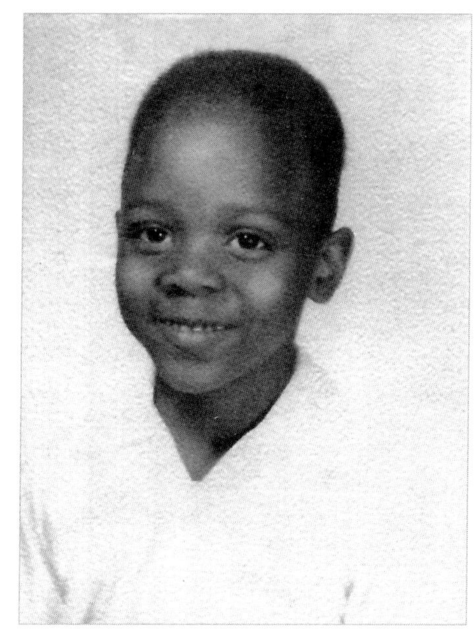

A formal portrait from about the time I was six.

My father, Eddie Bailey, whom I got to know well only later in our lives.

My uncle, Lilman Crossland; my mother, Elizabeth Crossland; and my grandfather James Crossland.

Sitting by a stream of crystal clear water near the Caribou Ranch recording compound in Caribou, Colorado.

Members of my last band in Colorado, Friends & Love: Winston Ford, (vocals), my first wife, Janet, Carl Carwell (vocals), me, and Julius Carey.

Al McKay, Maurice White, me (behind the cymbal), and Verdine White in 1972.

With my oldest son, Sir Bailey, during a visit to Denver in 1973.

A family meal with Janet and Sir in our first decent apartment, in a neighborhood called Tara Hills near Culver City, California.

Drummer Ralph Johnson, guitarist Al McKay, and me in the engineering booth at an EWF recording session for our album *Head to Sky*.

Singing and drumming during a tour in 1973, between our albums *Head to Sky* and *Open our Eyes*. I began to assume a more prominent role on vocals as the band grew more successful.

With Maurice and Sir at Caribou Ranch in 1974, during the recording of *That's the Way of the World*.

With Janet in Colorado in 1974.

Sharing a duet with Jessica Cleaves, who joined EWF as a vocalist in 1972 after leaving the Friends of Distinction.

With my childhood friend Henry Colbath during an Earth, Wind & Fire concert in Hawaii, just before the birth of my daughter Trinity.

With Maurice White in 1975, singing "Keep Your Head to the Sky."

In 1975 EWF toured Europe with Santana to promote *That's the Way of the World*. In London, from left to right: Larry Dunn, Verdine White (far back), me, Ralph Johnson, a musician from Santana, Don Myrick, Ndugo Chandler, Al McKay, Andrew Woolfolk, Michael Harris, and Lou Saterfield.

With Andrew Woolfolk, a versatile horn player with whom I worked early in my career in Denver, and who later joined EWF on saxophone, in 1975.

Al, Verdine, Andrew, Ralph, and one of Santana's players during the 1975 European summer tour.

On tour with EWF's keyboardist Larry Dunn, another old friend from my Denver days.

Freddy White (left), Ralph Johnson (center), and me (right) posing during a Latin Percussion photo shoot.

In Hawaii in 1975—Chico Woolfolk, Andrew Woolfolk, Larry Dunn, me, Carl Carwell, Al McKay, and Johnny Graham.

Me, Larry Dunn, Freddy White, and Al McKay during a sound check in Hawaii.

Backstage the gang gets ready to play—Al McKay, Ralph Johnson, Andrew Woolfolk, and Larry Dunn.

EWF toured America almost nonstop during the late 1970s. Al McKay, Maurice White, and Andrew Woolfolk on the tour bus that took us across the country.

In Honolulu in 1980 with Janet and our kids: Sir, Trinity, and Creed.

de force jam with Afro-Cuban percussion, Larry's organ and Fender Rhodes electric piano, plus a CTI Records–style trumpet solo. By combining those distinctive jazz layers with bouncy, funky guitars and Maurice's creative melodies, our sound tightened up.

We posed shirtless for the cover art of *Head to the Sky,* sexy and silly young men with a whole lot of energy who were just plain crazy. None of our waistlines measured more than twenty-nine inches. Jessica, who was at the center of the photo, was our little princess, until she began missing gigs and getting sidetracked with certain substances. Eventually Maurice had to let her go. Everybody loved Jessica like a sister. She was the sweetest thing with those beautiful eyes and her great voice, and I was sad that we weren't able to work it out. Jessica wound up being the last female core member of the group, as after her departure Maurice decided to discontinue the female vocalist role and go on with just the guys.

While Earth, Wind & Fire aspired to lift our listeners with hope, humanity, and positivity, 1973 signaled the start of a new sociopolitical era. The World Trade Center became the tallest building in the world as Richard Nixon, during the Watergate scandal, announced to the American public, "I am not a crook." OPEC nations began flexing their economic muscles and restricted the flow of oil to the United States, causing sharp increases in gasoline prices and signaling the arrival of blocks-long gasoline lines, and American troops were finally withdrawing from Vietnam and coming home.

The 1973 release of *Head to the Sky* heralded the beginning of our Earth, Wind & Fire station wagon tours. In those days we were playing a lot of college gigs to younger, jazz-loving audiences. We performed at a large outdoor show for a New York City college on its campus. It was the first time such a big crowd turned out to see us. Once we began to hear "Evil" on the radio, we figured things were moving forward.

For these tours, there were no more U-Haul trailers or vans for us. Instead we would fly to the East Coast and rent four or five station wagons. We carried our gear, drums, amps, and guitars, loaded up our own luggage into the back of each vehicle, and took turns driving. Ralph loved to drive. While Larry wasn't the greatest, I was a pretty decent driver. Johnny and Al drove a little whenever they were needed, and Verdine, well, forget it. We would cover the entire East Coast this way, checking into Holiday Inns, setting up at the venue and performing our act, then leaving for the next town in the dead of night. We were young and could handle the rigors of the road, motorcading from town to town, college to college.

Although I was an experienced road warrior—I was used to loading and unloading drums and Hammond organs from back when I traveled all over Colorado playing in small groups—I had never had the best sense of direction. One time when we had a gig on the northeast side of Washington, DC, we hung out afterward at a late-night party until about four in the morning. I was in charge of driving the band back to the Holiday Inn, but the Northeast, Northwest, Southeast, Southwest addresses got me so confused that I was completely turned around.

It was funny at first. Everybody laughed at our being lost and that I had no idea where we were. After driving around in circles, we'd end up back where we started, right near the Washington Monument. Then we found ourselves in the midst of heavy early-morning rush hour traffic. By then, the guys were so angry at me that I wasn't allowed to drive again for quite a while. After another late-night gig, I stole the car keys and hid them. It took the band all night to find them, and we didn't get back to the motel until almost sunrise, when we had to check out and leave again. I thought I was being funny, but nobody else did.

None of us was a novice in terms of touring, and we weren't averse to bunking two to a room, except for Maurice, who would book himself into a suite or his own room. We were so young, traversing the country, ordering room service, and ODing on cheesesteaks in Philly and buffalo wings in Buffalo. Luckily, the station wagon era didn't last for more than a year or so, just until we could afford to hire a roadie or two.

Maurice did not hang out with us after the shows but would take a car back to the hotel while the rest of us were out and about in search of parties. There were very few occasions when that he spent free time with us as a group. Apart from the age gap, Maurice had been a well-traveled musician with Ramsey Lewis, and was already road-tested and worldly while we were going through our early, partying phase. Unless we were in Manhattan hanging out with VIPs, Reese would make himself scarce while we were out chasing women, smoking herb, playing chess, or getting our hair braided.

Being on the East Coast was a different world for me. I had never been called a nigger in all my life until the time we got stuck in New Jersey on one of our station wagon tours. We had gotten seriously lost on the New Jersey Turnpike, and when we stopped at a filling station to get gas and directions, the people there would not sell us any fuel. I was so green that at first I thought they must not have heard my request.

"Excuse me, sir," I said, but they just sat there, looking at me as if I were crazy. The attendant muttered under his breath as I walked away. But being from Denver, I didn't know any different. I guess I should have sensed the weird vibes and left, but I went back to the door and repeated myself.

"Excuse me, sir?"

The guy snapped back at me, "I said, nigger, get outta here!"

Dawg! I only wanted to know how to get to New Brunswick, and there I was, a grown man, crushed. That hadn't ever happened to me in Colorado or California! I'll never forget how demoralized I felt. The man didn't even know me. How hurtful. I got back in the car and told the guys what had just happened. We were silent all the way to the hotel. Still, it was a different dues-paying experience than that of our R&B chitlin' circuit predecessors, who drove from coast to coast and throughout the Deep South, routinely putting up with the adverse racial climate across the country. At least we didn't have to endure that.

Back off the road and between recording sessions we had the hottest of jam sessions, which kept us sharp. Larry and I—and now Andrew—practically lived on top of one another on Blackwelder Street. Ralph used to come over and hang out with us, and we would play our instruments all day whenever we didn't have any gigs or recording planned. I found an old Wurlitzer piano, and somebody else gave me some vibes.

We drank carrot juice, and used aloe vera skin cream, a medicinal herbal remedy originating in North Africa. At one point the entire band tried becoming vegetarian. That didn't last long. Verdine got into transcendental meditation (TM) through Bob Cavallo and his wife, who hooked him up with a retreat in Laurel Canyon.

We were becoming an insulated—and opinionated—bunch. To us, groups like Harold Melvin & the Blue Notes were drill-team doo-wop stuff, "shoo-shoo-pa-doop." Being young and cocky, we soon got our clocks cleaned and learned a valuable lesson.

One night we opened for a band at the Armory in Washington, DC. We came out and did a flower-child set to polite applause and felt we had done all right that night—until Parliament Funkadelic came onstage and funked us right out of the building! We got our pants blown off! Funkadelic revved up a hellacious groove amid a thick cloud of smoke. The party got hot and heavy from the very first song. The whole venue was transfixed, with a packed house of nothing but black folks swaying from side to side. It was a different experience for me! It's something we laugh about nowadays, but at the time, we weren't used to getting knocked off the stage so severely. After the gig we sat around our motel rooms, moping and feeling hangdog. Then Maurice said, "We've got to go home and rehearse!" Thinking about it now, EWF didn't have the chops to compete with a band like Parliament Funkadelic. Getting our asses handed to us was the best way for us to learn to toughen up our sound.

While we were making progress live and in the studio, we hadn't yet developed the sharp edge that EWF is now known for. Since getting blown out at the Armory, we still chuckle (and cringe) whenever someone has the audacity to call Earth, Wind & Fire a funk band. But it was the Armory show that helped us go home and face the fact that we needed to inject some elements of funk and swing into our sound. Once we returned to LA we practiced our butts off, recharged, and got it together. While being upstaged had been a tremendous shock to our systems, it didn't happen again.

16

MIGHTY, MIGHTY CHARLES STEPNEY

With our lineup settled in and two Columbia albums under our belts, Maurice had met his early crossover goals. He had two strong attributes that made him a great bandleader. Number one, he was relentless and would not give up or throw in the towel when dealt a setback or disappointment. He could turn bad news to his advantage. Second, Reese knew how to bring in reinforcements when he felt it was time to raise the bar. In the winter of 1973, as we repaired to Caribou Ranch Studios in the foothills of the Rocky Mountains to record our third Columbia album, *Open Our Eyes,* he also wanted to add an extra dimension to our arrangements—and he knew just who to call. It was his hope that this new team member, an old friend and associate from his Chess Records days in Chicago, would vault us into rarefied gold- and platinum-record sales status and bring the material and our performances into a tighter focus.

Looking back, had Charles Stepney not been introduced into our ranks, there would have been no Earth Wind & Fire, or certainly not as we currently know it. This man made that much of a difference. As Maurice told me recently, "Charles was a very talented individual who made a great contribution to EWF, and through EWF, to humanity."

Charles was a genius, a musician, songwriter, producer, engineer, and arranger all rolled into one. I know the term "genius" is overused, but not in this case. Charles was the creator behind the studio band Rotary Connection, an esoteric ensemble that mixed soul, pop, avant-garde, and psychedelia into a progressive sonic stew. In 1970 Stepney brought Rotary Connection vocalist Minnie Riperton into the studio to record an amazing solo debut called *Come to My Garden*, which harvested an R&B/Top 40 crossover hit of the same name. (Like EWF, Minnie landed a record contract with CBS. After a couple of big hit records, she died in 1979 after a fatal bout with breast cancer.)

Even before I joined EWF I had been a huge fan of Minnie's, completely enamored of her incredible vocal range and her sweet harmonic styling. Perry Jones, Larry Dunn, and I loved listening to *Come to My Garden*. Now Charles Stepney, the man behind her music, was playing on our team. I regarded his joining the EWF team as an act of divine intervention. I was so caught up in Minnie's magic that I felt blessed to be mentored by the same guy who had guided her star!

Physically, Stepney was an unassuming black man. He was a bit of a frumpy guy and reminded Larry and me of Yogi Bear. Charles looked more like a math teacher or a scientist than a record producer. He stood about five-seven and, the consummate studio rat, smoked like a chimney and drank lots of coffee, but wasn't a drug user. He was a devoted family man and avid father, not a wild man by any stretch. Charles was a grounded individual—grounded like a rock—and very wise. He could say very little and still communicate quite a bit. His talents as a brass arranger and orchestrator were out of this world, and he banked major credibility with the studio musicians with whom he worked, including giants like Muddy Waters and Howlin' Wolf. In addition to his work with Rotary Connection, Charles produced a couple of "artists' artist" albums by elite Chicago guitarist-folksinger Terry Callier and jazz/R&B session player Phil Upchurch. In 1968 Stepney also produced two albums by Ramsey Lewis for Cadet Records, which is probably where Maurice experienced the Stepney magic firsthand, watching how the man could write orchestrations seemingly right off the top of his head, including a trio recording entitled *Maiden Voyage* and a charming record Ramsey cut accompanied by the Chicago Symphony Orchestra (with Moog synthesizer) called *Mother Nature's Son,* featuring Ramsey's interpretations of songs from The Beatles' self-titled 1968 release universally called "The White Album."

Stepney also produced another influential work on Cadet called *Freedom Means* by the Chicago R&B group The Dells. This very eclectic and unusual album features an angst-ridden, heartbreaking ballad called "The Love We Had (Stays on My Mind)" as well as some strangely middle-of-the-road, R&B-sounding covers, including Bread's "Make It with You" (which we also covered), Burt Bacharach and Hal David's "One Less Bell to Answer," and a medley combining Rod McKuen's "If You Go Away" with the theme from *Love Story.* The Dells and their burly baritone lead singer, Marvin Junior, had a sound that influenced Kenny Gamble and Leon Huff to sign Harold Melvin & the Blue Notes to their Philadelphia International soul label. As you might recall, the Blue Notes featured a young lead singer named Teddy Pendergrass, a baby version of Marvin Junior!

With his no-sun studio tan, Stepney lived like a hermit and wasn't exactly the picture of health. He worked in his four-track studio, tucked in the basement of his Chicago home—a nondescript single-family dwelling he shared with his wife and kids—composing and combing through technical manuals and constantly tinkering in his "writing room." Whatever technology was new in the world of recorded music during the 1970s, Charles was up on it. If he couldn't play a particular instrument, he would buy one, take it to his basement, and sit there until he mastered the darned thing. Charles was also a consummate songwriter, conductor, and musician who played vibes, keyboards, and piano. He could not only talk the talk but walk the walk, and showed us exactly what to do and how to do it.

If Maurice was the mastermind of EWF, Charles would become the gale force behind the creator. His contributions in the studio were incalculable. During the *Open Our Eyes* sessions, he taught me how to sing a song that I had cowritten with Maurice called "Devotion," one of the early pieces that expressed the band's spiritual side. The lyrics of "Devotion" were inspired by my going to catechism class when I was a boy attending Catholic school. (Catechism is like Sunday school for Catholics, except that you attend every day in the summer.)

Charles went over the entire structure of "Devotion" with all the musicians. The man had perfect pitch. He could break down and show Maurice and me the exact voicing we needed to further polish our seamless harmonic vocal arrangements. He would also strengthen and rewrite certain rhythms. Because jazz changes were important to everyone in the band except for Al McKay—who would comment on the "funny style chords" we were coming up with in our songs—instead of having Al play the whole chord and its extensions, like Larry did, Charles would tell Al to play part of the chord, but instructed him specifically as to which two notes to omit!

It was amazing to watch Charles work. I recall his coaching Andrew Woolfolk through a driving Coltranesque soprano saxophone solo on a short, free-jazz passage we called "Spasmodic Mood." During those sessions Andrew was having problems navigating the song's changes. Charles broke it down by suggesting that instead of tackling the complex solo as a whole, maybe Andrew should concentrate on one particular scale. Afterward, he worked through Andrew's intricate bebop solo note by note until Andrew got it right. It was as if Charles had visualized the whole thing in his head beforehand.

Stepney was also our Minimoog specialist and technician. He was the one who did our synthesizer programming, which had to be tediously dissected note by note because, at that time, the keyboard wasn't polyfunctional (or polyphonic), meaning that we couldn't play multiple notes and chords on it the way we can today.

Charles was a visionary, a philosopher, a father figure to the band members, and a big brother to Maurice. Maurice respected him as he did no other human being, and Charles was one of the few men Reese would take advice, criticism, and direction from. Maurice respected Stepney because Stepney wasn't intimidated by him. If Maurice wanted to do something in the studio that sounded wrong, Charles would scold him, "Now, Rooney, we don't do that." Surprisingly, Reese was okay with that, though woe be to the band member who tried the same maneuver. Charles also encouraged us to write songs and put together music that incorporated more than just our individual parts. Our drummer, Ralph, would often sit with Charles at the piano, working on augmented chords and musical ideas.

Stepney became our George Martin and our Quincy Jones, making sense of what was floating around in our heads. One cold day Maurice and I visited him in Chicago as he toiled amid the cigarette butts and coffee cups in the basement of his house, tinkering with the postproduction tracks for *Open Our Eyes*. One song Charles played us on the four-track tape recorder he used to store musical ideas was a funky little number he called "Tee Nine Chee Bit." After filling up all four tracks, Charles would bounce them around and remix them.

Together Maurice and Charles had fire and swagger; they were a dynamite team. It was plain to see that the new songs on *Open Our Eyes* that featured Stepney as engineer, arranger, and producer were getting tighter and tighter. Charles was leading us toward scoring that elusive hit record!

Which is what happened with "Mighty, Mighty," a tune that Verdine and Maurice cooked up. Not only did the song unfold with a catchy hook in the chorus, but Charles overlaid my multitracked vocal parts in a way that would become a key ingredient of Earth Wind & Fire's signature sound. Combining Al McKay's thick funk chords and riffs with Andrew Woolfolk's interwoven saxophone fills and countermelodies, "Mighty, Mighty" became a multifaceted, creative success. Hallelujah! Although the song peaked at number fifteen on the Billboard R&B singles charts, in my book the song qualified as our first bona fide hit! *Open Our Eyes* wound up staying on the Billboard album charts for thirty-seven weeks.

We followed up "Mighty, Mighty" with the soulfully introspective "Devotion," which featured another layered vocal performance by yours truly. By now I was feeling extremely confident with my role in the band. When I first heard the finished version of "Devotion," I was so impressed with the synths and chord changes that Stepney had added that I concluded that the song wouldn't have been effective without them. Charles was hearing elements of sound in his head that nobody else had imagined. Two other tracks on *Open Our Eyes,* "Kalimba Story" and "Drum Song," marked an important recording milestone for us: the debut of Maurice's African thumb piano, which he first discovered during his stint with the Ramsey Lewis Trio. The *kalimba* would come to represent a significant and exotic recurring musical ingredient for EWF. (Kalimba would later also be the name of Maurice's personal production company.)

Recording *Open Our Eyes* in Nederland, Colorado, at the opulent Caribou Ranch was a Rocky Mountain homecoming. The studio was a converted barn getaway built by James William Guercio, the producer and manager of our labelmate Chicago. We were one of the first bands after Chicago to record there. Hundreds of famous albums have been cut there since, including Elton John's *Caribou, Captain Fantastic and the Brown Dirt Cowboy,* and *Rock of the Westies.*

The funniest thing about *Open Our Eyes* is the cover photo. I'd rank it one of our worst. Maurice decided he wanted a group shot taken in the high altitude and thin air of the Rockies. There we were, early in the morning, standing in the mountains, frozen to the bone! Looking at the picture of us wearing our colorful costumes and robes, you have no idea how bitterly cold it was up there! If you could only see the snot running out of our noses as the photographer said, "One more time." And if that wasn't bad enough, something then went wrong with the camera's original exposures, so we ended up having to go to the Rockies twice! If you look closely, you can see by the looks on our faces how pissed off and unhappy we were. When the photo rushes from the session were sent to us, we were in Germany on tour. The art department needed someone to sign off in a hurry, or we would miss our album release date. When Joe Ruffalo showed me the final cover photos, I was mortified. I looked as if I had just come from a mortuary. The label tried fixing it, but we only looked worse. Even with the airbrushing and touch-ups, I definitely looked as if I were ready for the casket. I cried the first I saw the original finished cover.

Cover art aside, the album, buoyed by our first hit, "Mighty, Mighty," sold 500,000 copies. *Open Our Eyes* became our first gold record and our first hit album for Columbia! By then Earth, Wind & Fire had two Warner and three CBS releases, and it's hard to imagine a major label today being that patient in waiting for an artist to succeed. One of the main reasons we had chosen to record for Columbia Records was that, back when Perry Jones was still struggling for recognition at Warner, Clive Davis had already built an impressive black music division within a major label structure. Consequently the success of black record executives came about in part as a result of Earth, Wind & Fire's success and the crossover groundwork we helped lay during the early 1970s. The corporate atmosphere was a-changin'. African Americans were making inroads inside corporations like Xerox, IBM, and now CBS Records. That way once Clive's promotion staff set out to acknowledge black radio stations, specifically black program directors and general managers, the African American promotion men found they could better relate to black disc jockeys and music directors. Powerful black programmers and music directors had certain domains:

You needed Frankie Crocker on board at WBLS in New York, or Georgie Woods at WDAS in Philly, and Rodney Jones, who ran WVON in Chicago, on your side. These were the men who had to be on board, playing our records.

We knew our fan base had to start with black listeners in major R&B markets like Philadelphia; New York; Chicago; and Washington, DC, or risk fading away. Our strategy was to establish that firm R&B (or urban) base and then expand. Maurice had envisioned that, however, when he refused to sign with African American–based companies like Motown, Stax, or, for that matter, Chess.

Unfortunately, just as we gained a valuable, creative ally in the studio with Charles Stepney, we would lose our most important supporter on the record company front. Between the releases of *Head to the Sky* and *Open Our Eyes,* Columbia Records dismissed Clive Davis and escorted him out of the building in connection with an internal investigation concerning fraudulent invoices processed by someone within the company. Replacing Clive as label president would be the hard-nosed Walter Yetnikoff, who would send the label into a whole new, frenzied era while across town Clive would launch a competitive giant, Arista Records, the label that would be responsible for such pop successes as Whitney Houston and Barry Manilow. With Clive, the man who signed us, now gone, would we have the necessary corporate allies to become the crossover band of our dreams?

With the combined talents of Cavallo-Ruffalo, Columbia, a road crew headed by Leonard Smith, and producer and arranger Charles Stepney, we had built an organization that finally had gone gold. And while we maintained our strong roots in the R&B community, our music was becoming edgier and more socially aware. We felt the need to cross Maurice's message of spirituality and positivism over to a deeper, wider, mainstream American audience. Right around the time of *Open Our Eyes,* we opened for Sly Stone at Madison Square Garden in New York. We killed him that night.

By then he was done, though, and our time had come. I recall that during that gig, Verdine flew up into the air in a harness, and the audience went nuts.

To keep in touch with my roots during this heady period, I made a pilgrimage to Denver, drove my car up into the mountains, and reconnected for a few days, breathing in the clean mountain air. Being in Colorado again made me aware of the stark contrast between who I had been back in Denver and who I was now in Los Angeles. But as I continued to discover myself as an artist and performer, in the mountains I pondered many questions: Who am I? What's my style? What is my fashion? What do I want to look like? What's my swagger? One day it all came to me, basic and direct: If I concentrated on becoming the best I could be, no one could do it better than me. If I was secure enough in my abilities, I could become myself without reservation or fear of intimidation of being "found out" or exposed. It was up to *me* to discover and enhance the better parts of myself. I visualized myself as a shining star. This would be an image that I would ruminate on for quite a while, and a theme that would soon emerge as the central inspiration for one of my best songs.

17

SHINING STAR

Between 1971 and 1976 Earth, Wind & Fire would release seven major-label releases, which meant we were constantly caught up in the cycle of recording and writing songs. After *Open Our Eyes* struck gold, we returned to the Caribou Ranch with our team in late 1974 to make our crucial follow-up album. This time we arrived with a new band member, Maurice having decided we needed more edge on the drums. As Reese put in more and more time writing and producing, he found less time to devote to actually playing the drums himself. He soon hired a logical successor—his younger half-brother Freddie White.

Freddie made his bones as a professional drummer at age sixteen playing with the late, great singer-keyboardist Donny Hathaway. You can hear Freddie on Hathaway's finest record, a 1972 Atlantic release simply titled *Live*. *Live* is a record respected and revered by Donny's fans and fellow musicians alike. Hathaway had a sweet, soulful singing voice, and a rousing, rhythmic keyboard style in the spirit of Stevie Wonder and Brian McKnight. He was also a monster bandleader. *Live* is ridiculously funky and tasteful. It contains cooking versions of Marvin Gaye's "What's Going On," John Lennon's "Jealous Guy," and his signature live and audience-driven magnum opus, "The Ghetto." Side one was recorded live at the Troubadour in Hollywood, and side two was cut at the Bitter End in New York City. Maurice's Chicago friend Phil

Upchurch plays guitar in Hathaway's band on side one, and Cornell Dupree plays on side two, while Freddie drums on both sides. In addition to playing with Hathaway, Freddie also drummed briefly for Lowell George and Little Feat when he moved out to California from Chicago. Freddie's credentials were very impressive. He wasn't merely gravy-training on his older brother's name. Prior to his joining the group, whenever we'd visit Chicago, he was just Verdine's little brother. I had never suspected that he was such a gifted musician.

Combining Ralph and Freddie on drums was a fantastic idea. I liked playing with two drummers, and they meshed well. I had wondered how Freddie's joining EWF would impact Ralph's role, but apparently Ralph had a thick enough skin about it so that once they got the ego stuff out of the way, it was back to the groove. Besides, Ralph was a survivor. When he was first hired, on occasion Ralph and Maurice clashed. But soon they realized that in terms of playing, each musician had his own approach. The same rule held for Ralph and Freddie.

Since Maurice recorded a lot of the drum parts himself in the studio, Ralph wasn't as active in the studio sessions. Reese orchestrated the tracks and was often the creator of the music, so he knew exactly how he wanted things played. Bringing Freddie in stirred the pot a little. Maurice employed Freddie mainly because he needed a more sustained, steady, and consistent groove. While Maurice himself was jazzy and fiery and could groove, as could Ralph, Freddie's beat was downright infectious. As a singer I loved how Freddie put it down in a whole new style. He was part of the new school of drummers of the day, with more of a solid beat. Maurice came from another era and could swing. Ralph, a West Coast groove player, had a smoother style of keeping the beat. Freddie relied less on fills and lived solidly "in the pocket."

Adding my congas to the mix was a whole different thing. Congas don't matter a lick until you have the groove already locked down. If the foundation and essential groove isn't solid, the extra piece of percussion just adds noise. With the rhythms firmly in place, my percussion would be the icing on the cake. And that's what made EWF "tick-tock."

Adding Freddie and Al McKay and taking out some of the jazzier elements while injecting more R&B and edgy groove, our sound was taking on a different fire during rehearsals. We now had the perfect rhythmic blend for the new music we were about to record at Caribou Ranch. I could sense our next record was going to be a killer! This was to be the album that would become our breakthrough, *That's the Way of the World.*

After enlisting Freddie White on drums, the second new weapon in our creative arsenal was the addition of a mixing and engineering studio ace named George Massenburg. As our sound became fatter and more complex with the addition of strings, brass, and orchestral arrangements, we needed more clarity, punch, and polish in the mix on our albums. That's where Massenburg came in. It was Bob Cavallo who first suggested, on Lowell George's recommendation, that we bring him to the Caribou Ranch. When Cavallo first contacted Massenburg, who came from Baltimore, he was living in France. It was difficult reaching him in Europe, as in those days you couldn't just phone somebody in Paris. (It took six months for residents to obtain phone service!) So we sent George a letter asking him to work with us. George accepted and flew out to the States—to the Caribou Ranch and Los Angeles—just in time to record *That's the Way of the World.*

Returning to Colorado energized me. Maurice and I became inseparable there, cowriting songs. We had some very special moments composing lyrics and discussing life together at Caribou. I had my two-year-old son, Sir James, with me, and Maurice and I would go out for walks in the countryside. Reese would open up and talk about his younger days growing up in Memphis, and we would compare childhood experiences. There were no distractions as the lyrics, philosophies, and music flowed out of us effortlessly.

We didn't have any typical songwriting process but just grabbed pen and paper and went at it. We'd often switch roles as to who had the responsibility for the music and who wrote the lyrics. Composing can be a very cerebral and curious process. I have a theory about different plateaus of creativity. I believe lyrics and melody come from three levels: surfacing from a third power to the second power, and then upward to the first (and primary) power of our creative consciousness. When we composed songs, I'd hatch an idea buried in the third power of my mind—the intuitive level. As I began writing, I would woodshed the ideas back and forth to Maurice, bringing the song up to the second power—the development level. With the tweaks, rewrites, and changes we completed the process at the first power, the completed level. While I may have written most of a given song initially, without Maurice being the yin to my yang, I could never have brought it to full fruition by myself.

Though some may use a different terminology, I suspect that's how most cowriters collaborate. The seed of an idea can begin in the lowest layer of the psyche. You can't quite spell it or draw it out completely. Then, as someone else throws out ideas, the song begins to take shape as you start to isolate what in the material works. Finally, once the body of the song and the concept are fully intact, the process speeds up considerably, and soon you're able to polish it off to its final first layer.

Ideas for a song come to me in waves: The first verse. The hook. Chorus and bridge. I might realize that the third verse is actually the most powerful part of the song, so it becomes the opening. Once the reassembled song unfolds, it's almost done. When writing lyrics, I need a seed plot—the body of the song—clear, strong, and succinct enough to spark its energy.

Charles Stepney used to say that originality comes in three waves: imitation, assimilation, and creativity. How, as youngsters, do we learn to speak or walk? First we imitate the steps or sounds that we take from different sources. Then we assimilate them into our own bodies. From them we begin to create our "brand," our walk, our own voice. That's how we learn to do anything, for that matter. We walk our walk only after we have imitated who and what we see. In music, you can create something that's different, but it's ultimately a product of the twelve keys of the scale.

It sounds basic, but the creative process is much more interesting if you actually have something to say. A song is easier to write if you have an idea to convey. You can come up with great music and riffs all day long, but if you don't have a message, how can they be the basis for a great song? The core strength of a song comes from the central theme of its lyrics. "Shining Star" is a good example. The theme of "Shining Star" is that we are all special in our own way. It became an important song to me because of the time I spent asking myself, *What will it take to one day succeed?*

The message? I can become that shining star, and that tune became our first Top 40 crossover hit. It was a hallelujah moment cowritten with Maurice and Larry that set me ablaze creatively. Typically, once we hit the studio with a song, we didn't know what was going to happen to it or what Maurice might add to it. In the case of "Shining Star," Maurice began his magic by bringing the band in and explaining everyone's parts. When he played back the completed track for Bob Cavallo, Bob said, "You've got your first number one record."

To Bob's credit, he was astute about assessing a song's hit potential. He would often take Verdine and me out for walks and talk to us. I don't know what he would tell Maurice and the others, but he would urge us, "You guys gotta take it to the next step!"

Just before we sent the final master of "Shining Star" over to the record company, it underwent one more round of tweaks. Massenburg and Cavallo sneaked back into the studio in the middle of the night, bringing Freddie White in with them. On the drum track, they had Freddie hit the second and fourth beat of each measure, hard on the snare. Those touches made "Shining Star" much more pop-friendly, giving it a bit of a rock beat. The next day Bob called Maurice into the control room to play back what they'd concocted.

Maurice was pissed off at first, but after he listened to the track a few times, he told Bob he couldn't hear a difference. But *I* knew. Maybe he didn't want to let on, but Maurice could hear it. Once the song shot straight to the top of the charts, it was no longer an issue. We had our first across-the-board number one hit record on Top 40 and R&B—simultaneously! I didn't mention anything to Maurice about the last-minute snare hits. I was pleased that my message of personal success hit the airwaves worldwide while Bob, George, and Freddie's two- and four-beat punches brought that sucker home!

18

TTWOTW (THAT'S THE WAY OF THE WORLD)

Making *That's the Way of the World* was the happiest time for Earth, Wind & Fire. We had the team solidly set up and we were exceeding our expectations. Everybody was in high spirits playing together in the studio. This was right before the floodgates burst and the pop craziness began; the band was in the honeymoon phase of its relationship. Everything was in place: We knew our roles, and we were ready for whatever was about to come our way. Or so we thought. Maurice was working on ideas for making the live stage productions more elaborate and theatrical. We had made enough noise both on the touring front and in the record stores that people knew we were for real.

Columbia was excited for us to deliver the new record and hired one of the hottest music photographers—a lensman named Norman Seeff—to take our pictures for the front cover. Each band member was photographed individually, with Seeff shooting each of us in midair while jumping up and down on a trampoline, so that as he snapped our photos, we were in various states of flight. Afterward he cut out each black-and-white character portrait and arranged them all across a clean white gatefold album cover. It's interesting looking at that cover. Almost everyone is in motion—me, I'm doing the boogaloo. Maurice has both feet firmly on the ground with a satisfied grin on his face. Like the Zen master, he's in control.

This was the first record on which I could stretch out and compose ballads. As a writer I was creatively on fire, having cowritten five of the eight songs. Al McKay's scintillating opening chords and riff on "Shining Star" were phenomenal. Although "Shining Star" shot straight to number one on the charts, the love ballad I sang lead on and cowrote, "Reasons," was soon to become one of our top signature standards. On "All About Love," Maurice expounds his doctrine of positivism, preaching that we are as beautiful as our thoughts. Reese then mentions astrology, occult sciences, mysticism, and world religions—introducing EWF's message of universalism—in order to promote understanding of the inner self. With swelling strings and brass from Charles Stepney's deft charts, the song expands into a big production piece.

As happy as I was with the band, I was also becoming a perfectionist in the studio while cutting tracks with the other band members. I was death on the other guys if they made mistakes. I had no mercy—none at all. Finally Charles approached me one morning at breakfast in his fatherly way and spoke with me about my behavior.

"You know, Phil, it's only music."

"What are you talking about?" I asked, perplexed. Music was the driving force in my life—and I knew how important it was to him. But Charles insisted.

"It's only music, Philip. Music is not more important than relationships," he said.

More wisdom from Charles: There's a way to do things, but there's also a way to bring out the best in people without tearing them down. People are more important than the task at hand. This would be a vital lesson I would take to heart at a later stage of my career.

As we toiled on our new record, Earth, Wind & Fire became involved with another movie project. Following the success of

Sweet Sweetback, we hooked up with another filmmaker, a producer-director named Sig Shore. Shore had previously directed a few commercials and made some films about skiing but had achieved cinematic success as the producer of *Superfly,* the red-hot blaxploitation movie that sold more than thirty million dollars in tickets. Curtis Mayfield's famous soundtrack spawned three crossover hits and sold more than a million copies. Shore had sold Maurice on the idea of working together on a film that would feature our music, with *That's the Way of the World* as its official soundtrack album. In Shore's film, also called *That's the Way of the World,* the movie's protagonist was a hot record producer named Coleman Buckmaster (played by Harvey Keitel) who, according to the story line, worked with our band on his label. We costarred by playing ourselves, known as "the Group."

Of course, we had never acted in the movies before, and I think we did a fairly admirable job, considering we were all celluloid rookies. I recall filming some scenes in New York City. We performed "Happy Feeling" and actually cut the song in a roller rink during one of the takes. Although we recorded it again once we got back in the studio, we ended up using the original take because it felt so much better. In one scene of the film, Keitel's character, Coleman, shows a piano player some notes in the studio. As the piano player plays the chords, we see that it's Charles Stepney.

Making *That's the Way of the World* (the record) was a spiritual experience for me and took all of us out of ourselves. It was as if God had been guiding us through the record. When Maurice played us the finished mix and sequence of the finished album, I thought we sounded like angels, and the strings sounded like heaven. I was profoundly moved.

It didn't go as well on the movie front. Unbeknownst to me, our managers were very unhappy working with Sig Shore. Bob felt that Maurice and the band had held up our end of the deal, writing some great songs, but the movie was another story. It turned out that Shore had sold us a bill of goods about a lot of things. He promised he was going to hire a big director, but ended up directing the film himself. (Maybe that's what he had had in mind all along.) He was convinced that he had created something extraordinary and special and that it was going to make his career as a major Hollywood director.

When we attended a screening of the film in Los Angeles, we were shattered. It was a lousy movie with a bad story line, to boot. The quality of the record stood so far above that of the movie, it was embarrassing. Verdine started to cry when the film ended. We were extremely concerned that Sig's dog of a movie would damage our careers.

Then an angry Cavallo took us aside. "I know you guys are hurt, but I want you to know I'm going to fix this."

The unfortunate part of our original arrangement was that we'd made a deal with Shore granting him a piece of our record, while we would own a piece of the action on his film! Just as Bob had liberated us from our Warner Brothers record contract, he now sprang into action with Shore. He arranged a meeting with Sig, who began by bragging about how great his new film would do, so Bob challenged his ego and Hollywood vanity.

"If you're so confident," Bob told Sig, "why don't you take back our piece of the picture, and give us your piece of the publishing on the record?"

"Done," Sig said.

Cavallo quickly had all the rights to our songs reverted back to us. Thank God. Bob was so relieved. Once the film was released, it played on only a handful of screens around the country, and died in just a few days. Even though it was distributed by United Artists, Keitel wouldn't promote or talk about the film, and it soon vanished.

That's the Way of the World (the album) became a milestone for us upon its release in March 1975. It went on to sell three million copies and won a Grammy for Best R&B Vocal Performance by a Group. The album, along with "Shining Star," topped both the

Billboard singles and album charts simultaneously and garnered two more mass-appeal EWF hits! Hidden in small type on the back cover of the album was the message that *TTWOTW* was the original soundtrack for the Sig Shore production. Nobody cared one way or the other about the film.

Meanwhile, back on the creative front, Charles Stepney was feeling dissatisfied with the production credit he had been receiving. Maurice did have an odd way of crediting producers on our records ("odd" being a generous description). While Charles had elevated our game on *Open Our Eyes,* it was Joe Wissert who had been credited as coproducer alongside Maurice. Although Stepney was named as "associate producer," Charles was the man. As Reese and Charles took over the producing helm, the music got too deep for Joe, who became "executive producer."

Charles had since graduated from "associate producer" to "coproducer." He wasn't the kind of person to be overly concerned about his credits and billing. One of the reasons he went along with them at first was because, to him, it was about the music. That would soon change. Charles was given cowriter credits on some of the songs, and the arrangements and synthesizer parts that he contributed from his basement studio became very much a part of the overall Earth, Wind & Fire sound, inspiring Maurice and me to write great lyrics to accompany them. For instance, on "See the Light," which I cowrote, Charles added a unique 7/8 time signature along with some stylish trills on the lush strings and orchestra. Charles's presence was also strong at our sessions, during which he seriously challenged us younger musicians; nobody was immune when he screwed up. Once, although Ralph was laying down a fine, smooth drum track, Stepney stopped in the middle of the tune and mashed the intercom button.

"Rooney, you need to play on this one, man."

Young Ralph slunk out of the room and headed back to the Rocky Mountain resident cabins.

At other times Stepney would nearly knock Larry off the

keyboard bench, moving over to finish a part Larry was struggling with. Instead of exiting the studio, Larry would stand behind Stepney to watch and learn as Charles finished the track. Although Larry felt like a bumbling Barney Fife looking over Charles's shoulder, he sucked it up and benefited from the rejection.

"I'm gonna get it," Larry would sigh. "I may not have the feel on this one, but I'll have it the next time."

But Charles was feeling growing resentment over his credit as coproducer for the *TTWOTW* sessions and believed that our records should simply have been credited with "Produced by Maurice White and Charles Stepney." In LA one day, he came to visit Larry in Culver City, to hang out. Larry used the visit as an opportunity to surprise Charles and give him his gold record for the album. When presented with the framed award, Charles appeared lukewarm about it. After Larry vibed him over his indifference, Charles perked up.

"Don't get me wrong," he confided to Larry. "I'm appreciative of the accolades I get from you folks, but I've done a lot more and greater music than just Earth, Wind & Fire." Charles then reminded Larry, "your credit is worth much more than the money that you make from it.

"Let me ask you a question," Charles continued. "If one cat is a producer, and the other cat is a producer, then what the fuck is a *co*producer?"

Especially with the success of *TTWOTW,* Charles Stepney had changed the game for us. He had given us polished hit songs, and though we were writing tunes on our own, he brought us enlightened arrangements. We became like his sons, and he was like our father. Whenever he spoke, we listened. When he said something didn't work, we stopped playing it. We had that much respect and admiration for him.

Soon I began asking myself, *How long will he be with us?* I felt torn between two camps: respect for Charles's immense talents and contributions to our sound and loyalty to Maurice as our leader. I guess that's the way of the world.

19

RIDICULOUSLY FINE

With *Open Our Eyes* gaining gold-record status and *That's the Way of the World* racking up triple-platinum sales, we knew the band was ready to crest. Prior to this breakthrough, we were featured as an opening act on quite a few concert tours, eclipsing and catching headliner bands off guard or sleeping. War, for instance, was never the same after they toured with us. We also opened up for Curtis Mayfield and a funk band from Brooklyn called Mandrill, which had difficulty following us. Our craziest cobilling was an eight-week tour with Uriah Heep, a Spinal Tap-type hard-rock band from London. Although we were not compatible with Uriah Heep's brand of British "art" rock, the audience cheered loudly for us when we exited the stage—as loud as when the headliners hit it.

As their opening act, we brought heat unto "the Heep." Uriah Heep felt the love we were getting from their audiences. They opened their show with a long organ intro, and one night Larry learned the part note for note and played it to start off our set before we went on. The crowd cheered. Then we chanted, "The Heep can't take it! The Heep can't take it!" By the time the tour rolled into Oklahoma, their road manager informed us, "Look, you guys gotta go."

On April 6, 1974, we were booked as part of an eight-band

show at the California Jam rock festival held at the Ontario Motor Speedway in Southern California. It took over an hour to get from our hotel in Anaheim to the stage at the speedway festival grounds, even though we took a helicopter to the gig. We went on second, right after Rare Earth, a Motown rock band known for their hits "Get Ready" and "I Just Want to Celebrate," songs that I had sung during my Top 40 days back in Denver.

The Eagles came on after us, followed by Seals & Crofts, Black Oak Arkansas, and Black Sabbath. At nightfall Cal Jam hosted its headliners, Deep Purple and Emerson, Lake & Palmer. (I have the framed poster of that memorable gig on my wall.) Unlike Woodstock, Cal Jam was very organized and featured multiple stages. The massive crowd—250,000 people had turned up—was orderly, and is technically one of the biggest audiences we've played for in the United States. Although I don't think that performance changed the course of our careers, Cal Jam was definitely a great opportunity for us to gain extra exposure playing among the white rock and roll acts featured on the bill.

I enjoyed the nonstop touring circuit. Being a young road warrior, I was more than happy to be constantly traveling. In 1975 Janet gave birth to our second child, a daughter we named Trinity. While I was working, Janet and the children happily settled down in a house in Los Angeles. EWF became my synergetic family. I spent more time with them than with my own brood.

The thrill of touring was enough to keep our band members euphoric for quite some time. Whenever things got too serious, wherever we traveled, Larry Dunn would play the role of band jokester. He kept everyone in stitches with his wry comments and energy. Nobody tried to throw Larry into the pool—he had been lifting Hammond B-3's since he was thirteen years old. Andrew Woolfolk was also a jolly prankster. He might fill your hotel room trash can with hot water and balance it atop your bedroom door, just waiting for you to return late at night. We had a lot of fun on the road, more fun than serious times, caught up in a whirlwind of fantasy.

We lived modestly, doing what we loved for a decent salary, starting at about six hundred dollars a week with enough per diem cash and pocket money to get by. Nobody seemed strapped for funds or swimming in debt. Housing and apartments were affordable. Accountants and financial managers came into the picture. For instance, if one of us needed to lease a car, someone in the manager's office would set it up. It may not have been a Mercedes—maybe a Volkswagen or an Audi—but we could sign the papers and get on with it.

Larry Dunn became our de facto musical director at age twenty-one. Being a member of Earth, Wind & Fire became a structured job. In preparation for long tours, we would show up at our rehearsal studios in Los Angeles every day at 12:30 and work until 6:00 in the evening. For the first two or three weeks, we would split up and rehearse the basics with the rhythm section—Verdine, Freddie, and Ralph—along with Al, Johnny, Andrew, and Larry. Maurice and I would work out vocal arrangements in a separate room. Afterward we would all converge on the big stage for a few days of final run-throughs. We needed to be in good physical shape in order to perform the required stage moves and song segues. By opening night we were tight, or as Bugs Bunny used to sing: "We knew every part by heart."

As for costuming, we no longer had to create our onstage wardrobes. No more buying our clothes from Capezio's and army-surplus and used-clothing stores. By this point Maurice had found and hired Martine Colette, a professional costume designer, to create our stage wear.

Martine was a very eccentric lady. She lived by a dam where the 210 Freeway in Los Angeles ran into the San Fernando Valley. When Janet and I first went over to her house to pick up my costumes, she had a tiger living in the backyard! And poisonous snakes, too! I found out that Martine was an animal-rights activist, and when people brought exotic animals home from overseas and didn't know how to properly take care of them, they would call her, and she would pick them up and care for them. When Sir and Trinity were little, we would visit Martine and her wonderful zoo animals, which she had in cages around her home. Martine would go on to found a wilderness preserve in Southern California, a 160-acre animal sanctuary called Wildlife Waystation. She is still its director today. Martine later adopted Michael Jackson's chimp, Bubbles, but I first knew her as the original costume lady for EWF.

One day while we were on the road, Maurice announced that we needed to add horns to our live show. Hooray! We were tired of Larry having to play the horn parts from our records on his keyboards, and Maurice wanted the pizzazz and the authentic "zaps and pows" of a real, live horn section. He hired a kicking group composed of his old Chess Studio buddies: saxophonist Don Myrick, Michael Harris on trumpet, and the inimitable Lou Satterfield on trombone. Maurice, Sat, and Don had a long history together back in Chicago, and Lou had played bass on Fontella Bass's "Rescue Me" alongside Maurice in the studio. Originally we wanted to call them the Earth, Wind & Fire Horns, but Maurice was advised against it, so they became The Phenix Horns. Although they were formed as a separate entity, they fit hand in glove with our sound. Myrick and Satterfield created the most awe-inspiring, complex horn charts in memory. Don and Sat also worked with Charles Stepney on our arrangements. Even today they're nearly impossible to replicate onstage.

The Phenix Horns were older, close to Maurice's age. Don Myrick, the spokesman of the three, was beyond special as an instrumentalist, on a par with many of the great jazz saxophonists, like Wayne Shorter or Paul Desmond. He would teach me bebop songs line for line so I could scat to them. Satterfield was like a grandfather, very witty and funny, and in addition to being a fierce musician, he was very knowledgeable about Afrocentric culture. Michael Harris was younger than Don and Sat and had a playful, wild streak to him. Michael was a very gifted trumpet player but was later replaced by Rahmlee Michael Davis.

Because the Phenix Horns were Maurice's contemporaries, they, too, boasted more life experience than we younger members, and we looked to them for guidance. Sat had been Verdine's bass teacher back when Verdine was a teenager. A Buddha of musical knowledge, Sat had a series of off-the-cuff one-liners that I still recall today, borderline malapropisms packed with wisdom. One of my favorite Sat sayings was: "Don't let what you're thinking mess up what's really going on!"

Sat also used to say, "Son, you've got to pay for your fun and folly," meaning there are consequences for everything you do. Nothing is free, and one day there's gonna come a bill. It was a prophetic warning, considering my conduct on the road concerning the ladies.

From the first day Janet and I were married, I had little intention of remaining faithful. As a child I didn't witness much faithfulness in my parents' generation. With Janet back in Los Angeles, I was free to play the field and hook up with the finest-looking women in every city and town. As our live concerts gained popularity with many adoring female fans, the temptation to stray from the path of marriage proved too much to resist. Soon I had a woman in every port. The glitz and glam of being an Earth, Wind & Fire member felt like a combination of Mardi Gras and a three-ring circus. As soon as EWF hit a city or town, I began my womanizing routine.

On one tour in Germany, Don, the sax player, and guitarist Roland Bautista had an argument over one particular groupie and were going at it. When Maurice caught wind of the situation, he yelled out, "Hey! Hey! What's going on?" Then he got real serious. "Look! Are we here for the music or the bitches?"

Larry replied drily, "The bitches!"

There was a pause, and then everybody, including Reese, just fell out with laughter. That incident became a running joke with the band before we would go out onstage.

One day we landed in Philadelphia in our thirty-passenger charter jet. As we filed off the plane, I spied a gorgeous woman in the airport lounge who was . . . ridiculously fine! Supermodel tall and statuesque, she had a beautiful face and a lithe body to match. EWF band members were as alert as hound dogs when it came to sniffing out female talent, and once we got off that plane, everybody's gaze veered directly to her. Typically, if I noticed a lady I particularly fancied, I would alert Leonard—our road manager, Bafa—and give him the signal.

Well, the lady came up to my hotel room, and as we lay there afterward, she reached over and asked me, "Can I use your phone?" As she made her phone call, it was clear that she was speaking to her dude and telling him that she would be with him shortly. As she hung up the phone and got dressed, she remarked candidly, "You know, when I first saw you get off that plane, I said to myself, 'Oooh, I just got to have *him*.' "

Alas! The hunter became the hunted. Although I had been through this scene many times before, this particular time I felt . . . *so cheap!* The joke was on me! I felt so small, as if I were an inch tall.

I told Maurice what had happened. We could talk about anything; inspirationally, he was my brother, father, and homey rolled into one. Writing songs like "Devotion" and "Shining Star" together, we shared a deep, single-minded belief in ourselves. That's what made us such seamless writing partners.

After my experience with the ridiculously fine girl in my room, we wrote the song "Reasons" together. Maurice and I penned what became a classic tune in response to the multitude of women on the road. Today, when people tell me how much they love "Reasons," or when they admit that they got married to that song, I'm always surprised because it's not a romantic song. It deals with the physical love and passion of a one-night stand, and the mind games and illusions that occur at the time.

Didn't anyone bother to listen to the lyrics?

20

JUPITER! JUPITER! WHAT IS THE ANSWER?

By now we had become so famous that on tour we couldn't enter the front doors of a hotel to check in but had to sneak around the back. Security would escort us from the plane to the hotel to the gig, back to the hotel, then back to the plane and then on to the next city. One day at a hotel in Atlanta, we arrived to find a horde of fans, mostly women, waiting for us. As I headed toward my room, a female fan ran up to me in a seeming panic.

"Jupiter! Jupiter!" she pleaded, referring to a song we had begun performing in concert, "What is the answer?"

I gazed at her with a genuine feeling of compassion. "You know, baby, it's just a song." Then security grabbed her and led her away, leaving me confounded. Jupiter? What *was* the answer?

That song, which I had cowritten with Maurice, Verdine, and Larry, would later appear on the *All 'N All* album. As she was led away, I repeated to myself, *It's just a song!* But to this woman it was much more, as if something we had composed held the key to the secrets of the universe. The incident gnawed at me, forcing me to realize that I hadn't a clue about spiritual wisdom. In fact, I was about as dense, spiritually, as you could get. And to think that our most die-hard fans thought that we held the answers to the mysteries of life. That woman was actually searching for meaning in her own life, and she thought that I had it! That struck me and stopped me in my tracks. I hadn't bargained for the responsibility of all this.

At the time I was okay with Maurice's brand of pluralistic universalism and harmony. Although Maurice had been raised by his grandmother in the Baptist Church, according to our music, all religions and philosophies held equal authority on the path toward salvation, and even the artwork on our albums conveyed that message. For example, the inside gatefold for *All 'N All,* created by Japanese sci-fi illustrator Shusei Nagaoka, depicted twelve golden iconic symbols resting on twelve pedestals with an open holy book in front of them. These symbols included a Star of David, a cross, a menorah, a Buddha, and the caduceus (the symbol of medicine: intertwining snakes on a staff surmounted by wings). There were also two Egyptian symbols—the Eye of Horus (signifying a unified cosmos) and the ankh (suggesting eternal life). This amalgamation of sacred iconography typified Maurice's approach to universalism.

At first I had been so swayed and influenced by his spiritual views that during one trip home to Denver, I had informed my mother, "You need to take that white Jesus off your wall. How do you know the Bible isn't just the white man's book created to keep black people down?" Yet at the same time, I was uncomfortable with that pre–New Age stuff. While Larry and I had been raised as Catholics, and we were afraid of the hocus-pocus astrological ideas, Reese and Verdine went to readers, psychics, and soothsayers. All of that was part of the LA landscape at the time. (Remember First Lady Nancy Reagan and her personal astrologer, Linda Goodman?) While the band did get into transcendental meditation, mysticism gave me the creeps. I didn't want any soothsayer telling me what was going to happen to me. What if they told me that I was going to kick the bucket? Who wants to hear that kind of premonition?

The Jupiter incident in Atlanta might have shook me up as much as it did because it drew attention to how much mysticism actually surrounded me. Looking back, my telling my mother that Christianity was a way of keeping black people down only revealed that I was the one who was lost. I enjoyed the trappings of success, and although I was jetting around the globe in private planes and selling out big arenas, I was troubled. I didn't really know anything about Catholicism except for the routines of going to confession and attending catechism as a child. Nothing had stuck, spiritually. I talked to Larry about it, and he agreed that all he had gotten from the Catholic Church "was sore knees because I didn't understand Latin." I had also attended the Baptist church with my mother, where I'd see people shouting and falling down and stuff when I sang in the choir.

Los Angeles was like going to another land, another planet. It's not a spiritual place, but a very hedonistic one, and I had become infatuated by what was going on around me. I was like a kid in a candy store, buying anything I wanted, eating as much as I wanted, anytime I wanted it, and in all the different flavors and colors. In LA everything was at our disposal, and with people living this seemingly decadent life, many of us thought it was going to last forever, and that there would be no consequences and no end to it. You got caught up in its illusion, a high that was very much a lie. But being in your twenties, you didn't focus on it from that perspective; you simply got swept away by it.

This wasn't the first time that these issues had unsettled me, which leads me to the story of how I first got saved. I attended a church service in Chicago at the Life Center Church of God in Christ on Fifty-fifth Street and South Indiana Avenue. The Reverend T. L. Barrett was the resident pastor. Along with Larry Dunn and Andrew Woolfolk, I had decided to pay a visit to Barrett's church because we had heard that the Life Center was a very popular place, and that its congregation drew lots of younger folks. Plus, there was a host of fine-looking ladies who attended the Life Center, and that was good enough for me, as I was always on the prowl.

On the Sunday that we attended the service, Barrett preached about the dangers of making decisions while reacting in the heat of anger and pain—a subject I could heavily relate to. During the sermon Barrett quoted a New Testament passage, Matthew 11:28: "Come to me, all who labor and are heavy laden, and I will give you rest. Come learn from me. For my yoke is easy and my burden is light."

When I heard that verse, I cried uncontrollably, cried as never before in my life. I couldn't stop weeping, and it didn't matter that people were staring at me! I couldn't hide my involuntary tears, and it was through that experience that I began to seek out an understanding of the Bible and my core Christian beliefs. That was the moment I gave my heart to Christ. Once I had that epiphany in Chicago, I prayed, *God, I'm going to stop trying to determine what is true or not true. Instead I'm just going to ask you to answer these questions in my heart.*

Not long after the Jupiter incident, I got on a plane back to Los Angeles and was seated next to a lady, a complete stranger. She turned to me and asked me a question out of the blue.

"Do you have a personal relationship with God?"

That marked the first time I had encountered witnessing of that kind.

"A personal relationship with God?"

I thought about that word, "relationship." I had said my Hail Marys and had been confirmed in the Catholic Church. But a personal relationship with God? Not really.

"You mean, like, do I speak to God, and does he speak back?"

The woman nodded.

I didn't have that kind of relationship with God.

When I got home I told Janet about the religious questions I'd been asking myself, and she revealed to me that, coincidentally, she had been out looking for a home church for us. We ultimately found one after much searching. I met Dr. Billy Ingram, one of the young associate pastors at a church near our home. (This was before Billy earned his doctorate degree.) Because he was my age, Ingram taught the youngadults' ministry. We became fast friends, and when he left and founded the Maranatha Community Church on Martin Luther King Jr. Boulevard in Los Angeles, I became a charter member. Dr. Ingram was an author, educator, poet . . . and a percussionist, just like me. We had a lot in common, and we were very close friends for many years. (On March 8, 2011, Dr. Ingram died unexpectedly of a massive heart attack. To this day, I miss him.)

Back on the road and on another flight soon afterward, I discovered that there was one seat left open on the plane, right next to a priest. I used that opportunity to continue my spiritual search and asked the priest some pointed questions about adultery. He listened to my queries and then stopped me in the course of our conversation.

"You know, Philip, let me explain: It isn't about not committing adultery any longer so that you won't go to hell. Jesus already died for that. It's about your not violating the relationship!"

Here was that poignant word again: "relationship."

My seatmate on the previous flight had spoken about a personal relationship. Now this priest was talking about violating a relationship while explaining that God loves us. I began to savor the concept of having a relationship with God, which is what I had been searching for when I was first converted in Chicago with T. L. Barrett. It started to make sense.

In 1975 we went on tour in Europe with Santana to promote the release of *That's the Way of the World*. We were the opening act and given only twenty minutes to do our thing, which felt strange considering how big we had become as a gold and platinum act in the United States. Santana's crew had a large timer set on the side of the stage, strictly counting down our allotted time; when the clock flashed red, it was our signal to get off. Every night it was as though the clock got red faster, almost as soon as we started playing. At the time we had the number-one record straight across the board, and we were the *opening* act? I think it partly had to do with the inability of the music industry to equate a top-notch African American band like ours to conventional superstar rock acts like The Who or The Rolling Stones. Sometimes the racism was more overt. One critic from London even wrote something like, "I don't like black bands, but you can't say these guys aren't good."

Leon Patillo was a young vocalist with Santana who had a deep interest in the Bible. I didn't know that Leon was a devout Christian when he approached me and introduced himself.

"What's that under your arm?" I asked him, pointing to the book he was carrying.

"My Bible," Leon replied.

"Know anything out of that book?" I asked him.

Leon did.

"Then why don't you teach us?" I suggested.

During the rest of the tour, after each concert Leon regularly conducted Bible study with Larry, Andrew, and me. Larry had had his own spiritual awakening when, prior to the Santana European gigs, he enrolled in a transcendental meditation program. I approached him about it at the beginning of the tour. "Ooh, Larry," I teased him, "you've got that same look in your eyes as Maurice and Verdine have!" While cruising through Europe on the tour bus, Larry began chanting his mantra until he heard a voice inside his head abruptly interrupt him.

Stop doing that!

According to Larry, he was told by the voice, *Tomorrow you will be stopping at an army base in Germany*. The next day our bus arrived, as predicted. Larry was then ordered by the voice to buy a Bible at the base bookstore. He dutifully bought a little white Bible, the same one he used to study with Leon, Andrew, and me.

We concentrated on the New Testament, and would meet in Leon's room or in one of ours. I used an annotated Dake's Bible, which T. L. Barrett had recommended I pick up. The four of us managed to work our way up through the book of John. (After recording three bestselling albums with Santana, Patillo would leave the band in 1978 amid his strong religious beliefs.)

At that time I was beginning to open up to new ideas. This being my first international tour, everything around me was brand-new. I inexplicably felt a heightened consciousness and awareness of experiencing God in a personal way. It was a memorable and pivotal experience, and the first time I had explored the Bible as the sole source of my truth.

Having strayed from EWF's universalist tenets and more toward traditional Christian values, I began asking myself questions like, *Is Jesus who he says he is? I'm open. Please reveal it to me.* The idea that I needed a savior to atone for my sins—based on the premise that God gave us his son, Jesus, to save us and that we couldn't save ourselves—was something I believed and embrace to this day.

So I prayed that God would make me known to his will, his way, and his truth for my life. Although I was saved in Chicago, I still needed to embark on a spiritual journey of discovery. Change would occur through a chain of events in which God revealed himself to me in a way that enabled me to wholly embrace Christianity and the Bible as the central truth and key to my salvation.

I had clearly reached a fundamental impasse with Earth, Wind & Fire. While our audiences viewed us as a spiritual force, I realized our perceived mysticism no longer held water. Once I was introduced to true spirituality, a line in the sand was drawn as to how Maurice and I related to each other.

On the way to Germany during the European tour with Santana, Maurice had noticed a few of his band members with open Bibles in the back of the tour bus, and confronted us.

"Whaty'all doin'?" he asked.

"Studying," I said.

"Studying what?"

"The Word."

"What word?"

"The Word of God," I told him.

Maurice grimaced. "Hmm. That's funny, because God never wrote no book. The white man wrote a book to keep black people in bondage."

I could see Maurice was irritated as he walked back to the front of the bus.

Maurice and I had come to a parting of the ways in our beliefs, but it's not as if we had a huge falling-out over religion. Prior to my conversion, my gaze fell in the shadow of Maurice's gaze. Now that I had seen the Christian light, my life changed, and the dynamic of the band also changed as other members embarked on a similar spiritual journey, though maybe not on the same scale as mine. I believe God speaks to you on the level that you've reached. He will find you wherever you are. He'll find you on the big arena stage. He might find you on the showroom floor or in a corporate cubicle. He might find you while you're incarcerated. There's a lot of ways God reaches out to us, and that's how he found me.

I guess if there was a copilot in EWF, it was me. My relationship with Maurice differed from everyone else's, and I had always had strong praise for his ability to raise humanity's perceptions through our music by elevating spiritual consciousness and awareness of the divine as a positive force. Maurice accomplished that on many levels, promoting self-improvement and self-esteem. Through his leadership we impacted many people's lives by strengthening and encouraging them through our lyrics and songs. That's not to be trivialized in any shape, form, or fashion.

However, conflicts over spiritualities did arise. While I was deep into my new awakening, we were recording a song called "Diana." Maurice had written it as an homage to the Greek goddess of hunting, the moon, and childbirth. It had a lead vocal part that I had to lay down in the studio. I found I couldn't sing a song to a pagan

Greek goddess. It was something I felt uncomfortable doing, so I summoned the nerve to confront Maurice about it.

EWF managed to cut the song, though it ended up in the vault, and was released years later. At that time, Maurice recognized that my conversion was real, and he respected me for it. We now held different spiritual beliefs, though I still considered Maurice to be as sensitive and responsive to different points of view as he had always been. It was his choice to make "Open Our Eyes," the title track on our third Columbia album. And we did write "Devotion" together, which was based on subject matter straight out of the Word.

Still, things had changed between us. Up until my conversion, Maurice had been my personal guru, but once I changed course, I saw the effect it had on our relationship. At the same time the dynamic within the band itself was starting to alter, and I could see its members beginning to grow apart. I sensed change on the horizon for EWF, and matters would indeed soon come to a head.

My faith would be tested greatly when my mother passed away on June 16, 1975. The previous summer I had had a premonition that I would have to prepare myself for her not being around much longer. Although she wasn't ill at the time, I felt that I had to start dealing with the inevitability of my parent passing on. At the time my mother would speak about dying in melancholy tones. She had lived a laborious existence that would have put wear and tear on anyone. I think she had various illnesses and was not being properly diagnosed or cared for, primarily because she refused to go to the doctor for checkups or various ailments.

She was in her seventies when I lost her. One day she suffered from bad headaches and high blood pressure, then got very sick and started throwing up. She suffered a major stroke, and never regained consciousness. She slipped into a coma and was in the hospital for a week. Looking back, it was the best way to go, because had she recovered, she would have remained in an unconscious state.

I was in Los Angeles when I got the news of her stroke. I flew to Denver and spent the week in the hospital at her bedside. I was holding her hand and sang a song to her—"The Lord's Prayer"—on the day she passed away. That day will be forever etched in my memory. I swear she opened her eyes at the end of the song, and then I saw what looked to be a mist pass through the corner of the room. Denver was very windy that day, and when I opened the window, I saw a rainbow stretched across the sky.

I stood next to her casket and sang at the funeral. I had asked T. L. Barrett to fly in from Chicago to deliver the eulogy. After the funeral I went back out on the road. During such intense grieving periods, I believe God puts you into a metaphysical capsule and protects you from the sad realities around you. I remember I didn't cry before and after the time she died, but later, on the plane, I broke down and sobbed uncontrollably. I couldn't stop the tears from flowing. It was one of those delayed reactions.

My mother had toiled all her life, and—like mother, like son—many of her skills rubbed off on me. She taught me how to iron my butt off. Today I can clean a house like nobody in this world. Even today when women try to iron my clothes, I look at the result and say, "Hmm. That's okay, I'll do it myself." I was glad that my mother could see me succeed before she died, and while she was very proud of my accomplishments, I'm not sure she necessarily ever came to understand the music business. If I had told her I wanted to move back to Colorado and get a job in the civil service, her response would have been, "Baby, I think that's good," and not, "What the hell are you talking about?" Her generation believed in working hard and following the rules, and if you had an honest job and kept at it until your retirement, then you did well.

21

SING A SONG OF SPIRIT AND IMAGINATION

The bigger EWF got, the more I reflected seriously on my family background and the effect it had had on my ability to forge relationships with my wife, Janet; my mentor, Maurice; and women in general. As a child, I developed an innate coping mechanism to make up for my mom and dad's split and especially for my father's neglect. I found that the damage and emptiness I felt often played itself out in my inability to trust others and open myself up to important intimate relationships. I remain in a constant state of healing and learning because of that brokenness. Much later I wrote about it in a song called "Lonely Broken Hearted People," which described the passing on of those coping skills to the next generation.

> Can we help a lonely broken hearted person?
> See their tears become their laughter,
> Paint the canvas of their hearts
> With the colors of the rainbow.
> Change their frown into a smile.

With the band out on the road, though, I continued my devilish diva ways. Just as in my days with Friends & Love, I expected no less than perfection from myself and total dedication from everybody else. One day we played an amazing gig with Stevie Wonder and Patti LaBelle at the Pine Knob Music Festival in Michigan. It was hot and crazy enough being on the bill with two of my idols. We'd gotten a great reception, which was amazing. LaBelle brought it on, followed by Stevie Wonder. I recall sitting on the stage about thirty feet away from Stevie. He sounded absolutely remarkable to me. His singing and background vocalists were letter perfect. I went back to the hotel after the show, where all the guys were elated. Yet there I was, walking around, pissing on everybody's parade, pouting, moaning, and spouting crap like, "We sounded like shit. Our vocals were out of tune and we played too loud and too fast!"

Maurice called me over and pulled me aside.

"You acting like a bitch."

"What?"

"You actin' like a bitch! I understand you want things to be perfect, but you gotta give it time! Stevie has been doing this a lot longer than we have. And we will get there. Meanwhile, you can't be pouring water on everybody's fire! Those guys did a fantastic job, and we got a great reception. Let them celebrate!"

I stood embarrassed and humbled. "I'm sorry."

The time came for the daunting task of following up *That's the Way of the World,* and Columbia Records wanted a record . . . and quick! Since we were living out on the road, we decided to record the band live, to try to capture the magic we were feeling on the stage. We hired a remote-recording crew to follow us around the United States. Maurice also had five polished studio tracks he wanted to include, and the result was the Christmas 1975 holiday release of *Gratitude*. The record featured live songs from performances in Chicago, Los Angeles, St. Louis, Atlanta, Boston, and New York City, as well as the first cities that had embraced us, namely, Philadelphia and Washington, DC.

Gratitude marked the recording debut of the Phenix Horns, who excelled on the studio tracks as well as on the concert material. The

Horns would soon become the strongest part of our signature sound. Production credits were split. The live tracks on *Gratitude* were produced by Maurice and Joe Wissert, while the studio pieces were produced (not "coproduced") by Reese and Charles Stepney. The arrangements were credited to both Earth, Wind & Fire and Charles Stepney. George Massenburg's squeaky-clean mixes and engineering remained on board as well.

One of my favorite tracks on the record is a studio song I cowrote called "Sunshine," in which I incorporated the recurring image of a shining star in the lyrics. Also featured was the chart-topping pop and R&B hit "Sing a Song." Like "Shining Star," it featured sparkling rhythm guitar work by Al McKay. The group vocals I coarranged were pretty slick, too. Maurice's seductive lead vocal on the ballad "Can't Hide Love" gave us another hit single that March.

I was thrilled when Columbia scheduled a special midnight release of *Gratitude* in December 1975, which took place at Tower Records on Sunset Boulevard in Hollywood. A long line of eager fans stood waiting to purchase the first pressings of the record. Like *That's the Way of the World, Gratitude* would quickly be certified triple platinum by the RIAA, debuting on the album charts at number one. The album topped the Billboard album charts for three weeks and was number one on their R&B album chart for six weeks! We had reached a pinnacle of crossover success.

In the early years of EWF our primary audience was African American. But after two triple-platinum records and three R&B/ Top 40 double-format hits ("Shining Star," "That's the Way of the World," and "Sing a Song"), we began to notice our core audience shifting dramatically. We were drawing a lot more white fans because of the realities of disposable income. Whites, who could more easily afford the tickets, tended to order their seats in advance; traditionally black audiences were more likely to "walk up." Looking out from behind the microphone, I also saw a lot more

Latinos and mixed couples. It was gratifying to see Maurice's Concept growing demographically.

One effect of our crossover success was to help put more African American music industry executives on a faster career path. The major-label infrastructure at Columbia had patiently molded us into a major act, but our breakthrough created a ripple effect, boosting the presence of black executives within the corporate music structure. Or as Maurice reminded us, "It's all about economics. Black radio is expanding, and the labels want to profit by it." More important, we became one of the first modern black bands beyond the rock crossover success of Sly Stone to prove that African American music and musicians could have an explosive impact, from niche gold status to mainstream platinum, not only on R&B audiences but on all types of music lovers—black, white, Latino, Asian older adults, and beyond, both domestically and internationally.

With the release of *Gratitude,* a familiar face rejoined our ranks when my old friend Perry Jones returned as a road and tour manager. After Perry had returned to Denver, he became involved with a nightclub, held down a Sunday night radio show on KFML, and opened up a record store. He also worked again with Barry Fey, the biggest concert promoter in the Colorado market. Perry helped book us at the Denver Coliseum, where we sold all 10,500 seats. My "homecoming gig" was one of our biggest-drawing shows on the tour. Afterward Perry hosted a hotel get-together with the band and met with Bob Cavallo out on the deck of the penthouse. Bob was very happy with the results of the concert, and a few months later Perry got a call from Maurice inviting him back as a tour manager. It was great to have him around again.

Now capable of consistently drawing five-figure arena crowds, we were poised for our biggest road trip yet. My perception was that larger halls were just another venue to play: tonight a 10,000-seater, next year maybe a 20,000-seater. That was great, as long as we were making steady progress, and that's how I saw it: as a step-by-step process. I wasn't particularly in awe of the numbers. As long as we pushed onward, we had no choice but to keep moving forward.

We kept the growing Earth, Wind & Fire hysteria in check as best we could. Don't forget, we were younger than most musicians. Groups like Led Zeppelin and The Who were older and more road-experienced and cocky, so they did more of that hedonistic, crazy hotel-wrecking stuff than we did. That's not to say mischief didn't follow us. We were a bunch of twentysomething guys with a whole lot of energy having fun. But I was so into the music, I just rode with it. I liked the good life too much to jeopardize it by acting the rock-star fool. Besides, Maurice wouldn't have stood for it.

While the easy women and temptation were still out there, the music remained foremost for me. The Concept had worked. We hadn't been created by a record label or some Svengali manager, like the Monkees or New Kids on the Block. While we did have creative and organizational help from Columbia and Cavallo-Ruffalo, we had shaped our own personas and destinies.

During this period I became pretty much an absentee father and husband. When Sir was little, he could barely comprehend what I did for a living. All he knew was that I wasn't there at home, which was unfortunate. I think back to my childhood days when my mother was too busy working to show up at my school concerts. As a parent I now sympathized with the situation and forgave her.

Whenever I did get home, say, for birthday parties for the kids, I might be in the other room asleep, resting up for the next gig or show. As a result, I missed practically all of my children's back-to-school nights. I also wasn't there for Sir's or Trinity's school dances. That was Janet's job, to get them prepped for life, and to raise them.

There were some fringe benefits for the kids in having a famous dad. They got to wear EWF stage costumes for Halloween! Trinity had the prom dress of a lifetime, and Sir got to drive my Mercedes to his prom. (I'm only just now hearing about their driving exploits while I was gone.) While there was no substitute for their having a full-time dad, my kids enjoyed having nice new cars at an early age and went to great schools and took incredible vacations. While it wasn't my choice to neglect them, being away from the family was the nature of the profession. If I was on the road performing, it's because that's what I did for a living.

I became more of a supervisor than a father, telling Janet what she needed to do or what I expected to be done. It was an unintentional impulse, since I was accustomed to having staff on the road seeing to my needs and getting things done on a timely basis. I was so used to a highly mechanized routine that when I got off the road, I had trouble readjusting to "real life."

Janet stayed with me through some tricky times. When I came home to Los Angeles from touring one night in 1978, I had a confession to make. I told Janet, "I have something to tell you. I'm having a baby."

At the time Janet was pregnant with Creed, our third child. "I know," she said. "We're having Creed."

"No," I said. "I mean, I'm having another baby." And I had to confess to her that I had had an affair on the road with Jeanette Hutchinson from The Emotions and that she was pregnant with my child.

Janet threw a huge fit, so I put her out on the front porch to cool off.

Janet had her hands full raising our kids. (In addition to Sir James, who was born in September 1971, and Trinity Donet, who was born in March 1975, we would have Creed Ellington Bailey, named after my heroes Creed Taylor and Duke Ellington, who arrived in January 1978, and Philip Doron Bailey, who was born in August 1981.) As a mother, she was strict in terms of discipline. The children didn't dare cross Janet or lie to her, but when it came to social activities, she was more permissive than I was (when I was around). When I was in town, the family adhered to a stricter, more regimented set of home rules, and once I left to go out on tour, it would revert back to Janet's way of running the household and being more lenient.

Looking back, I realize that Janet suffered as a result of my extramarital activities. She was a great mom, but she would hibernate in her room a lot, going through down periods and dealing with her sadness, especially after my affair with Jeanette. She was dealing with her own life issues of raising the children and running a household without me. After we moved the family back to Denver for a few years, Trinity had memories as a young girl of sharing a large brass bed with her mother. She would pretend to be asleep but listen to Janet weeping on the telephone and discussing with her aunt Debbie the different women I was involved with at the time. After a while, Janet began to smoke weed and drink E&J brandy to numb her sorrows.

As Janet suffered through the rejection and the isolation she was thrown into, she also started using street pharmaceuticals to mask her pain and hanging out with people who were far beneath her. I was the "main dude" in the Bailey family and within our social circles, and as my wife, she lived in my shadow. She probably should have kicked me to the curb, but in our reality, we both felt that once you got married, you stayed married, no matter what. Besides, Janet felt she didn't have the necessary job skills or a college education to start over. What was she going to do with four children without a husband? Divorce scared the hell out of her. Staying together made sense. But with Janet using, and me womanizing out on the road, we drifted further apart.

In August 1978 Jeanette gave birth to a daughter she named Pili Asabi Foluke Titilayo Bailey, whom I affectionately call "Pili." Pili is a Swahili name, meaning "second born." The rest of her name translates to: Asabi—she is a choice birth; Foluke—placed in care of God; Titilayo—where happiness is eternal. Janet was pragmatic about the situation. She decided there was nothing she could do about it, so she accepted it. Whenever I wanted to visit with Pili, Janet insisted that I bring her to the house, and nowadays she's part of the extended Bailey family. Pili and I are very close. Today she's a successful career woman who has college degrees and is happily married with a son, who is my seventh grandchild.

For six years straight the band was almost always together. Not a day passed that band members—particularly me, Verdine, Larry, and Maurice—didn't talk, exchange musical ideas, or check up on one another three, four, or even ten times. Under Maurice's leadership, whenever we traveled, we kept pretty much to ourselves. While it wasn't intentional, the EWF troupe was a close-knit one, a cult of sorts guided by our ethics and idealism. We were either touring, writing, or preparing new material and arrangements for the future, or in the studio.

Things were moving so fast, a year felt like a month. With very little spare time, we had little opportunity to stop and smell the roses and enjoy our accomplishments, let alone share them. Maurice didn't necessarily run a profamily organization. For instance, there weren't any relaxing Earth, Wind & Fire barbecues. We didn't fraternize outside of the music. There weren't any picnics or parties or family get-togethers to celebrate our success. That stuff didn't happen.

The sold-out arena tours started around 1977, and the days became more and more of a blur. For security reasons we'd book an entire hotel floor, sequestered and isolated on one level in order to get us to the concert hall and back efficiently. Out on the road Verdine lived in his hotel room with his extensive wardrobe. Verdine loves his clothes and carried the most luggage. With four or five wardrobe changes a day, he had a different look going. Larry lived more like a hermit, a typical night person. Even during the day, he kept the curtains pulled tightly closed or covered the windows with a bedspread so he could sleep all day. Later we'd go out together to the clubs until two or three in the morning. With arrivals, departures, sound checks, and show times carried out with military precision, our movements were constantly accounted for. We couldn't just walk out on the street or go anywhere unless the outing was prearranged.

With a total of sixty-seven people on the payroll and seven or eight tractor-trailers to haul our equipment and a propjet and buses to transport us, we whirled from city to city. Large-scale production effects had been added to our arena shows, with lights and explosions. Drums levitated! Once the big money came streaming in, Maurice put it back into the show, creating spectacles never before staged. He hired both the late, great magician Doug Henning and the famous illusionist David Copperfield as consultants, enhancing our show with state-of-the-art magic tricks and theatrical effects. Earth, Wind & Fire needed to be spectacular and cutting-edge at all times.

I wasn't concerned about the extraordinary costs required to put on such extravagant shows. For example, Henning and Copperfield had concocted a magnificent and extraordinary opening. Before we came out, the house darkened, and you could hear these incredibly loud rumblings and frightening sounds. It was symbolic of the elements of the universe erupting. Then, after three loud crashes on a gong, came the booming voice of Leonard Smith:

"Presenting . . . Earth . . . Wind . . . and Fire . . ."

Nine tubes rose up from the fog-filled stage. Inside each pod was a member of EWF, "hibernating" and wearing a beautiful cape. After another large explosion the tubes disappeared, the fog cleared, and we emerged accompanied by a prerecorded bed of *kalimba* music! We danced around the stage, flashing the grand capes like matadors. Even our managers and roadie crews went bananas. They'd seen it in rehearsal and were still cheering! The screams from the crowd during this segment were so loud it was sometimes unbearable. One time Bob Cavallo was sitting in the middle of the house, right in the vortex of the noise, and the opening roar was so loud he dropped down to his knees and covered his ears.

We had built a substage under the stage proper so that we could perform sensational magic tricks, such as disappearing and reappearing throughout the show. We would climb up inside pyramids, and then the pyramids would explode and shatter, only to reveal us safe and sound, standing out among the audience. Our timing had to be perfect. We rehearsed over and over to the letter in order for everything to go off without a hitch. The magic tricks never had a major misfire or miscue.

There was one trick where we were ushered into a spaceship by a group of androids. The spaceship would fly upward and dangle over the stage. People would be literally shaking! It was priceless seeing the looks on their faces when the androids converged at the front of the stage, took off their masks—and were us! How did we do it? Out of respect for the magicians, we signed a waiver not to divulge Henning's and Copperfield's secret art forms. It's best to keep the mystique.

We did have a few screw-ups. In one of the productions we would stand under a flying laser eagle and a giant floating globe. The stage was raked sharply to allow us to look down on the audience. The road crew would spread sticky Coca-Cola on the floor so that our feet stayed in place when the lights burst on. One night they forgot to put the soda on the floor and instead turned on the fog machine. As the fog wetted down the raked floor, we ran out and lost our balance, stumbling and bumbling around the stage. Satterfield flew up in the air feet first, landing hard on his ass. Larry and I burst into hysterical laughter at Sat's expense.

I regret not having film footage of those monumental shows. It was not yet the video era, so not a lot of film exists in the archives. We never hired a professional movie crew to capture our performances. Plus, Maurice didn't like TV. He was a purist, and during the late 1970s television sound wasn't that great. Plus, television studio hands wouldn't let us mix our own music. If you were doing live television, the guy in the control booth opening and closing the mics would be the same person in charge of mixing your extravagant sound needs. Maurice, the audiophile perfectionist, wanted it done right or not at all, and I had to agree with him. Even though we did shows like *Don Kirshner's Rock Concert* and Burt Sugarman's *The Midnight Special,* whenever we could, we'd go in and fix what was wrong or listen beforehand and mix it right. As big as Earth, Wind & Fire were, in the long run our lack of television exposure cost us. Our fan base could have been much bigger if more people had known how amazing an experience our live appearances truly were! Due to our lack of film and video exposure, the band did not have a definitive face, like The Rolling Stones had with Mick Jagger and Keith Richards, for instance. We should have been branded better visually, especially during the span of our hit records.

To keep our standards high we also began to use topflight stage directors and choreographers. At my suggestion the band flew out to New York to meet with George Faison, the famed Broadway choreographer of *The Wiz*. I had seen the show in New York, and its pacing and energy were so tight and dynamic that I had excitedly told Maurice about it.

Soon Faison was instructing us on how to move around and dance more eloquently onstage. We weren't a band that was into choreography—until George came on the scene. He taught us double pirouettes and so many moves that we felt like dance students, and I still remember the long, grueling rehearsals. Damn, man! What did this have to do with the music? But it was necessary to get us to where we had to be. Our goal was to move so naturally onstage that we weren't thinking about it. George also advised us on the set list with regard to pacing and timing. He monitored the patter between songs and the way we would close each show. George was responsible for teaching me how to hit my mark.

Next we hired the acclaimed Hollywood costume designer Bill Whitten to create exotic, one-of-a-kind glittering outfits—some costing as much as $20,000 apiece. They made our stage entrances quite an exhibition. Bill was a flamboyant and eccentric character who had also designed wardrobes for the Jacksons, Elton John, Michael Jackson, and Neil Diamond. He wore fancy brocade slippers and a tunic and had flowing shoulder-length hair. He would scour the world in search of fabrics, spend months detailing the costumes, and then bring his creations over with his helpers, ordering us, "Try this on. See how this looks on you." He had an incredible imagination, and was way out there! He once dressed me as a royal Egyptian pharaoh in full regalia—gold lamé and chains with intricate crystal and rhinestone beading dripping from the fabric. Bill's creations looked astounding under the bright lights. We employed a wardrobe crew backstage to help us in and out of the quick costume changes. Louis Wells, our current wardrobe adviser, was then a young man fresh out of college, and worked with Bill Whitten during that period. us.

Although Cavallo was against our spending so lavishly on costumes and onstage productions, money was no object when it came to the Concept. Out on the road EWF was a dominating force as pop, R&B, and rock fans thronged to our shows. We were selling out the Los Angeles Forum five nights in a row, followed by three or four consecutive nights at Madison Square Garden in New York and the Spectrum in Philly. Leading up to a tour, Maurice would rehearse (and pay) the band for about six weeks. To expend that much prep time today would be cost-prohibitive. However, at the time, nobody felt overly concerned about our finances. At least not yet.

By the spring of 1976, we began work on our next album, set to be titled *Spirit*. "Getaway" would be the breakout single that opened the album, another multiformat hit. The second single, "On Your Face," would do okay as a midcharting record on the R&B charts. In addition to our success on the Top 40 and R&B airwaves, adult/contemporary radio, aimed at older listeners aged thirty-five to fifty-four, began to heavily embrace Earth, Wind & Fire, particularly our ballads. While airplay on "adult" radio wouldn't spark the megasales that Top 40 or R&B—later dubbed "urban radio"—did, adults would join our loyal fan base for years to come.

During the recording of *Spirit,* Charles Stepney ramped up his arrangements in Chicago on six of the nine tunes. Meanwhile, Larry had written the music for a new song in Los Angeles. After we finished recording it at three in the morning, we commented on how beautiful it sounded. Yet Larry seemed strangely melancholy. Originally titled "I Gave You Love," Larry's song would serve as the title track for the new album once Maurice added lyrics to it and renamed it "Spirit."

While we were recording in Los Angeles, Charles suffered a heart attack, but kept right on working. He was taken to Central City Hospital in Chicago. Verdine had a buddy who was a doctor there, so we checked up on Charles regularly. I remember Verdine telling Maurice and me that he hoped Charles would get some much-needed rest.

Then, on May 17, 1976, after cutting basic tracks at Hollywood Sound, we got the phone call: Charles was found dead in his home in Chicago by a family member. We were floored by the news. His death would affect us both personally and professionally, altering our course tremendously.

Ordinarily, today when people suffer from heart disease, having a coronary artery bypass is a fairly standard procedure. Had Charles undergone such a routine operation, he would have been fine, but the procedure wasn't nearly as common then as it is now. Back then, when someone like Charles suffered a heart attack, the odds were far greater that he would be stricken again. And that's exactly what happened.

We finished *Spirit,* which indeed has a heavy spiritual aura, after Charles's passing. Charles had suspected he was in bad health—he was a diabetic and had a problem with high blood pressure—and had suggested that if anything were to happen to him, his friend Tom Tom Washington could step in as our arranger and orchestrator. Washington was a skilled producer, arranger, pianist, and drummer from Chicago. He masterfully arranged the title track in Stepney's absence. While "Spirit" is very gospel-oriented, and is a glorious song honoring Charles, the tune I love the most is "Imagination," which has a celestial, even angelic, sentiment that reminds me of Charles.

The powerful bridge on "Imagination," with its rich layers of vocals and orchestrations, makes the hair on the back of my neck stand up. "Imagination" is also one of my finest vocal performances on record. Although it wasn't a commercial hit record, it's one of our very best songs, and sadly, it was the last song Charles arranged for us. *Spirit* was ultimately credited as "Produced by Maurice White and Charles Stepney." Charles had finally posthumously attained the proper production credit on a full album that he so rightly deserved. Had he lived, he might have become a more prominent arranger and producer than Quincy Jones.

The entire band flew to Chicago to attend Step's funeral and to pay our respects to his widow, Ruby. We didn't know how Maurice took Stepney's death, as he didn't cry or grieve in front of the band. My guess is that he internalized it. While I'm sure Charles's death shocked him, he wasn't the type to openly express his feelings. Instead he reacted through his actions, and from that moment on, our studio output would spiral to gigantic proportions.

22

GOT TO GET YOU INTO MY LIFE

When we were booked to coheadline at a stadium in Kansas City with the Commodores in 1977, I decided, on a whim, to search for Eddie, my elusive father. It's not that I was necessarily on a serious emotional quest to locate him; it's just that I had heard he was living in Kansas City and I was in town. It was as good a time as any to reach out and contact him. In the phone book I found an Edward A. Bailey in the listings, so I phoned him cold. Bear in mind that I had had no contact with him since I was three years old.

"Hi, this is Philip, your son," I announced. "I play with a group, and we're in your town."

Eddie hesitated, apparently speechless. How could he not have been blown away?

"I can't believe this," he uttered in disbelief.

So I invited Eddie Bailey—my dad!—to our stadium performance. Our show was to be held at a packed outdoor stadium in front of thirty-five thousand people, with both the Commodores and EWF at the top of their games. I think Eddie knew what Earth, Wind & Fire was, and I suspected he might even have heard about me through the press. He was sincerely taken aback when I told him what I was up to, brought him to the gig, and slapped a backstage pass on his shirt.

From that experience we struck up a casual relationship. I had a day off the next day, so I made arrangements to visit him at his home. One of the first questions I had to ask was about that night in the blizzard with the crowbar, and how he had threatened to kill my mother. He confirmed the story my mother told me. He had gone back and forth, torn as to whether or not he was going to leave his first family for my mother, sister, and me. After the military stationed him to Idaho, here was his chance to make a move, and my mother rejected him. When I pressed him as to why I never became a part of his life afterward, he simply replied, "Philip, you don't always do what's right at the time, you do what is expedient."

The huge plus in my reaching out to my father was that I felt incredibly proud to be able to introduce him to Maurice and Verdine and say, "This is my dad." I had known Maurice's stepdad and Verdine's dad, Dr. Verdine Adams Sr., the podiatrist, and in some ways, he became my stand-in father. He even used to work on my feet. But that day in Kansas City was a surreal moment. To have Maurice meet him, smile, and tell me, "Man, Philip, you look just like him," was a special moment. Plus, Maurice was right—I did look more like Eddie than like my mother.

We talked about what he had been up to. During his hitch in the service, Eddie had been a photographer and a clerical worker. He confessed a deep love for music and owned an extensive two-track tape library of jazz albums that he recorded from radio shows. With jazz being my first musical love as a kid, it was uncanny that, as we slid past the rough and uncomfortable part of meeting again and exchanging all that "where have you been all my life?" stuff, to have the same tastes in music felt right. Backstage after the show, Eddie grinned and told me, "Son, you're a chip off the old block."

Eddie Bailey died a few years later, in the 1980s. I have no idea how I ended up with an Irish name like Bailey. One day I must trace my ancestry and find out.

All 'N All, Earth, Wind & Fire's ninth album, was released in December 1977 and became the supreme party-down record for our fans. Maurice's ongoing interest in many world religions and mythologies became the central themes for the album: holiness and mysticism, not politics.

It was Al McKay who came up with the title. During the sessions, in the summer of 1977, he asked Maurice, "What are you going to call it?"

Maurice hesitated. "Hmm . . . *All* . . . something."

"How about *All in All*?" Maurice looked over at Al, and his eyes widened. That look meant that you'd hit on a good idea.

The bass-popping funk of "Serpentine Fire" was another smash hit. Flanked by the punchy Phoenix Horns and featuring Maurice's feisty lead vocal mixed with my silky falsetto on the chorus hook, it earned us another R&B number one song as well as a Top 10 crossover hit on the pop side. The album's second track, "Fantasy," gave the album a solid one-two punch. "Fantasy" had an airborne feel to it. We became renowned for our soaring group vocal arrangements, and a song like "Fantasy" was a terrific vehicle for Maurice and me to multitrack our vocals throughout the verses. Laying them down in the studio was a painstaking process, but well worth it.

Recording in Hollywood, we were sequestered for days. Janet would visit me in the itty-bitty studio we booked off of Cahuenga and Sunset boulevards, which Maurice would block out for entire days and nights to cut vocals. Recording proved to be too tedious for visiting spouses like Janet and Larry's wife, Debbie, who would end up curled up and asleep on the couch in the control room. Once the instrumental tracks were nailed down, not many of the band members stuck around for our vocal overdubs. Even Verdine limited his visits, waiting until his brother finished his vocal parts before he stopped by. We seldom let any outsiders in because the process was so laborious that we couldn't handle distractions. Maurice and I would go over and over and over the same vocal parts, angling for a very specific blend. If it wasn't perfect, we would start all over again. This was no time to party or get stoned in the studio.

Ironically, the tighter the studio sound got, the more isolated and separate we became as a group. Rather than the band playing together live in the studio like we used to with Charles Stepney, we would often cut our parts separately. As a producer, Maurice was such a taskmaster that guys like Verdine didn't want people watching in the event he made mistakes while laying down his bass parts. Arrangers like Tom Tom 84 and Jerry Peters now handled the string and horn parts, and engineer George Massenburg kept the mix and sound pristine. With Charles Stepney gone, Maurice doubled down on the production duties and enlisted Verdine and Larry as his production assistants. Maurice would credit himself as sole producer for the record.

We were consistently selling out our shows as Maurice and Cavallo-Ruffalo kept up the grinding cycle of record and tour, record and tour, record and tour. When we sold out the fabulous Forum arena in Los Angeles, where the "Showtime" Lakers played roundball, our success wasn't lost on the members who grew up in Southern California. Ralph Johnson had watched it being built in Inglewood where he played outdoors as a child. One of his proudest moments was taking his parents to see EWF at the Forum.

All 'N All coincided with the massive popularity of *Star Wars,* which was released in 1977. When Maurice first saw the film, it rocked his world. He was just as hooked on the *Star Wars* mania as the kids lined up outside the movie theaters, watching the film for the fifth and sixth time.

"We gotta do something like that," he told the band, which is why we featured a pyramid spaceship onstage, combining it with a love of the metaphysics of Egyptology. Stylistically we mixed fusion, jazz/pop scat, and funky soul into our sound. When we were cutting *All 'N All*'s instrumental jam, a track called "Runnin'," we were originally going to perform it with Freddie and Ralph on drums. Somehow, though, we couldn't get the rhythm right, so Verdine, Larry, Maurice, and I worked on it, and we were cooking on that song! It sounded like something off a CTI record. Maurice was playing drums with his shirt off, and that's the first time I noticed him showing strain. He was exhausted, digging from the bottom of the well, but we got it together after a few takes. "Be Ever Wonderful," the album's ballad finale, was one of those songs that Maurice wrote during a sound check. The band would try out new grooves before live gigs, as Larry Dunn remained the master at tinkering with unique chord progressions that separated us from more standard pop groups.

All 'N All was the most difficult record we ever made. We didn't have Step around, and we weren't giddy kids anymore, either. Being in the studio with Step was like having your dad around. But with gold and platinum momentum behind us, we had to get this record right: The game was intensifying as the stakes were getting higher.

In addition to the music, we were refining our dancing and working on even more ambitious visuals and special effects, and trying new costumes. The color combinations that Bill Whitten came up with for our wardrobes were ever more eyepopping. Move over, David Bowie and the Spiders from Mars! We were dressed in glitzy skintight outfits splashed in loud chartreuse, aquamarine and turquoise, blood red and cobalt blue, and glittering silver and gold fabrics with matching knee-high platform boots. One extraterrestrial-looking outfit I wore was doused in lime green with yellow and red trim, topped with bright purple boots.

Every morning we would work out with choreographer George Faison, doing calisthenics and rehearsing our dance steps. We would take the afternoon off, then rehearse the music and the show later that night. Between the recording and the live rehearsals, nobody worked as hard as we did—not even the top rock and roll bands of the day, like Fleetwood Mac and Queen.

After *All 'N All* sold its first million copies, we were approached with another movie project, this time a feature highlighting the music of The Beatles. Because the Bee Gees and their manager,

Robert Stigwood, were also to be involved, Bob Cavallo thought it was a great idea. *Saturday Night Fever,* which featured the Bee Gees' music, was a blockbuster movie that fueled the disco era in America during that time. Stigwood and his producers told Maurice and Cavallo they wanted us to be in the new film and to help with the soundtrack. It would star Peter Frampton and the Bee Gees, with other top bands—Aerosmith, Alice Cooper, and EWF—performing covers of famous Beatles standards, and would be called *Sgt. Pepper's Lonely Hearts Club Band.*

While in New York, I saw an EWF "billboard" beaming across Times Square on the giant outdoor Trinitron. We were on our way to Sam Goody's music store to pick up some sheet music for a Beatles song when Reese asked Verdine, the band's resident Beatles fan, which one we should choose to cover. Verdine answered without hesitation, "Got to Get You into My Life." We bought the sheet music, and later we met with George Martin, The Beatles' famed producer. George told us we could arrange and perform the song any way we chose. Although I suspected George didn't know much about our music, Maurice wanted to apply the indelible EWF stamp on whatever we turned in. "I want to do what *we* do," Maurice told the band as we prepared to cut the tune.

We were on a stopover on tour in Denver when we set up the session to cut "Got to Get You into My Life." Reese called Larry from his hotel suite beforehand and told him, "Larry, we're going to be in this movie with all Beatles tunes. I need to meet you downstairs in the convention ballroom." The road crew had gotten us a piano and a turntable and speakers. We put on The Beatles 45 for a listen. Larry learned the chords in one sitting.

"Now I need one of those crazy intros."

We cut the song—overdubs, horns, and all—in one day. Maurice and Larry worked out the frenzied but tight arrangement featuring Larry on electric piano with the Phenix Horns and Al McKay doing the crazy unison horn and guitar lines. Because Freddie had broken his ankle, Ralph played drums. Maurice laid down a swinging syncopated lead vocal. Next I cut some falsetto parts over the top. We mixed it the next day.

Maurice couldn't get over it. He had been getting a bit too carried away, going overboard on arrangements since Step died. When the song was completed, Maurice turned to Verdine: "Man, that's got to be the biggest damn fluke—"

"That's no fluke, Reese," Verdine insisted. "Don't you get it? That's a number one record! And this time you didn't get a chance to overproduce it by adding eighteen other horns and thirty-six more string players."

Cavallo was so proud when he first heard it. We didn't just cover a Beatles tune, we transformed it, the EWF way. The folks at Columbia Records went crazy, and so did Paul McCartney, who wrote the song. Everybody was pleased.

We completed "Got to Get You into My Life" six months before the movie came out. At the time the Bee Gees were as hot as a firecracker, and the *Sgt. Pepper's* film was supposed to be their next big thing. Michael Schultz, the film's director, was an African American who had directed hit movies like *Car Wash* and *Cooley High.* (Today he's a successful TV director.)

After the studio showed us a rough cut of *Sgt. Pepper's Lonely Hearts Club Band,* we realized—*ouch!*—what a lousy movie! We knew the film would be a loser from the get-go. Even the singing was out of synch! When the vocals came on, we squirmed nervously in our seats. At first we thought, *It's a rough cut and they'll fix it in postproduction.* But it was out of synch at the premiere! The other songs, by Aerosmith and Alice Cooper, sounded too similar to the original versions. This film had "flop" written all over it. It was destined to be yet another EWF bomb at the box office, the same scenario as *That's the Way of the World,* except five years later! Bob, Verdine, and I sat in the screening room afterward, stunned and disappointed. This time nobody cried. We knew what to do in this situation.

After the screening Cavallo-Ruffalo sprang into damage control mode. Columbia rush-released our single, and by the time the movie hit the screens, we were already number one straight across the board—pop, R&B, the whole enchilada. As the movie inevitably tanked—along with the other singles—soon after, the Robert Stigwood Organization's RSO record label and movie empire went down with it.

The Bee Gees were pissed! They wouldn't speak to us because they thought we stole their thunder. Although Barry Gibb is cool with us now, back then they gave us no love at the gala premiere. There was a red-carpet welcome for Robin, Maurice, and Barry Gibb, but by the time EWF got off the plane, they had already rolled up the red carpet! But we were the ones with the number one record.

After "Got to Get You into My Life" hit in August 1978, we scored a quick follow-up with one of our best songs. We first released "September" as a single that November. It was written from a groove that Al McKay had worked up at a sound check one day and then made a demo track of in his eight-track home studio. After McKay played Maurice the demo—twice!—the first words out of Maurice's mouth were "Do you remember?" Al saw that trademark smile on Reese's face, and knew he had struck gold. Maurice later brought in a lyricist, Allee Willis, to help finish the words. "September" kicked in effortlessly across the radio airwaves.

The Best of Earth, Wind & Fire, Vol. 1, featuring hits like "Got to Get You into My Life," "September," "Shining Star," and "That's the Way of the World," was a hot Columbia holiday release that December and ultimately sold five million units. During that time Maurice had scored a bonanza deal that Cavallo-Ruffalo had negotiated for him. Starting with the release of *The Best of Earth, Wind & Fire,* Maurice formed ARC Records, a CBS-distributed label bankrolled with more than ten million dollars from the Columbia Records war chest. Technically ARC had previously existed as the American Record Company, a label entity from 1904 to 1908, in the infancy of the record player. The insignia of Maurice's new ARC—the American Recording Company—would now appear above the familiar red Columbia Records logo on future EWF records.

Maurice would debut more artists under the ARC banner, including another Ramsey Lewis record to follow up the successful 1974 soul jazz classic *Sun Goddess,* which Ramsey had made with Maurice and Stepney in 1974. Ramsey's first ARC record, *Tequila Mockingbird,* would be coproduced by Larry Dunn and include guest appearances by Verdine, Al, and Johnny Graham. Maurice would next introduce two new artists to the ARC roster, a talented young female vocalist named Deniece Williams and the hot-looking female trio The Emotions.

Fueled by the money he scored from Columbia Records to debut ARC, Maurice built himself a lavish headquarters for ARC that we called the Complex. When Maurice renegotiated his deal and was resigned by Columbia, Reese scored his boatload of money from CBS to set up his new musical empire. The Complex, situated near Pico Boulevard and Corinth in West Los Angeles, was a center for offices, a recording studio, and rehearsal rooms. Reese spent gobs of money to remodel the building. I believe he changed the new carpeting in the Complex more than once because he didn't like how it looked once it was installed.

Shortly afterward we signed new contracts with Maurice's company on account of his new pact with Columbia. Then, when Maurice scheduled his big gala opening of the studio and record company, the members of the band were not invited! Not only were we not part of the festivities, we didn't even get a share of any of the ARC money.

On January 9, 1979, we appeared at the United Nations for a high-profile concert on behalf of UNICEF (United Nations International Children's Fund), a benefit entitled "A Gift of Song." We performed "September" at the General Assembly in New York City. Rod Stewart, ABBA, Olivia Newton-John, John Denver, Kris Kristofferson and Rita Coolidge, and Donna Summer also took part, and while some of the artists, like ABBA and the Bee Gees, cheated and lip-synched their songs, the concert raised a million bucks. I remember how aware I was that we were within a whole new power circle, even though we had been enjoying our share of massive and influential pop-culture success.

A few weeks later, on February 15, Earth, Wind & Fire snared three Grammy Awards—Best R&B Vocal Performance by a Duo, Group or Chorus for *All 'N All;* Best Arrangement for Accompanying Vocalists for "Got to Get You into My Life"; and Best R&B Instrumental Performance for "Runnin'," the instrumental we had slaved over in the studio.

The most perplexing thing about the Grammy Awards ceremony was that, when we won ours in the 1970s, the R&B categories were not televised. Our Grammys were simply announced and awarded prior to the telecast. We earned seven Grammys—and not a single televised acceptance speech. Our Best R&B Vocal Performance by a Duo, Group or Chorus in 1979 didn't make it onto the airwaves. How ridiculous was that?

While we were ecstatic over the accumulating accolades and awards, I started to suspect the band members were being kept in the dark about Maurice's business dealings. At recent shows a distinct separation vibe had been going down. After each concert Leonard Smith would usher Maurice into a private limo and off they'd go. We didn't see Reese at the hotel, and he began to hang out with the band members less and less. Although I didn't realize it at the time, change was imminent, though not necessarily in a good way.

23

THE WHITE BOY BEHIND THE BLACK VELVET CURTAIN

Despite the momentum of *All 'N All* and the additional infusion of hit singles like "September" and "Got to Get You into My Life," we still felt the loss of Charles Stepney, especially in the songwriting and arranging departments. Maurice was feeling pressure to fill the void and to keep our winning streak going. We needed a new personality to help energize our musical inner sanctum.

Enter a twenty-nine-year-old piano player from Victoria, British Columbia, named David Walter Foster. Foster had migrated to Southern California and had begun playing around the Los Angeles music scene. In 1974 he was hired to play piano for the house band backing up the first live performances of *The Rocky Horror Picture Show,* which began its first long-run engagement at the Roxy in Hollywood. After a year and two weeks he was promoted to music director of the production. *The Rocky Horror Picture Show* turned out to be a fortuitous stepping-stone. Foster would later meet young session musicians like David Paich (son of the great West Coast jazz arranger Marty Paich) and Jeff and Steve Porcaro, who would help Foster break into the tight ranks of the LA studio musician scene.

Between 1975 and 1979 Foster became a much-sought-after studio musician. Even though his studio pay quickly graduated from ordinary "demo" scale to single scale and double or triple scale, he would soon experience the potential downside to being a busy on-call session player, and risk getting burned out.

In 1978 Foster and David Paich cowrote the disco hit "Got to Be Real" for songstress Cheryl Lynn. By the end of the seventies, Foster's ambition was to phase out of his role as a hired-gun session man by scoring a gig with Earth, Wind & Fire as a songwriter, arranger, and studio hand, hoping that could help clear the way for him one day to become a successful record producer and songwriter.

David had long been an enormous fan of Earth, Wind & Fire. In December 1975, when Tower Records in Los Angeles stayed open past midnight to allow our fans to be the first to purchase a copy of *Gratitude,* he stood at the front of the line. At that time, in addition to his session work, David was also a journeyman keyboardist for a pop group called Skylark, which scored a one-off hit on Capitol Records called "Wildflower." He next formed an album-rock trio called Airplay with guitarist Jay Graydon. Many of the backup musicians who played on Airplay's lone album would later unite to form Toto. An ex-hippie from Northern California named Bill Champlin, who had played in his notoriously funky San Francisco rock band, the Sons of Champlin, would also contribute background vocals.

Foster and Graydon sat down with Champlin and wrote the melody and lyrics for an extraordinary song that would forever change the course of David's musical career, as well as ours. "After the Love Is Gone" was one of those once-in-a-lifetime songs cast in the style of "You've Lost That Lovin' Feeling" by the Righteous Brothers. Foster and Graydon wrote the melody while Champlin wrote the lyrics.

When Foster and his friends finished writing the tune, David performed the piece—sitting on a bed—for one of his music industry friends, a woman by the name of Carole Childs. (Childs would later join the David Geffen Company as an A&R executive.) When David finished the song, she was floored.

"I've got to introduce you to Maurice White."

Childs set up an audition for Foster at Sunset Sound Studios for Maurice and the band, and to play us his new song. Maurice had already told Verdine and me about this new kid he wanted to check out. David recalls sitting down at the piano, his heart nearly pounding out of his chest. He had been an admirer of EWF since its inception, and here was his big chance to plug a song for us.

Admittedly David wasn't that great of a singer, but I knew right away that "After the Love Is Gone" had the makings of a major hit. In our business, song is king. It's what creates careers. You can take a lesser singer and give him a great song and make him a shining star. There was magic in the room when we first heard it, and while everybody felt the vibe, you never knew for sure what would transpire further up the management/record company chain of command, and whether they would love it or not. Foster waited for the verdict from Maurice.

"We're going to record that song," Maurice assured Foster, looking him in the eye and smiling.

David replied, half dumbfounded, "When?"

"Tonight."

That night we retreated to the studio and rolled twenty-four tracks on David's song.

Our treatment of "After the Love Is Gone" would levitate from verse to chorus. Maurice's steady vocal on the lower registers smoldered throughout the verses, counterbalanced by the soaring falsetto parts I provided on the chorus, which contained the hook of the song. By the time the song reached its climax, highlighted by a searing bebop-styled saxophone solo by Don Myrick, it had become a tour de force.

"After the Love" was not an easy piece to sing, and from a strictly technical standpoint, you could make the argument that it is flawed. Its overambitious architecture demands a multioctave range, and theoretically, to do it justice one person can't perform the entire song alone. Maybe it should have been sung by a female vocalist with a higher and wider gospel range. Luckily EWF had the necessary combined range and vocal firepower to handle it. We solved the inherent problems in the song's structure by having Maurice do the verses with me singing the chorus, enabling us to capture the breadth of its notes and emotions. (It wasn't the first time Maurice and I had to double up roles to rescue a song.)

After the fruitful collaboration on "After the Love Is Gone," Maurice invited David to join him and the band at Reese's twelve-acre compound in Carmel, California, for a writing session to compose more new material for the upcoming *I Am* album. Maurice's Carmel estate was awesome. It had three houses on it—and not just casitas or guest quarters but full-blown houses! Maurice's was the largest, a very homey and warm single-level, Mediterranean-style home. The furnishings and spiritual artifacts were carefully arranged according to feng shui principles. Freddie had his place, while Verdine stayed in the third house on the property. The estate had multiple swimming pools and plenty of land, with orange groves and vineyards. While it didn't have an oceanside view, the beauty of the trees and countryside was exquisite. I know Reese had spent a whole lot of money on the property. For example, after putting up rich mahogany walls, he plastered over them when he decided that they weren't what he wanted. I also believe some people took him for a financial ride. The front door alone cost $35,000. We occasionally did some rehearsing up there in a small room, and at other times some writing. Only a select few band members were invited to spend time there. While the rest of us were thrilled to be buying our first homes in our early twenties in nicer areas of Los Angeles, Maurice lived in Bel Air and enjoyed the luxury of a sprawling Carmel estate as his retreat.

To say that Reese and Foster's writing session was prolific would almost be an understatement. In a single sitting, from 7:00 p.m. until 7:00 a.m. the next morning, they sat at the grand piano in Maurice's living room and wrote eight more songs for the album.

The creative process opened an artistic floodgate. There were no musical rules. Together David and Maurice would create the germ of a song and then compose a few noteworthy hooks with the aid of a cassette recorder. Foster took his place at the piano and began playing various lines and phrases. The key was to be musically adventurous, to cast the creative chains of the writing process aside, the same methodology Maurice and I used to collaborate on songs like "Reasons" and "Devotion." Anything goes! There was no attempt to adhere to any musical formats or to stay within certain commercial boundaries, be it R&B, pop, black, white, or beat-oriented dance music. Song was king.

"Just play, and I will sing along. Whatever you want to do, do it," Maurice told Foster.

The more adventurous the two got musically, the more Maurice thrived, and the more he encouraged Foster to flesh out the various musical ideas that came pouring out. It was as if the music were flowing through them and not from them, a very liberating and productive experience for the young Canadian. As is typical in many pop-songwriting collaborations, Maurice and David labored primarily on the music. Soon after, Maurice would dispatch lyricist Allee Willis to finish the bulk of the words.

Especially striking was how much leeway Maurice was willing to give David in order to keep the process moving. Foster, whose main diet at the time was fast food and grilled cheese sandwiches, managed to score a hot dog during the wee hours of the morning, a very unlikely entrée to be consumed at Maurice's healthy compound. Foster's sitting at the piano with a hot dog in one hand and a cigarette in the other were major taboos that Maurice abhorred. Yet he tolerated David's bad habits in order to not break their concentration by having Foster leave the piano to go outside and smoke.

The majority of the songs for *I Am* came from that one writing session in Carmel. From there we took the material to band rehearsals in New York, and later to the studios in Hollywood—which were in three different locations in Los Angeles: Sunset

Sound, Hollywood Sound Recorders, and Davlen Sound Studios. George Massenburg engineered all sessions using his proprietary EQ (equalization) system and tight microphone techniques, keeping the sound crisp and clean.

Foster played acoustic piano on nearly every song and keyboards alongside Larry. In order to keep his piano sonically isolated, he performed his piano parts behind a thick black velvet curtain enlisted to prevent sound leaking in from the drums and the bass. During the sessions, when *Jet* magazine dropped by to write a feature about us, we joked about "keeping the white boy behind the curtain so that nobody could see him."

Foster also helped to arrange and coarrange most of the nine tracks. In addition he turned us on to Jerry Hey, a remarkable horn and string arranger who would help us fill the Charles Stepney void. Like Step and Tom Tom 84, Jerry was a master at creating super-tight horn and string charts. He had done some fine arrangements on Michael Jackson's *Off the Wall* album. Arranging in the late 1970s meant no synthesizers or computer programs. It was a pen-to-paper operation, much like what Mozart and Duke Ellington had accomplished centuries and years earlier.

Foster was so proud of his work on *I Am* that he wanted to impress his studio friends with the headway he had made within the group. While later working on an Alice Cooper session with Jeff Porcaro and David Paich, he sneaked into the studio vault and pulled out the twenty-four-track tapes for *I Am* and brought them up on the studio monitors to play them for his friends.

Besides "After the Love Is Gone," *I Am* featured a bevy of tight, catchy hits, with "Boogie Wonderland" being the most commercial tune of the bunch. That song, written by pop songwriters Jon Lind and Allee Willis, was originally presented to Al McKay, who was in the studio recording an ARC act, Curtis the Brothers, for Maurice and Cavallo-Ruffalo. During that time we had vowed we would never cut a disco song. The first time and last time I visited Studio 54 in New York City, I felt utter disdain for disco, because so many of the songs sounded monotonous, fueled by robotic beats. After Al cut an instrumental track for "Boogie Wonderland," it was Cavallo's idea to hand the tune over to EWF.

When we agreed to cut "Boogie Wonderland," Maurice and I decided that if we were actually going to record a disco number, we would pull out all the stops and do it our way. The arrangements and orchestrations were punchy, our response to the dreaded disco era. It was Al and Maurice's idea to use a slamming female trio, The Emotions, that had just joined Reese's new ARC label, to augment the groove. Influenced by German producer Giorgio Moroder's immaculate beat-driven hits with Donna Summer, we took it a step further and featured three layers of vocals, with Maurice singing lead, plus The Emotions, and my voice added to the top of the heap. Cutting "Boogie Wonderland" was actually a quick no-brainer. The four-to-the-floor kick drum at about a hundred twenty beats per minute, plus the high hat on the upbeat, automatically made it disco, while Verdine kicked in a walking disco bass riff augmented by David Foster's flashy piano intro, punctuated with traces of Latin percussion. I actually found Allee Willis's lyrics to be deceptively deep and cerebral and I've grown to love the tune, which we use to open our live shows today.

While David worked with us in the studio, Foster was amazed that the more we added to our studio tracks, the better our music sounded! For most artists and producers, adding superfluous instruments and vocals weighs down the sound and obscures the vocal performances. With EWF, the more guitar parts, vocal harmonies, keyboard fills, and horn and/or string charts we added, the better and richer our sound became. It's one of those intangibles about the magic of Earth, Wind & Fire's music. Our arrangements are busy—there's always something going on—yet there's clarity in that busyness. The golden rule in producing popular music is "Don't let anything get in the way of the vocal." We break that rule all the time, which is one aspect of how we achieve our unique sound.

At the conclusion of the *I Am* sessions, David was informed that if EWF released their versions of his songs, Maurice would be entitled to a piece of the publishing royalties. David, realizing his rookie bargaining status, agreed. He received good news with the bad. Because he had worked so diligently on the album, Maurice gave him a half point's credit on the album—which amounted to one-half percent of the album revenues. In addition to being paid session and arranging fees, David was compensated as a cowriter on six of the nine tunes featured on the album, as well as given a small share as a producer. To the chagrin of many of the band members, David ended up getting what no one else in the group ever received—a healthy piece of the action from an EWF album!

24

"MAN, THE TUNES IS PISSED . . ."

As a major African American superstar act grossing amazing ticket sales all over the world, Earth, Wind & Fire began to be publicly criticized. We were scolded by the NAACP for not hiring enough African American stage hands and road crew. Not only were we spending a tremendous amount of money to buy, operate, and transport our sound, lights, and staging, but we also hired highly experienced and expensive technicians who had worked with other large touring rock bands, mostly white bands like Electric Light Orchestra and Emerson, Lake & Palmer. These were the high-roller acts that featured levitating pianos and drums that spun around. We needed a special caliber of stagehand capable of entering an enormous empty shell of an arena like Madison Square Garden and hanging our vast array of speakers, lights, and hydraulic stage gear. We didn't hire on the basis of color, but qualification. Looking back, perhaps we should have been more diligent in employing personnel from the African American communities.

Touring was a lucrative but also an expensive proposition. Maurice—or more specifically, the band, through its revenues—shouldered a lot of the financial responsibility. At that time we hadn't yet attracted significant corporate sponsorship to help offset our touring costs. Our three ring circus/Mardi Gras atmosphere onstage—along with our outrageous, glitzy costumes—had helped put us on the map. If we had been more frugal and cut corners, we might never have made it. We needed to spend money in order to make money to keep the show on the road, and at the time we were just one African American group competing with a cascade of established white rock and roll bands that had an economic advantage over us in terms of access to financial and tour support.

The people who were disgruntled about our stage crews weren't aware of the bigger picture. Our management responded to the NAACP's charges by reminding them that EWF regularly collaborated with many African American promoters in copresenting our concerts. The problem of black promoters getting edged out has been a touchy issue in the concert business for years. Maurice and the Earth, Wind & Fire band and management regularly used black radio programmers as cosponsors of our shows. We didn't hesitate to turn to noted African American promoters like Billy Sparks, Quentin Perry, and the late Louis Grey to help present our concerts. The anger from the NAACP would subside later, and in 1994 Earth, Wind & Fire would receive an NAACP Image Award and be inducted into their Hall of Fame, which honors outstanding people of color in television, movies, music, and literature.

With the 1980s creeping up on us, a new musical invention called the Linn drum machine would greatly impact the process of recording popular music in the studio. David Foster was the first guy to take Roger Linn's prototype over to Maurice's place to have him check it out.

"This is the future of recording," David told Reese, and with one press of a button, they marveled as a clear, piercing, and snappy synthesized snare drum hit emanated from the digital machine. Maurice and Foster were fascinated with the device, and Maurice would use it for our next album, *Faces*. From that point on technology would profoundly influence Maurice's methods of production, and the new era of drum machines and polyphonic synthesizers would greatly affect our communal vibe as a studio band.

With the multiplatinum success of *I Am,* and for all of its hits and crossover success, there was discord brewing within the band. *I Am* had more of a pop sound than some of the musicians were comfortable with. Al and Larry felt that we were shedding some of our identity, drifting away from a more dominant R&B sound with the increased use of outside session players. Given *I Am*'s Grammy awards and accolades, many music fans view it as the pinnacle of EWF recordings. Others within our inner sanctum look back on earlier albums, like *That's the Way of the World,* with much more fondness, not only for its strong repertoire and arrangements but also for its era of close band camaraderie. Personally, I choose *That's the Way of the World* as our definitive release.

Faces was recorded during 1980 with Maurice back at the producer's helm alongside engineer George Massenburg. As usual, Maurice was thinking big. *Faces* was an ambitious seventeen-song, double-set vinyl extravaganza cut in various studios in Los Angeles and Hollywood, as well as at The Beatles' producer George Martin's opulent Air Studios in Montserrat in beautiful tropical Antigua, nestled in the West Indies. While we recorded at Montserrat, I took time out to teach my older son, Sir, how to swim in the warm West Indian waters.

The rhythm tracks on *Faces* were intricate, sometimes complicated, but built on a nice solid groove. Our signature horn parts were punchy using Jerry Hey's arrangements. As on *I Am,* lots of outside players returned, including percussionist Paulinho da Costa and Toto guitarist Steve Lukather, keyboardist David Paich, and the talented Porcaro brothers (Jeff on drums and Steve on keyboards and synths). David Foster also returned to contribute on a few tracks, but did not participate to the extent he did on *I Am.* Meanwhile, band members muttered that Maurice's sessions were beginning to sound overproduced with his growing legions of string players, background vocalists, and percussionists. The title track, for instance, is a sprawling tour de force of exotic, driving rhythms and big-band sounds—much like the CTI records I enjoyed as a youth, featuring dozens of players and singers.

We had always been big fans of the Great American Songbook and classic twentieth-century songwriters like Cole Porter, George Gershwin, Duke Ellington, Billy Strayhorn, Jerome Kern, Hoagy Carmichael, Irving Berlin, and Richard Rodgers. We weren't so caught up in ourselves that we didn't recognize the need for outside help, and we used some very fine lyricists to cowrite our tunes. When crafting tunes like "Fantasy" from *All 'N All,* we often wrote with lyricists like Brenda Russell and Eddie del Barrio after we had finished the basics of a song. Those were the days when our songs had three or four different sections to them, so we wanted to keep the quality of our lyrics edgy and forward-moving. On *Faces* Maurice and I concentrated on our craft as songwriters by collaborating with talented wordsmiths like Roxanne Seeman to polish our songs and take them to the next level. Roxanne Seeman cowrote "Sailaway" on *Faces* with me, and we would work together on more songs later on.

For all its grandeur and glory, *Faces* was not a financial success for us—and it wasn't because we didn't get the promotional street support from Columbia Records. In terms of quality, it's a great record. But as a double album, it got lost due to its sheer volume of material. Although *Faces* became a gold record, it didn't have an identifiable smash single; audiences had trouble finding a simple sing-along hit like "September" or "Shining Star." Looking back, we should have concentrated on cutting that elusive, radio-friendly, catchy song and then released half the material from *Faces* in order to make it one great album.

Also working against us was the fact that in 1980 the entire radio and music industry was in transition. The megahits and multiplatinum sales of Michael Jackson's 1979 album, *Off the Wall,* would later affect our own standing and status at Columbia. Jackson's tremendous dominance of pop culture throughout the 1980s was just beginning, and as a result (and partially to our detriment), the executives at the Sony label group were starting to mobilize behind him.

Plus, during the making of *Faces,* disharmony had begun brewing within the band. Shortly after the album's November 1980 release, Al McKay became increasingly more vocal about his unhappiness with Maurice. As a result, session players Steve Lukather and Marlo Henderson performed many of the guitar solos. McKay's presence was felt less and less, and through his discontent I could see cracks in the band's infrastructure. Al was unhappy that there was now a very evident large financial abyss between Maurice and the other band members, and he felt that the rest of us weren't getting paid enough. He would often try to gauge the other guys' reaction over the matter and once pulled Larry Dunn aside and said, "You know, if we all pull together, we can get on Maurice and nip this whole inequality thing in the bud!"

Larry, being the youngest member, responded that he didn't care about the money; he loved the music. Besides, Maurice was such a nice guy.

It turns out that Al had a point. We signed a separate EWF production contract. That meant that technically, we were signed as a band to Maurice's production company. Al was the first to say, essentially, "Hey, guys, we better go and have a talk and let Maurice know that this arrangement has got to change."

Al knew more about the pitfalls of the music business and what to watch out for than I did. He was the first to see that our situation might not be as rosy as we thought. For my own part, I didn't realize what was happening. I just knew that life as a musician was grand. I was making money playing in front of thousands and thousands of people, attracting fame if not fortune. At twenty-nine years of age, I wasn't thinking enough about the business end. I figured that while Maurice took most of the financial and creative risks, things would take care of themselves.

Some of the band members took offense at Al's awakening.

Earth, Wind & Fire was their life's passion. They loved Maurice and believed that everybody was going to become a millionaire. As long as band members could buy houses for themselves and their parents and loved ones and drive nice cars, we were satisfied. Some went to Maurice and warned him that Al was causing trouble within the ranks, but by then it was too late: Al was on his way out.

We were in Argentina on a South American tour in 1980 when Al announced that he intended to quit. It was raining like crazy that day, and we were sitting around the hotel, playing chess. Al told Andrew and Larry, "This is my last tour. This is it."

Andrew and Larry looked at Al like he was nuts. "Are you crazy?"

When we flew to Mexico City for the next step of the tour, Al passed separately through customs along with my wife, Janet, and Larry's wife, Debbie. Afterward the promoter, along with a hospitality interpreter, came and rounded up the rest of the band, took our passports, and walked us through customs. Nobody came over and told Al to join us.

We played a large stadium gig the next day in Mexico City, and the crowds went crazy. Since there were four days before our next gig in Mexico, the plan was for the group to fly back to the United States for some time off and then return to Mexico. Once we got to the airport, though, none of the band could leave Mexico, as our passports hadn't been given back to us after we initially cleared customs coming in—that is, except for Al, who had his passport with him.

When Al arrived back in Southern California, he was given strict orders to immediately fly back to Mexico and join the rest of the band. Al, not seeing the logic, didn't pack his bags. Then he received a phone call from Ralph Johnson.

"Oh, man, the Tunes is pissed . . ." ("Tunes" being short for Rooney Tunes.) Ralph handed the phone over to an irate Maurice.

And that's how it ended. Reese fired Al over the phone, and a few days later McKay got the letter informing him that he was officially terminated. In Al's mind he had already quit and had anticipated his dismissal.

After that tour we headed back to the States and then on to Montserrat to finish the *Faces* album. It was a sad time for us to lose Al, our "rhythm master," but a relief to him, once it had gotten too intense and unbearably ugly for him to continue.

25

THE MEETING

The three-album era between 1981 and 1983 proved to be a tenuous period for Earth, Wind & Fire. Guitarist Roland Bautista had rejoined the band in 1981 to replace Al McKay. With Bautista back on board, we recorded a dance number called "Let's Groove" for the *Raise!* LP, our eleventh Columbia release. It was a catchy duet I cut with Maurice, whose voice was heavily bathed in synthesized vocoder effects. In June 1981 BET, the Black Entertainment Television cable channel, premiered its first entertainment series, *Video Soul,* and "Let's Groove" was the first piece they played on the air. *Raise!* also included a silly futuristic song called "Evolution Orange," cowritten by David Foster, which he says was one of the worst songs he had ever been part of.

By 1983 the rest of the band members were finally waking up to the fact that EWF's fortunes weren't benefiting everyone in an equitable way. The more I looked into it, the more distressing the situation appeared. We were at the peak of our careers, selling out the Los Angeles Forum for five nights and scoring Grammys and other awards, yet I was making $2,500 a week, an impressive sum at the time, but small in the grand scheme of things. I didn't have a clue as to how much money Maurice was generating from the total picture of record sales, publishing, ticket sales, concert grosses, and merchandising. Then one day I ran into a musician friend who was playing with Michael Jackson at the time. During our conversation he mentioned that he was making $10,000 a week working for Michael as a sideman—four times what I was being paid as a band member! And were the lighting guys, the bus company people, and the trucking employees making more than the band members?

My God! I had no idea that other musicians were making that kind of money. I suspected that I fared better than some of the other members because I was getting publishing royalties from the songs I had cowritten. Also, at year's end, because I was a key man in the band, when management dispensed annual bonuses, I would get extra compensation.

Along with Michael Jackson's meteoric rise in popularity, another awesome talent had appeared in our rearview mirror. Prince was a hot musical commodity, and many labels were courting him. One of the first people to spot Prince's potential was my old friend Perry Jones. After Perry had briefly returned to work for us as a tour manager he departed again to strike out on his own as a concert promoter, helping Maurice and his booking agents stage some of our concerts in the United States. Around this time Perry received a call from Mo Ostin's office at Warner Brothers Records asking if he knew about a rising young performer named Prince. Perry told Warner that he was familiar with Prince, whom he had met during one of our concerts. Perry did some advance work for Warner to help get Prince on their roster.

By the time Perry made overtures to sign a management deal with Prince, the diminutive artiste had already migrated to—guess where?—Cavallo-Ruffalo! Once again Perry's management ambitions were derailed by Bob Cavallo, Joe Ruffalo, and Steve Fargnoli, who had signed a deal to become Prince's personal managers. By 1979, when Prince recorded his second album, it produced his first crossover hit, "I Wanna Be Your Lover." (Fargnoli died in 2001.)

Cavallo now had a hot new star to look after in addition to

Maurice and EWF—something Reese was not enthusiastic about. By this time solo acts were becoming a big thing on the urban music scene. While Cavallo still viewed Maurice as the visionary in our band, he regarded Prince as the most unique individual artist he had ever met. After securing representation for Prince, Cavallo attempted to sign him to Maurice's ARC Records. Unfortunately Columbia dropped the ball badly when they sent a senior A&R representative from New York to Los Angeles to speak with Prince ahead of Cavallo. The executive made a major faux pas when, in attempting to woo Prince to ARC, he told him, "I can get Maurice White to produce you." That remark killed the deal, since Prince had no intention of having anybody but himself produce his records. By 1983, with Prince's career skyrocketing with gold and platinum records, Cavallo's firm was entrenched in the arduous task of bringing Prince's movie *Purple Rain* to the silver screen.

Earth, Wind & Fire was one of Prince's earliest inspirations. As a youth he had attended one of our arena shows in Minneapolis and was completely bowled over. Prince later admitted to Cavallo that upon seeing our concert, he was pushed back in his seat in amazement. According to Bob, he asked himself, "How could I ever equal this?" Later, when Prince came to Warner Brothers, he contacted Ostin and asked him to hook him up with the folks who represented Earth, Wind & Fire. Ostin referred Prince to his old friend Bob, which helped cement a professional relationship that would last for nine years. After that, Maurice White and Cavallo-Ruffalo would amicably part company.

Between 1981 and 1983 we released three marginal albums on Columbia. After *Raise!* came out in November 1981 we released two other albums on Columbia, *Powerlight* in March 1983, and *Electric Universe* the following December.

After *Faces* the band had effectively become glorified session players for Maurice in the studio. All three releases were blandly flavored with Linn drum machines and Yamaha DX7 keyboard synthesizers. The rest of the band members were clearly disenchanted, and the vibe was not good. When we were together, the cold distance and isolation that had arisen was clear in everyone's body language. We would drop in to cut our parts and split, and we spent less time on the road. The group camaraderie had evaporated, and Maurice called the creative shots. Even George Massenburg was no longer working with us. Maurice had also begun writing with other people, and since he and his new cowriters had already prepared the songs, I basically became just a session singer. Maurice and I would lay down our background vocals. Bang! Done! That was the vibe through all three of those records. Although we won another Grammy award—Best R&B Vocal Performance by a Duo or Group—for "Wanna Be With You" from *Raise!,* our momentum had stalled.

I penned only one song on *Raise!*—a midtempo, loping, funky piece ironically titled "I've Had Enough," which I wrote with Greg Phillinganes and coproduced with Maurice—and between *Powerlight* and *Electric Universe,* I contributed only one song. "Straight from the Heart" (another unlikely title) was a soppy ballad on *Powerlight.* After that record came out, Maurice cut the Phenix Horns loose. Don Myrick, Lou Satterfield, and Michael Harris were now free to tour and record with other major acts, and were snapped up by Phil Collins and Genesis. The party was over. After eleven years, were we lucky that it had lasted as long as it did?

All this creative inertia finally led to what is darkly described by Earth, Wind & Fire members as "the Meeting," which was held at the end of 1983 after *Electric Universe* was released—and flopped horribly. There are varied accounts of the Meeting. Some say it took place over multiple sit-downs, others say it was one explosive event. Here's how I remember what went down.

In late 1983 Maurice summoned the entire band to the Complex. He began by saying, "Guys, I've decided that I'm going to put Earth, Wind & Fire on the back burner. We're going to stop touring. You guys need to do whatever you want to do in the meantime. Columbia doesn't want an album from us. They want me to do my solo album." Maurice disbanded the group straightaway. It didn't happen gradually over a few months. It was over immediately. That was it. The band members were caught completely unawares. We had no time to prepare.

It was a shock, a wake-up call beyond description. At that point I was thirty-two years old. Lord have mercy, life had just gotten deadly serious. The $2,500-a-week salary that I had been counting on, and which I had comfortably lived on, was no more—done, over and out! How would I deal with it?

It happened rather unceremoniously. We each received a letter in our pay packets advising us to remove all of our personal possessions and musical gear from storage, otherwise they would be sold out from under us. The band owning its own sound and lights had created a huge financial burden and tied up a lot of money, and we had also paid a quarter of a million dollars for wardrobes. Now the equipment and road cases were to be liquidated! Tragically, the wardrobe cases containing the grandest costumes went with them. Most were not rescued. Years later I was contacted by someone who had bought one of the wardrobe cases for a few hundred dollars, wanting to know if I wanted to buy back the costumes! In hindsight maybe I should have, but emotionally, at the time, I didn't appreciate the legacy. I just thought it was over with.

We could have been forewarned that EWF was going to be disbanded. By using the term "back burner," Maurice seemed to imply that Earth, Wind & Fire was on hiatus. Walking out of that infamous meeting, that's not how I saw it. In my opinion Earth, Wind & Fire had broken up, and anybody who said differently was in denial. You don't tell people that you're going to sell all their stuff in storage when you go on hiatus. You don't stop speaking to band members for the next few years.

Who could have conceived how big Earth, Wind & Fire was going to be? Who could have foreseen our demise? Looking back, we needed a proverbial corner man, as in a boxing match. Had we still had Charles Stepney and Clive Davis in our corner—like Michael Jackson had Quincy Jones—we might have been able to make it through our creative malaise. Clive was wise, a sage. I learned a lot whenever I spoke with him.

The questions became, What happens next? How do you reinvent yourself? EWF was an archetypal band of the 1970s, and yet we didn't understand the dynamics of the 1980s. Michael Jackson understood the 1980s. Maybe the Concept didn't apply anymore. The world wasn't about peace, love, and positivism. The 1980s were about economics and music for cold hard cash. And we didn't anticipate the video world being as influential as it would become. We shot videos merely as promotional vehicles, while Michael Jackson premiered them as major milestone events. We both had our long string of hit records, but we dominated our era with spectacular concert events, while Michael Jackson dominated his throughout the multimedia age in people's living rooms.

In the end it was Maurice's decision to disband EWF the way he did. The managers worked for him, and not the other way around. Who knows if Reese realized what the consequences of his actions might be? He claims today that while the breakup might have appeared abrupt, it was not done impulsively, and that he thought long and hard before doing it, and was sensitive to the impact it would have on everyone involved.

My own belief is that Maurice was overwhelmed and overleveraged, and in response he panicked. Soon afterward he would shut down the ARC label, then split with Cavallo-Ruffalo and Massenburg. Was he in a space where he was sabotaging himself? It's what New Age guru Deepak Chopra calls "the fight-or-flight response." Reese took flight because the musical era was changing, and he reacted by fighting back with automatic anger and fear. Maybe he had too much static in his head, and his strong personality worked against him. After enjoying success as an outside producer working with artists like Deniece Williams, The Emotions, Jennifer Holiday, and Barbra Streisand, Maurice might have felt that he had become more important than the band.

I couldn't help but feel bitter. Bottom line, I was dumb, naïve, and inexperienced. On one level I was intimidated and afraid. On another level, I was shocked, appalled, and crushed with disbelief. On yet another level, I was in denial. But then the recovery started. At some point, you have to recover.

I made it through, grounded in my Christian faith. In retrospect, who could have known the best way to react and then emerge from a painful breakup? For me, I had to forgive. Not for anybody else, but for myself. I had to look inside myself and say, "Whatever is in store, God will continue to take care of me."

So I made my decision to go it alone. What would be in store for me as a solo artist?

I was caught in a real bind. I couldn't become a session player because I didn't read music like studio players, and I hadn't cultivated those kinds of connections. After singing and playing with EWF for eleven years, how could I go to somebody and say, "I need a gig"?

I went home and examined my personal assets. I had a house in Los Angeles that my family was living in, and another house in Inglewood, where my sister Beverly stayed. Janet and I had a twelve-unit piece of income property on Normandie Avenue in LA. When I went down to Pep Boys on Pico Boulevard to purchase something, my EWF credit card was rejected. I panicked! It was too much, so I told Janet, "Let's just move back to Denver. We can pare down our lifestyle by leaving California."

So we sold our stuff and moved back to Denver. But in hindsight, I saw that you can't go back home. I may have been overreacting, but we did move, and the family ended up staying there for four years. And that's where my children found out what community is about; we didn't have that same sense of neighborhood in Los Angeles.

For the rest of the band, the breakup was a nightmare. Some members lost their homes and fortunes, and some went into counseling after suffering nervous breakdowns. Even Maurice's brothers weren't immune from the axe. Maurice and Verdine weren't speaking to each other during this terrible time, and Freddie had moved on. Verdine became a record producer and directed music videos. For a while Ralph Johnson wrote songs and coproduced an album by The Temptations with Al McKay, which begat the hit "Treat Her Like a Lady," but he ended up working at the Federated Group on Sunset and LaBrea, selling stereo equipment. When Maurice's girlfriend came into the store to buy a stereo for Maurice's son, it was Ralph who had to sell it to her. He even did some work on a construction site.

Prior to the Meeting, Cavallo-Ruffalo had scored me a solo record deal with Columbia, and my first album, *Continuation,* which I had cut in 1983 with the late George Duke as producer, came out after the release of *Electric Universe.* The record was straight-down-the-middle R&B/pop and featured George Duke on keyboards and my friend Nathan East on bass, along with guest backing vocal support from Jeffrey Osborne and Sister ("We Are Family") Sledge. Jerry Hey arranged the horns. For my solo debut, I could sing in my tenor voice as well as my trademark falsetto.

As a result of *Continuation*'s modest Top 20 success on the R&B album charts, I had something to build on toward a future career. Becoming a gospel singer gave me another platform. In 1984 I recorded a gospel album for Word Records on their Myrrh label called *The Wonders of His Love,* which went gold and won a Grammy. I traveled on tour with pop gospel star Amy Grant, and refocused. I became wiser about band finances and how people were to be compensated. Sometimes I paid my sidemen more than I was making, and I played in smaller halls, but at least I was musically active.

26

EASY LOVER

In 1984, as I was preparing to work on my second album for Columbia, I launched my new post-EWF pop/R&B solo career with team Cavallo, Ruffalo & Fargnoli managing my musical affairs. Janet and the family were headquartered in Colorado, and I kept an apartment in Los Angeles.

I went to see Phil Collins play at the Forum in Los Angeles with his band Genesis on their Mama Tour that January. My former cohorts, the Phenix Horns, were playing with him, and Sat and Don, now part of Phil's musical entourage, had invited me to the show. Admittedly I wasn't that familiar with Genesis and Phil's music, but I was blown away by the concert. Internationally Phil was bigger than life and was playing everywhere. While I was writing and gathering material for my second record, I told Jamie Shoop, who worked with my management team, "I'd like to cover one of Phil's songs. Do you think I could get a song from him?" She was able to get in touch with him and found out that Phil was a huge Earth, Wind & Fire fan. One conversation led to another, and management suggested reaching out to him to see if he wanted to produce the entire album! Why not? It was worth a try.

Phil consented to do it—wow!—and as he and I had exchanged songs, I made plans to go to London. When I was getting on the plane to England, Roxanne Seeman, who had worked on "Sailaway" with me on the *Faces* album, brought me a cassette of a song that she had written with Billie Hughes called "Walking on the Chinese Wall." I took it with me. Ralph Johnson submitted a song he cowrote called "Go." Then Phil played me a song he had found called "Children of the Ghetto" and we added that to the list, too.

We spent a great deal of productive time writing songs and recording in London. I brought my bass player friend, Nathan East, along with me for the project. I told Phil he needed to get to know Nathan, because he was the ultimate cat! Nathan ended up working with Phil for many years, as well as with Eric Clapton. Nathan later joined the smooth jazz quartet Fourplay with pianist Bob James, guitarist Lee Ritenour, and drummer Harvey Mason.

Working with Phil was the best. We were the same age, and he has an easygoing personality and is unassuming and not egotistical in any way. For him, it was all about the music, and he wasn't caught up in the star thing that was exploding around him. We would just show up at the studio and roll tape, and after the day's work Phil would turn us on to some incredible Indian food joints around London—not to mention imbibing many pints of lager and lime. I started gaining weight when I was over in the UK, so I took tennis lessons and worked out in the gym when we weren't making music.

After we'd finished recording, we laid down the horn parts in Los Angeles. Of course I used the Phenix Horns and hired Tom Tom 84 to arrange them. Then it was back to London, where, as we listened to the finished tunes, we realized that we needed one more up-tempo song. I started singing a bass line in the studio, and Nathan jumped on the keyboards and added a part. Then Phil climbed into the drum booth, and after we laid down the basics, we finished up a rough mix of an instrumental track. Phil then took the track home that night and wrote the lyrics. When we came back to the studio the next day, Phil and I performed the duet. At that point, "Easy Lover" was done, and so was the album, *Chinese Wall*. It was released in the United States in December 1984 and in the UK in February 1985.

"Easy Lover" was one of the biggest pop records of 1985, and catapulted me to a whole new musical plateau. Oh, my God! I thought I had seen hit-record success with EWF, but it was nothing like this. Compared to the crossover track record of EWF, this was really the big time. The record was flying out the door like popcorn, selling 500,000 singles a week, and the record company promotion people were going crazy. It was wild. Wherever I was, driving all over the United States, even in the so-called flyover states between the East and West coasts, "Easy Lover" was a radio staple in heavy rotation on four different contemporary music formats—Top 40, urban, adult/contemporary, and album radio. The closest I had come to having such a monster hit was with "After the Love Is Gone." "Easy Lover" also did well internationally and stayed number one in the United Kingdom for four weeks. It was on *Top of the Pops* and BBC Radio One so often that every hipster in London and every clothing boutique in the UK were blaring the song. Later that year, we won an MTV Video Music Award, and "Easy Lover" was nominated for a Grammy.

Chinese Wall did well for me. It gave me autonomy, confidence, and authority in my own life and career. It also gave me a greater appreciation for the legacy of Earth, Wind & Fire and for what we had contributed musically. I could now view EWF from a different, more aerial perspective, after having been out of the eye of the storm for a few years.

I had become my own shining star, and I now viewed the music of EWF more objectively, realizing that its legacy was far bigger than the sum of its hit records. Maurice was right when he taught me to be true to the music and to the Concept. I discovered that our body of work was something I should be proud of. It had a lineage all its own, and it would only grow more valuable in the years to come.

When young musicians and singers ask me for professional advice, I tell them that in order to succeed in the arts, you have to love what you're doing more than you hate the changes and difficulties you're going to have to endure to survive in a business as wacky as the music industry. Case in point is what happened to me following the success of *Chinese Wall.*

The record executives at Columbia were elated with the success of "Easy Lover," and came to me with an idea for my third album. In 1985 the label sent me back to London, where we put together an all-star lineup of players to help me record my next batch of songs. The list of contributors was awesome. Joining me in the studio were guitarists Jeff Beck, Nile Rodgers, and Ray Parker Jr., keyboardist George Duke, and Phil Collins returning on drums. We recorded a few songs, and then Columbia sent me to New York City to work in the studio with two other hot production/songwriting teams: Full Force and the System. Later I met up with Nile Rodgers in Manhattan, and we cut another set of songs. I also went into the studio in Los Angeles with Randy Jackson, who had just become Columbia's new West Coast head of A&R.

This whole musical course played out for almost two years as we stockpiled more and more new songs. The reason the project was taking so long was that there had been multiple changes of personnel within the label, and responsibility for my record was transferred to different A&R staffers. Hence the stops and starts. Some thought that my third album should be more pop, while others felt it should veer stylistically toward an urban/R&B sound. As a result of the back-and-forth creative process, I was no longer touring and generating income to support my wife and four children, whom I had since brought back to Los Angeles from Colorado. Although I was becoming uncomfortable sitting on the sidelines and living off royalties, I didn't make waves or cause a stink about not having a follow-up record released in a timely manner.

Finally, in 1986 my third solo album, *Inside Out,* was quietly released. It was a hodgepodge of different directions and producers, and didn't chart the success of *Chinese Wall.*

Soon after I was summoned to a meeting with Randy at the

label's Century City headquarters. He hemmed and hawed nervously about the progress of the record's release and finally confessed that because of the many changes of label executives, including the appointment of Tommy Mottola as their new president, Columbia was making big changes. Randy talked about the label's shift of creative direction and suggested I meet with other record companies. He said that he had gone to bat for me with his superiors, but now I was being dropped from the label!

I put on my best front and smiled and walked out the door, sunken and depressed. I had waited all this time, and now I was immersed in a cash-flow crunch as a result of the downtime and broken promises.

I got into my car and headed back home. As I drove onto the freeway, I was flooded with and paralyzed by every negative emotion that an artist could suffer—anger, disappointment, rage, trepidation, resentment, bitterness, and fear. I was so scared, upset, and rattled that I pulled the car over. Then I simply bowed my head and prayed. I told God, "Lord, you've taken care of me and my family this far along, and I trust that you will continue to help me. Right now I feel horrible, but I'm putting my life into your hands with the fervent hope that this will work out in some way."

I soldiered on for a while doing a few musical collaborations, and years later, I turned on the radio and heard, out of the blue, a song by the newest hip-hop sensation, MC Hammer. Hammer had just scored a megamonster hit called "U Can't Touch This," a song that dominated radio and the MTV video channel. When his album *Please Hammer, Don't Hurt 'Em* came out, it featured the song I heard, which had an all-too-familiar riff and sample. It turned out that MC Hammer had covered an obscure song called "On Your Face," which I had cowritten with Charles Stepney and Maurice White. Hammer's album went on to sell nine million units! The publishing royalty check I received for one-third ownership of that song was staggering—and came just in time to meet my family's economic needs. Hammer also sent me a framed platinum album of *Please Hammer,* which hangs in my home studio. I looked at this whole roller-coaster ordeal as a journey of faith and trust in God.

During the whirlwind cycle of "Easy Lover" I had heard nothing from Maurice. He didn't call to congratulate me on my hit record. But, then, why would he call and pass on his good wishes? What was he going to say? He had kicked me out with no severance pay after eleven years' service, and at that point there was no contact between Maurice and any of the band members. Verdine wasn't treated any better than anybody else. The two brothers continued to speak rarely during the "hiatus."

One day Larkin Arnold, a Columbia vice president on the West Coast, ran into me at a CBS record function in Santa Barbara. Larkin asked me straight up, "Why don't you talk to Maurice? You guys have to get back together, man. You need to call him, and you need to put the band back together!"

I stared at him blankly and said nothing. Larkin got the message. Then he said, "Okay. I'm going to call him."

I can't honestly remember if I contacted Maurice or if he called me after Larkin broke the ice, but we did have a sit-down after not having spoken to each other in a few years. We talked about what it would be like if we got back together. Cut a couple of records and take it slow, on a trial basis? As Maurice and I spoke more seriously about the matter, I told myself that I needed to view the whole scenario as if we were entering a new era. I had to forgive Maurice and move on, but when we decided to re-form in 1987, I assured him that things were going to be different. My newfound success had put me on a different bargaining level. *Chinese Wall* had been certified gold in the United States in 1985, while Maurice's long-awaited self-titled solo debut on Columbia barely cracked 200,000 copies that same year. My solo success forced Maurice to deal with me as an equal—just as Phil Collins had treated me as an equal—and not as a little brother.

I no longer had to look up to Maurice as a mentor. I could look at him across the table as a contemporary and say, yes, maybe we can work together.

"I won't work for you," I told Reese, "but I'll work with you."

Of course I had felt anger and mistrust, as though I had been deserted when Maurice ignored me and the other band members and formed the ARC label without consulting us. But at the same time, I chose to live out my faith, and for my own good, I put it all in perspective. I could either let it go, forgive Maurice, and move on, or else I could live in a web of bitterness, like some of the other members were doing.

Once negotiations for an EWF reunion accelerated, I phoned Verdine and arranged a meeting between him, Maurice, and me. When we decided that we were going to give it a go, we reached out to Ralph Johnson and Andrew Woolfolk. I believe Larry Dunn passed when we gave him a call. Next we hired Sheldon Reynolds to be our new guitarist, and we brought in a fantastic drummer named Sonny Emery.

That was the new EWF lineup as we entered the studio to record *Touch the World,* which was released by Columbia in November 1987. The politically charged first single, "System of Survival," hit the R&B singles chart respectably. It was an aural homecoming of sorts. My falsetto made a return on the ballad "You and I," and Reese's *kalimba* was featured on the song "Thinking of You." Yet it wasn't exactly a feel-good, lovey-dovey reunion album. Because our audience's tastes had changed, we decided to go with more edgy material. *Touch the World* dealt with the burning social issues of the day, such as urban crime, the Iran-Contra political scandal, prostitution, and teen pregnancy on songs like "System of Survival," "Touch the World," and "Evil Roy."

Over the past few years I had experienced victory and defeat, acceptance and rejection. Now the next challenge was to weather an Earth, Wind & Fire comeback world tour. The urban/pop/R&B music world of 1987 was an entirely new and different landscape with sexy solo artists and "new jack swingers" like Keith Sweat, Babyface, Whitney Houston, Anita Baker, Luther Vandross, and Janet Jackson. With our latest album, we were moving in the opposite direction. How would we fit in?

We spent more than a half million dollars putting together a brand-new show, anticipating the throngs of people who would welcome us back in style. We spent crazy money on production, and Maurice secured new management with Jerry Weintraub, the superagent who also represented Frank Sinatra, John Denver, Neil Diamond, and other topflight acts. It seemed like a slam dunk, and everybody around us assured us that the fans would return in droves: "Oh, they're waiting for you out there, all right."

Instead we received a rude awakening. While we booked the same giant amphitheaters and arenas that we had played previously, the crowds that turned out were minuscule. We were selling only between two thousand and three thousand tickets per show. It was devastating, and we hemorrhaged money on the road. We had gone from reserving entire floors of hotels, flying on private jets, and having to be rescued by security and police to playing in front of empty halls with an overblown production budget. Maurice still owned the EWF entity, and for the first time ever he shared the financial truth with me: We were hundreds of thousands of dollars in rehearsal debt before the shows even started, and now the whole tour was deemed a severe flop. I had newfound compassion for what Maurice must have been going through. I was touched by his faith and confidence in me. We were brothers again.

I had horrible nightmares and scary dreams while we were out on the road playing those dreadful comeback gigs. It was a very dark and humbling experience. While we had a few good box offices in New York, Chicago, and Los Angeles, in the rest of the country we fared pretty poorly. The last straw came when we played a very bizarre show in Japan. It was a gig that took place during the "halftime" of an auto race. The promoters set up a giant stage in the center of the racetrack, where we were to perform. The crowd hadn't come to hear music, and the concert was a disaster. We were merely a sideshow in some out-of-the-way city. Afterward, on the way to the airport, Maurice and I solemnly looked at each other, crestfallen.

"You know what?" Maurice said to me. "I'd rather leave the legacy behind and let it be what it's gonna be, because this is not it." We both agreed.

But we stuck with it. In order to pay the bills, we booked ourselves on some "Budfest" package shows, sponsored by Anheuser-Busch, the brewers of Budweiser. The live dates featured a stable of younger R&B groups, like the Deele and the Time, some of whom were direct musical descendants of EWF. We played one night in Madison Square Garden with these new-generation urban acts. I suggested we do one of our sexy hits, "Can't Hide Love" from the 1976 *Gratitude* album. Maurice demurred, but we did it anyway, and the audience, especially the women, went bananas. As I hit the congas, I yelled over at Verdine, "I told you so, I told you so." This proved that our fire was not yet doused. We tore up the other acts on the bill. We were on a slow, gradual rise, committed to rebuilding our audience even if it meant going back out as an opening act again. Later we did just that when we went out on tour with Barry White, who was billed as the headliner, and EWF as "special guests." It helped us make our way toward playing the better venues again.

Next we set up a tour to help rebuild our European market, and did forty-four more shows. It was rough, but we had to tough it out. While out on the road overseas, I noticed that Maurice had tremors in his hands. As time went on, they got progressively worse, and Reese tried his best to hide them. I also noticed that he had begun taking strong medication. Then we experienced a very scary incident. In Amsterdam we were crossing an avenue on which trolleys were running. I looked over and saw Maurice standing in the middle of the road as a speeding trolley headed directly toward him. I grabbed him and pulled him out of the way just in time.

Maurice was diagnosed with Parkinson's disease around 1992 but didn't make a public statement about it until 2000 in *Rolling Stone* magazine where he said he was treating it with medication and had it under control. Parkinson's is a degenerative disorder of the nervous system, and the early symptoms include shaking of the limbs, cramped joints, and slow movement of the body. There is no cure, but its symptoms can be controlled with medication. Maurice had always been the picture of health and had taken such great care of himself. As long as I had known him, he ate healthy foods and took many vitamins.

Maurice hid his condition from the other band members as rumors of his ill health began to circulate around the industry. Certain aspects of his behavior made sense. Whenever we signed agreements, his handlers would escort Maurice into another room so that we couldn't see them holding his hand steady so he could sign the documents. Soon it was plain to see that while Maurice could continue to work in the studio and compose, he could no longer handle the latest rigors of the road.

The public announcement of Maurice's inability to tour was a major blow to Earth Wind & Fire's campaign to return to prominence and dominance. The obvious question became: What would happen to the group now that Maurice was no longer an active performing member?

27

WANDERING THE WILDERNESS

We were clutching at straws when we released *Heritage* in February 1990, our final album on Columbia. It's filled with annoying drum machines and inboard studio effects, and even special guests like MC Hammer (featured on two tracks), a prepubescent rap group on Motown called The Boys, and an aging Sly Stone couldn't rescue the dated and insincere studio sound of the record. Hip-hop was going full steam at the time, and there we were, figuring out if we could still play the game. It was our most disappointing record. Ugh.

In 1993 we left Columbia and signed with Reprise Records, the same Warner Brothers label group that had launched the original EWF back in 1971. With *Millennium,* instead of chasing the latest trends in urban music, we tried a back-to-basics approach. We brought in lyricists who had worked well for us, including Allee Willis, Roxanne Seeman, and Jon Lind. Maurice and I cowrote a love ballad with the great Burt Bacharach. In spite of the adjustments, the album was a dud, and we were dropped from the label.

That same year Don Myrick was killed. His death occurred years after we worked together. I don't know the whole story, but the cops were called out to his house because of noise or a disturbance. The police thought he pulled a gun, and he was fatally shot in his doorway. Don was unquestionably a very special talent. His best solos can be heard on "Sun Goddess," "After the Love Is Gone," and "Reasons." He never sounded clichéd, but had a swinging hard-bop tone that was right up there with Sonny Rollins and Ornette Coleman.

By the turn of the nineties we had become the children of Israel, leaving Egypt and wandering the wilderness. EWF had to pay penance for a few years until our fans, both old and new, could fall back in love with our songbook of hits. With Maurice no longer in the lineup on the road, we were unsure of our future The band didn't officially break up; we were in "pause" mode until further notice. Then an intriguing chain of events took place.

In 1994 I was performing solo gigs that included a few Earth, Wind & Fire songs in my set. That same year smooth jazz guitarist Russ Freeman from The Rippingtons and pianist David Benoit released a CD entitled *The Benoit/Freeman Project*. One of the songs on the disc was a version of "After the Love Is Gone," featuring vocalists Phil Perry and Vesta. At the time smooth jazz had a network of about eighty highly rated radio stations across the United States, including stations like the Wave in Los Angeles; WNUA-Chicago; WQCD in New York; and the genre's pioneer station, KIFM in San Diego, playing a mix of contemporary vocal and instrumental jazz.

Each year KIFM hosted an annual outdoor listener-appreciation party and concert at the beautiful Hyatt Regency in La Jolla, north of San Diego on the Pacific Ocean. Their Memorial Day weekend event featured signature smooth jazz artists like saxophonists Kenny G and Dave Koz. With Benoit and Freeman booked to perform in 1994, they contacted me to ask if I might be interested in joining them onstage as a special guest to sing "After the Love Is Gone."

After I told them I would do the guest slot, I wondered, *What if Verdine came, too?* At the time Verdine was working on a music project with the British pop funk band Level 42, but said that he would gladly come down to San Diego and do the show with me. The two of us jumped onstage, feeling a little nervous and uncertain about how it was going to go down. I ended up also performing a few snippets of Earth, Wind & Fire standards, and then Verdine launched into a stinging version of Ramsey Lewis's "Sun Goddess." At that point the crowd went wild. At the post-gig meet-and-greet, people were all over us. After signing a few autographs, Verdine and I looked at each other and came to the same conclusion.

"Maybe we *can* do this without Maurice!"

That show lit the fuse for what was to happen next. What we saw—and had missed on our prior comeback attempt—was that between 1983 and 1994 a new generation of music lovers had been getting turned on to us. After a ten-year cooling-off period our music had come back into fashion with a combination of original and new fans.

Soon after the KIFM gig Verdine and I had dinner with Maurice to tell him what had happened. We spoke about the possibility of using the name to tour. We felt the band needed to continue to uphold its legacy. The audience was there, and time was working in our favor. True, as youngsters we had had more energy, but as we'd matured, we now had the know-how and experience. Although it wouldn't be easy, with the right budget-conscious execution, we could possibly make this work again.

Next Verdine and I met with Bob Cavallo. Although he was no longer managing Maurice or the band, Bob had been getting calls from an agent named Jeff Frasco at Creative Arts Agency (CAA). He'd been asking Bob about us. "Can we get Earth, Wind & Fire to go out on tour again?"

Frasco assured Bob that CAA could build up enough demand on the concert trail to make it worth our while to perform again. The figures Bob mentioned sounded pretty enticing. Once Cavallo reached out to Maurice, Reese's curiosity was piqued, even though we knew it was out of the question for him to rejoin the band on the road.

"Will people come if I'm not there?" Maurice asked Bob.

"I think they will," Bob replied. "Hire an extra guy, and let Philip sing your parts."

While Cavallo brokered an arrangement with CAA, we held auditions and rehearsals. An associate of mine, Damien Smith, became our manager, and later we aligned ourselves with Irving Azoff's Frontline Management. The central lineup became Verdine, Ralph, and me as the original frontline triumvirate. We went on the radio to announce on Tom Joyner's nationally syndicated morning show the news that we were back. We performed live in the studio, and Tom heartily endorsed the concept of EWF going out without Maurice.

We negotiated a licensing agreement with Maurice so that we could legally use the name Earth, Wind & Fire. By 1996 EWF was back on the road without its original mentor and founder but with a full musical ensemble: guitars, keyboards, drums, bass, the five-piece Earth, Wind & Fire Horns (in place of the Phenix Horns), plus two supporting vocalists, one of whom was my son, Philip Jr. We drew up a hit-laden hundred-minute set and toured like bandits as the demand for our music got stronger.

Unlike our 1987 return we didn't play the arenas but cautiously booked ourselves into smaller theaters and medium-sized halls, cultivating our audiences, just as we had in the old days, except now we had infrastructure, a brand, and the music from which to build. It took us about three years, working our butts off, to convince the domestic and foreign promoters that we were for real, and that the band could still perform . . . and that audiences weren't going to throw apples at us when they discovered that Maurice was no longer standing up there with us.

As we blazed trails again, I had dinner one night with Richie Salvato, a longtime supporter who also works with Maurice. I hadn't fully embraced the responsibility of leadership within the organization until Richie told me, point-blank, "One of these days you're going to have to step up and accept the fact that you're now the leader of this band."

It was a come-to-Jesus moment. When I first joined the group in 1972, not in my wildest imagination had I ever had any intention or desire to lead EWF. Until Richie laid it on the line, I hadn't even considered the idea of my being the leader. But *somebody* had to lead, and that conversation with Richie was the nudge I needed for me to finally assume an active leadership role in the group.

Now with the power to hire and fire, what kind of leader would I become? A nurturer? A perfectionist? One who delegates? I wound up becoming all three, in some form or fashion. I'm very meticulous, yet I'm supportive. I inspire musicians to be their best. I don't get involved in power struggles. I don't bark orders. I'm the guy who watches over everything, and very little gets by me. I'm intuitive and sensitive and concerned about others in the organization—how they're faring and whether or not they're raising their game.

Auditioning musicians is a process that Verdine, Ralph, and I now do together. We listen and we watch, and each time we do there's a twinge in my chest that says yea or nay. In addition to reading their résumés, I watch how musicians carry themselves and how they get along with other people. Our organization doesn't have time for drama or craziness. If you need intimidation to motivate you, you're not the right choice. The music tells when it's time to make adjustments.

My leadership differs from Reese's in that I'm more pro-family, which we weren't under Maurice's reign. Looking back, neither Maurice nor I was practiced in the art of preserving family stability. When and where we grew up, family wasn't a priority. We didn't realize how important paying attention to family was. Looking back, surely we should have maintained a better balance between our professional and personal responsibilities. That has all changed. My daughter Trinity is my personal assistant, Philip Jr. sings the harmonies in the band, while Creed helps me archive the latest EWF images.

Verdine, Ralph, and I have a personal chemistry that works. Verdine creates attention everywhere he goes, and is at "ten" from the minute he steps on the stage. Even though I'm a loner, I like to think of myself as a consummate pro. I'm not an entourage guy. I like my space. Maurice noticed early on that, like him, I was a private person when we traveled as a band. It might have to do with having been fatherless as a kid. Most important, my identity is not wrapped up in EWF. It's what I do, and I'm very proud and thankful for it, but it's not who I am. That's an important distinction between me and the others.

Right now we're in an enviable position. The Earth, Wind & Fire songbook is two hours of hit songs that everybody knows and loves. At the same time we're always tweaking and balancing the set. Two shows at the Beacon Theatre in New York City can't mean the second night is a repeat performance of the previous night's show. Each gig and venue must have its own identity.

Songwriting, performing, and entertaining are about service. If you keep that in perspective, you can't wander too far off the path. It's only when you get too self-absorbed that you lose your way. You're there to play music. Whenever I feel the ego rising, I can hear my mother's voice telling me, "An honest day's pay for an honest day's work."

It's hard to believe, but since reforming back in 1996, we've reached more fans, young and old, without Maurice than we did with him from 1972 to 1990. We have six buses and four semi-trucks. With concert tours, foreign and corporate gigs, plus orchestral and classical dates, we work more than we did back in the glory days. Only now we're much happier and smart enough to slow down, enjoy our families, take a break, and be thankful for the opportunities that enable us to tour globally.

The Concept of EWF has been placed in my keeping. So far we've had almost two decades of renewed prosperity, which never would have happened had I fought over a share of the ARC money. In the long run, and by the grace of God, I have benefited instead by braving the elements of Earth, Wind & Fire.

28

AWARDS AND ACCOLADES

If you can even survive this crazy music business, then you qualify for awards. In March 2000, after seven years on the nominee list, we were inducted into the Rock and Roll Hall of Fame. (The *Los Angeles Times* figured we wouldn't get in because we were a disco act and an R&B band—a strange assumption, since we were always anti-disco!) EWF was introduced at the sixteenth annual induction ceremony at the Waldorf Astoria Hotel in New York City by Sir Paul McCartney, which was a high honor. Other acts inducted into the hall that year were Bonnie Raitt, Eric Clapton, James Taylor, The Moonglows and The Lovin' Spoonful. As is usually the case with such reunions, it had been a long time since the original EWF lineup stood together on one stage. Actually, we hadn't all been in the same room since Maurice delivered his fateful "back burner" speech at the Complex seventeen years earlier. The original nine—Maurice, Verdine, Andrew, Larry, Freddie, Johnny, Al, Ralph, and I—were rehearsed and ready to hit the stage for a brief set. The vibe went well, and we performed a short medley of songs, including "September" and "Shining Star."

To my dismay, the Rock and Roll Hall of Fame Museum display honoring us ended up featuring a small picture of the band and an outfit of Maurice's that none of us remembered him ever wearing. It wasn't a definitive portrait of EWF. Still, I was very honored to be included.

With age comes respectability, and also with age come the accolades. In 2000 we were invited to perform at the White House for President Bill Clinton. We played at a state dinner honoring King Mohammed VI and Princess Lalla Salma of Morocco. In July 2003 we were given a space on the Hollywood RockWalk. In September 2003 we were named to the Vocal Group Hall of Fame. In June 2004 the National Academy of Recording Arts and Sciences (NARAS), the people who dispense the Grammys, gave us the Signature Governors Award. In 2005 we received a BET Lifetime Award, and that same year we performed as part of the Super Bowl XXXIX pregame show and played in Russia for the first time. Many band members received honorary college degrees.

In June 2010 we were inducted into the Songwriters Hall of Fame, along with our friend David Foster, which was way cool because Phil Collins was also on hand to receive his Lifetime Achievement Award. Phil chose to sing "Easy Lover" at the presentation, which we performed together for the first time since we recorded it in the studio. The Songwriters Hall of Fame is an especially prestigious industry award, because the people selected are veteran writers with an impressive catalog of work. For us to be honored that year alongside writers like Leonard Cohen, Jackie DeShannon, and Johnny Mandel was stellar.

Over the past three decades I've released ten solo albums, which include the three on the Columbia label, three gospel CDs on Word Records, a few independent-label releases, and two recorded in 1999 and 2002 for the jazz label Heads Up. Today I'm actively touring as a solo artist and constantly on the road appearing as a guest on other projects with my musician friends.

Not everything that's happened in the new millennium has been joyful—especially on the domestic front. In 2001 Janet and I split up. We were married for thirty-two years and separated for five before we finally divorced. Fortunately our breakup proved to be positive for her, because through intense therapy and a Christian spiritual rebirth she was able to discover who she truly was. Afterward I began dating a young lady named Krystal Johnson who was half my age. We fell in love, and in 2002 we married. We had two wonderful sons, Jaleel Mikale Bailey, who was born in May 2004, and Jaylen Christopher Bailey, who was born in March 2006.

Sadly, my second marriage didn't work out. After having been married to Janet for thirty-two years, I saw my union with Krystal as a second chance to enter into a faithful partnership. I went into it with high hopes, coupling her innocence with my experience and the love that we had for each other. I looked at it as an opportunity to make things work the second time around. I relished the opportunity to start anew with Krystal.

Krystal and I split up in 2010, and as I picked up the broken pieces, I learned that, yes, you can master the mechanics of having great sex, but the ability to love and sacrifice for someone is a divine thing. If the relationship becomes more about the flesh than it is about the spirit, then you won't be able to sustain it. And, unfortunately, that's what happened with Krystal and me.

I was dejected when the marriage ended, and in fact, I truly believe that my breakup with Krystal was my first major heartbreak. Subsequently I went through stages of intense disappointment, embarrassment, and anger. One night while singing "After the Love Is Gone" I nearly lost it and became unglued onstage. The lyrics about the emotional aftereffects of a lost love haunted me. Oh, my God! I was living this, and I had to perform the song, and it was really tough.

On a positive note, it was another song that later ministered to me. I was performing "Sing a Song," and although I had written the lyrics, the words that night came back to me like a boomerang. I needed to sing that song to lift me up at that moment: The tune put a smile on my face because it speaks to me about how a simple song can change your outlook and mood in an upbeat way. I sang it with renewed passion—and a newfound revelation of its meaning—and I felt transformed.

Krystal and I have since worked through our estrangement. We have a friendly relationship that is healthier than ever. I see Jaleel and Jaylen all the time and am very much a part of their lives. Krystal and I are coparenting, and we're doing the best we can to raise our little men with the finest opportunities. Because I didn't have a father around, I'm determined to be an exemplary dad. Today, with my younger sons, I'm a lot different than I was with my first family with Janet. These days I'll change my schedule in order to be around for the important times.

I'm fortunate that I get along with my children so well, but as far as committed relationships with women are concerned, I'm still learning. I'm not proud of my past extramarital exploits. There have been a lot of emotional casualties along the way as a result, and in the end I guess I'm the biggest one. I have problems dealing with anger, and I have control issues, and I find that I sometimes overreact to the ups and downs of my emotions.

I believe certain traits of behavior are hereditary. For example, a person may be very needy and unable to find fulfillment, possibly because a father or a grandparent was that way. Or a person can be very sweet, but have deep-seated anger issues because his mother had a tendency to display intense rage. Studies have shown that children of divorce and/or dysfunctional parents have been hard-pressed in their later attempts to build successful marriages and unions. My unfaithfulness over the years was a major factor in my emotional shortcomings, and although Janet forgave me for my many indiscretions, including having my daughter Pili with another woman, it wasn't enough to salvage our marriage.

Janet is still a strong part of my life as well. Whenever she attends an EWF concert, we welcome her. I've known her since I was nine years old. We have four children and six grandchildren together, and she probably knows me better than anyone. We play an occasional round of golf together and talk about the kids, grandchildren, old friends, and our Christian faith. Janet wants to be a part of the lives of anyone I bring into my life. She has stood by me and my other children. Pili calls Janet "Mama Jane," and they speak every now and then. When Jaleel had difficulty with an asthma attack (as I did as a child), Janet went to the hospital to visit. She believes that given the energy it takes to be angry and bitter, why not use it instead to be supportive and get along?

And for me, all is not lost on the romantic front. I currently have a steady girlfriend, and we're growing together and letting things happen spontaneously.

One of our recent highlights on the road was our three coheadlining tours with Chicago in 2004, 2005, and 2009. Featuring three hours of music, the Earth, Wind & Fire/Chicago tours were among the highest grossing of our careers. The idea came about when we ran into members of Chicago backstage at a Portland show, and after attending one of their concerts, we realized that our material blended very well. Between our bodies of work and our many hits, we were able to bridge the narrow gap between die-hard EWF and Chicago fans. From the stage, I could sense that our audiences were tentative at first. Then by the end of the show, each group of fans was hugging the other and exchanging high-fives.

Another recent concert highlight took place in September 2010 when, for the first time, EWF performed live with a full orchestra at the Hollywood Bowl in Los Angeles. It was an important occasion, and festive enough to bring Maurice back into the spotlight. Both Hollywood Bowl concerts were sold out, and were among the highest-grossing events at that venue in years. We recorded them and filmed them for our edification.

For the Hollywood Bowl gig we incurred the initial expense of hiring someone to write orchestral arrangements of our songs, which now gives us the opportunity to visit other cities with symphony orchestras. For such engagements we'll generally do five or six pieces with just the band, while the rest of the songs utilize an orchestra. I find that classical players are the best musicians you can enlist on the road. Since then we've done a full slate of concerts in cities like Dallas, Akron, and Charlotte and look forward to one day playing overseas in esteemed cities like Prague and Vienna with their traditionally renowned philharmonic orchestras.

Like many blessed musicians, I've chosen to give back through a nonprofit entity I've created with my daughter Trinity called Music Is Unity. Music Is Unity (www.musicisunity.org) primarily serves recently disadvantaged foster-care youth who are dropped back into society as soon as they reach eighteen years of age. This is a tremendously underserved segment of our society that needs help. Quite often these "emancipated" youths are driven out of government and private social aid programs, and are frequently just handed their belongings and sent out to tackle life on their own. Many times they end up back on the streets, in jail, in prostitution, living under bridges, Dumpster diving, or having difficulty finding employment. Emancipation statutes can be callous and cold. Stuck in foster care through no fault of their own, these young people can get lost in the bureaucracy. That's where Music Is Unity can help.

As a father of seven children, five of whom are grown, I know firsthand that young people in their late teens and early twenties are still figuring things out, so I linked up with the National Foster Youth Action Network, and a portion of our ticket sales go to Music Is Unity. Grants are awarded to different organizations that are helping to fund foster care and instill policy changes. It's one cause I'm extremely passionate about.

Do you remember September 2013? Earth, Wind & Fire released *Now, Then & Forever* on the Sony Music Legacy label. This being our twentieth studio album—and our first album since 2005—*Now, Then & Forever* debuted strong on the Billboard R&B chart at number five, and at eleven on the BB pop chart. *NT &F* marked our highest chart presence in over thirty years!

The recording project was two years in the making, and I served as executive producer, along with Verdine as co-executive producer.

Like so many of our best recordings, *Now, Then & Forever* explores various genres of music, as well as the signature Earth, Wind & Fire sound that our fans respect and love. One of the lead tracks I'm especially proud of is a satiny ballad called "Guiding Lights," which was cowritten by my son Philip Doron Bailey (along with Darrin Simpson, Austin Jacobs, and Daniel McClain). "Guiding Lights," was recorded about one year into the project, and is one of six songs co-written by Philip Doron. It's pure vintage EWF at its best, and we're proud of this breakthrough release.

Over the past two decades we've played before presidents, kings, queens, prime ministers, and Olympic medalists around the world. We've performed at government functions for both political parties, and appeared at the 2002 Winter Olympics in Utah. And when Al Gore was awarded the Nobel Peace Prize in Oslo in 2007, we performed at a special reception for the attendees in Norway.

When Barack Hussein Obama was elected the forty-fourth president of the United States in 2008, EWF was chosen to perform at President Obama and First Lady Michelle Obama's first formal social function. We got the call from Desiree Rogers, the White House social secretary, who told us that the president had requested us for the Governors' Ball, which was just three weeks away, on February 22, 2009. We were there, no problem.

Playing for the president was quite a memorable experience. Dressed casually in a sweater and Dockers, President Obama strolled into the green room and hung out with us that afternoon during the set-up and rehearsal.

"What's going on down here?" he asked jokingly.

We took pictures of President Obama together with the band. Then the first lady came down with her assistant for more photos.

The president was pretty low-key during our visit. "I used to sing 'Reasons' in college," he confessed to me, "but I lost my falsetto."

We played the Governors' Ball that night with minimal

amplification and microphones. Just the drums alone, not to mention our horn section, could have blown the room away, but we put on a darned good show. As I looked out into the crowd, I knew that we had truly elected the first African American president of the United States when I saw President Obama, who was dancing to one of our songs, lift his hands up in the air and exclaim, *"That's my jam!"*

Bottom line—and I'm sure President Obama agrees—Earth, Wind & Fire makes you feel good, as music should. Our longevity has to do with the strength of our songbook and our body of work—for which I give Maurice his respectful props—produced over a rollicking forty-year period. It's become part of the weave of the creative fabric of American society, as well as the worldwide music continuum. While we don't travel on our own private plane like we did in the past, EWF still gets whisked off to exciting faraway lands: Africa, Asia, Europe, Latin America, and South America. After a humble upbringing, God has allowed me to see and experience so much through my music. He's had an intentional purpose for my life: to try to point people toward a God who loves us, forgives us, and doesn't give up on us.

I think back to when that lady on the airplane asked if I had a personal relationship with God, and I can now honestly say that I do. I've come to know God through the highs and lows. But getting to know God is a time-consuming process. You can't rush it along and jump from one state of grace to the next! Spiritual growth is slow and gradual, and takes discipline, but I'm on the path. Every morning I read the Bible and reflect, meditate, and pray.

As I complete this memoir I think about its subtitle, *Braving the Elements of Earth, Wind & Fire*. I'm reminded of the personal earthquakes of conflict in my life. I ponder the winds and torrents of adversity and prosperity that I have endured. I reflect on the fires that have consumed the many broken relationships along the way. But I try to let every experience make me better, instead of bitter. My goal has been to survive those elements, so that God can one day say to me, "Well done!"

Yes, I am a shining star, but I'm simply an instrument through which God shines. And I encourage my readers and my social-networking friends on Facebook and Twitter to be their own shining stars. Practice your craft every day and be ready when you receive your special calling. Life is precious and rich, whether you're jetting off somewhere or sitting in the most remote part of our beautiful world, watching the stars above. For me personally, I never became a musician for fame or material gain. I did it for the love of music. Even without the awards and accolades, I would still be singing and playing in some fashion or other. The gift I have to sing is God's gift. The love I have for music is something that he has given me. I see it as a means to an end.

INDEX